Cross-Cultural Studies in
Cognition and Mathematics

DEVELOPMENTAL PSYCHOLOGY SERIES

SERIES EDITOR

Harry Beilin

Developmental Psychology Program
City University of New York Graduate School
New York, New York

In Preparation

MARSHA B. LISS (Editor). *Children's Play: Sex Differences and the Acquisition of Cognitive and Social Skills*

Published

DAVID F. LANCY. *Cross-Cultural Studies in Cognition and Mathematics*

HERBERT P. GINSBURG. (Editor). *The Development of Mathematical Thinking*

MICHAEL POTEGAL. (Editor). *Spatial Abilities: Development and Physiological Foundations*

NANCY EISENBERG. (Editor). *The Development of Prosocial Behavior*

WILLIAM J. FRIEDMAN. (Editor). *The Developmental Psychology of Time*

SIDNEY STRAUSS. (Editor). *U-Shaped Behavioral Growth*

GEORGE E. FORMAN. (Editor). *Action and Thought: From Sensorimotor Schemes to Symbolic Operations*

EUGENE S. GOLLIN. (Editor). *Developmental Plasticity: Behavioral and Biological Aspects of Variations in Development*

W. PATRICK DICKSON. (Editor). *Children's Oral Communication Skills*

LYNN S. LIBEN, ARTHUR H. PATTERSON, and NORA NEWCOMBE. (Editors). *Spatial Representation and Behavior across the Life Span: Theory and Application*

SARAH L. FRIEDMAN and MARIAN SIGMAN. (Editors). *Preterm Birth and Psychological Development*

HARBEN BOUTOURLINE YOUNG and LUCY RAU FERGUSON. *Puberty to Manhood in Italy and America*

The list of titles in this series continues on the last page of this volume.

Cross-Cultural Studies in Cognition and Mathematics

DAVID F. LANCY

College of Education
Arizona State University
Tempe, Arizona

 1983

ACADEMIC PRESS

A Subsidiary of Harcourt Brace Jovanovich, Publishers

New York   London
Paris   San Diego   San Francisco   São Paulo   Sydney   Tokyo   Toronto

ACADEMIC PRESS, INC.
111 Fifth Avenue, New York, New York 10003

United Kingdom Edition published by
ACADEMIC PRESS, INC. (LONDON) LTD.
24/28 Oval Road, London NW1 7DX

Library of Congress Cataloging in Publication Data

Lancy, David F.
  Cross-cultural studies in cognition and mathematics.

  Bibliography: p.
  Includes index.
  1. Mathematics--Study and teaching--Papua New Guinea.
2. Cognition in children--Papua New Guinea. I. Title.
QA14.P25L36   1982   370.15'6   82-8794
ISBN 0-12-435620-6   AACR2

PRINTED IN THE UNITED STATES OF AMERICA

83 84 85 86   9 8 7 6 5 4 3 2 1

Thank you Dorothy, Nadia, and Sonia for your
almighty forbearance.

This work is also dedicated to the memory of
Millard Madsen, colleague, patron,
and very dear friend.

Contents

3
Cognitive Testing in Papua New Guinea   53

4
Intercultural Variation in Cognitive Development   73

5
Cultural Complexity   101

6
The Development of Counting and Classification Skills   137

7
The Limits of Mathematical Achievement   171

8
The Co-evolution of Culture, Cognition, and Schooling   195

List of Figures

List of Tables

Preface

Cross-Cultural Studies in Cognition and Mathematics describes a multifaceted research project undertaken in Papua New Guinea. Building on previous research, the author and his colleagues began in 1976 to examine systematically the relationship between the cultural background of the child and his or her pattern of cognitive development and acquisition of school arithmetic. Data were gathered in 10 highly diverse, traditional societies and two urban sites. These data were of three basic types. Various anthropological procedures were used to document indigenous mathematics and classification systems as well as general ethnography. Our aim was to prepare a formal description of cognitive activity characteristic of each of the 10 societies. In each site, children from two age and education levels were given a series of tests designed to uncover characteristic levels of cognitive processing. Our later analysis of these data sets considered possible relationships between the cognitive demands imposed by the society and the tests, respectively. A particularly strong relationship was found between the extent to which the folk classification system (as elicited with ethnoscientific techniques) utilized taxonomic principles and the child's readiness to use a taxonomic strategy on the cognitive tests. Exposure to formal education also had a profound effect on patterns of cognitive processing.

The third data set was drawn entirely from schools. Children in grades 2–6 were administered cognitive tests and mathematics tests based on the uniform curriculum currently in use. Additional data pertinent to assessing the quality of classroom instruction were collected. Relationships among cultural background, cognitive development, and mathematics achievement were established, and instructional issues appeared to be of equal or more importance in accounting for variation in achievement.

The first chapter sets the theoretical, practical, and political context for this work and provides a summary of the chapters to follow. The second chapter briefly describes Papua New Guinea as an independent and gradually Westernizing nation and as a diverse collection of unique societies. The third chapter reviews the essential literature on cross-cultural psychology and cognitive anthropology that was drawn on in establishing the present project. Chapter 4 outlines the design of the project, the research methods employed, and the results of the 10-site cognitive testing program. Chapter 5 parallels Chapter 4 in presenting data and analyses from our ethnographic studies and examines our major hypotheses relating culture to cognition. Chapter 6 reports the results of several in-depth follow-up studies carried out in a subsample of the original 10 sites. Chapter 7 is concerned primarily with mathematics achievement and schooling. The final chapter reviews theoretical issues raised throughout the book and moves toward a synthesis and advance on current thinking in several pertinent fields.

There are several unique aspects of this work. A concerted effort was put forth to obtain contemporaneous and complementary data on the culture of the child and his or her pattern of cognitive development. Although we did not neglect general cultural description, we focused on very specific aspects of these societies (e.g., indigenous mathematics, classification, children's games, etc.) which were hypothesized to have a direct impact on cognition. Furthermore, unlike most studies in cross-cultural psychology, our concern was not primarily to examine the effects of acculturation or to compare "primitive" and "Western" thought. Rather, we hoped to discover whether societies characterized equally by the absence of modern institutions (e.g., cash economy, political hierarchy, literacy, etc.) might not engender different degrees of cognitive development as a function of internal, traditional practices. On the other hand, we also replicated most of the important features of the cross-cultural literature. We used testing methods that had a respectable history in the field, and we examined the effects of age, gender, formal education, urbanization, social class, and nutritional status on test performance.

Because the project was conducted under the sponsorship of the Papua New Guinea Department of Education, educational issues were addressed to a degree unprecedented in research of this type. Not only were we able to attend to the interaction of schooling practices and intellectual development, we were also able to draw on our findings at various points for their policy implications. These were many and have resulted in the adaptation of completely revised national achievement testing and analysis procedures, special provisions for "disadvantaged schools," changes in the mathematics curriculum, and so forth.

I have attempted in *Cross-Cultural Studies in Cognition and Mathematics* to document thoroughly a particular research project and to place this project into a broader historical and theoretical context. Literature from both cross-cultural psychology and cognitive anthropology is extensively and carefully reviewed. Gradually the book moves from theories and ideas prominent in the 1950s and 1960s to more recent formulations influenced by developments in sociobiology and information-processing psychology. These sources are drawn upon to build a theory of the coevolution of culture and thought.

Two groups of scholars will find this book essential reading: cross-cultural psychologists and cognitive anthropologists. Readers with a minor interest in these areas and a major concern with child development, cognition, instructional psychology, mathematics education, classroom processes, human evolution, Melanesian studies, and children's play will also be rewarded. Care has been taken with prose and illustrations to achieve a high degree of clarity so that nonspecialists, including administrators in the Papua New Guinea Department of Education, will be enlightened—even amused—rather than intimidated.

Acknowledgments

In April 1976, I was appointed Principal Research Officer in the Curriculum Branch of the Papua New Guinea Department of Education. As the position had been unfilled for quite some time, education research under the Department's auspices was moribund, and there was no staff to administer. Consequently, my charge was to "get things going." The first task was to find some researchers. I recruited people from wherever I could find them. Students and faculty from the two universities were located, negotiations were undertaken, and funding was arranged. A small but steady stream of projects was started, with reports appearing in, among other places, *The Papua New Guinea Journal of Education* (which I edited). A few researchers were lured from overseas to work on high priority topics.

There was, however, one major constraint. Given the dearth of permanent research staff in the Department and the very small staff at the University, there were severe limits on the kind of research for which we could contract. Most researchers, either those already employed (as teachers or administrators) in Papua New Guinea or those who came to PNG solely to carry out research, had their own priorities or agendas. These might be adjusted slightly at the behest of the Department, but the questions asked were determined largely by the interests of the available researchers. One way around this dilemma was to design a large-scale study that would capitalize on the interests of a fairly large group of researchers and on some concerns of the Department. Thus was born the *Indigenous Mathematics Project*. The project had a cognitive development component at least in part because a sizable number of past (notably Max Kelly and Hugh Philp) and present education researchers in the country, including myself, had focused mainly on this. The project had an anthropological component because, for quite some time, introduction into the classroom of elements of traditional culture had been a priority of the Department. Each succeeding edition of the curriculum has looked more "home grown" and, among the readily available researchers, anthropologists were in the majority. The project had a mathematics component at least partly because, of all areas of the curriculum, mathematics had been influenced most heavily by an ongoing R & D effort. And, again, there was a large, if widely dispersed, cadre of specialists in mathematics education to draw upon. Finally, a growing departmental concern corresponded to an extremely able group of nutrition specialists and researchers at work in the country, many of whom were to work eventually with the project.

The planning and pilot testing phase was in 1976. We developed instruments to study cognitive development and recruited anthropologists and linguists to assist with various aspects of the ethnographic research. In 1977, research was carried out in 10 fairly unacculturated societies that sampled the great cultural and ecological diversity of the country. Toward the end of the year we began to survey mathematics achievement in a representative sample of community schools. In 1978, in-depth studies in a few societies were undertaken as a follow-up to the initial surveys. Data analysis and initial reporting were begun. Also in 1978, I began to share our results with colleagues in the United States, Australia, and elsewhere through a lecture tour and a presentation at the International Congress of Archaeological and Ethnological Sciences in Delhi. The web grew larger as we began to get input from individuals who had not participated in the actual research. In late 1978 and early 1979, Venina Kada and Bob Roberts began to survey carefully the practice of mathematics instruction. Much of the research undertaken from 1977 to 1979 was then replicated and extended by Randall Souviney during 1980–1981. In August of 1979, I left Papua New Guinea carrying reams of data which were to be augmented continually during the following 2 years as additional reports became available. An NIMH post-doctoral fellowship at UCLA gave me the freedom to begin a more fine-grained analysis of data, review of related literature, and write-up than had been possible previously. Patricia Greenfield, Wendell Jeffrey, and Millard Madsen in the Developmental Psychology Program helped me make the difficult transition from administrator–practitioner to scholar as I tried to portray the work undertaken in Papua New Guinea for a wider audience. Their support, both moral and intellectual, was invaluable and I shall always be grateful to them. The College of Education at Arizona State University has provided a congenial home for the last stages of this effort.

Nearly 100 individuals have a "piece" of the Indigenous Mathematics Project. With such a large cast of characters, I can do no more than single out a few of the critical participants for praise. Among the researchers who assisted with test data collection, Venina Kada, Hilary Pumuye, and Herman Taolam stand out for both the extent and the quality of their work. At the various sites we were often hosted by missionaries or anthropologists. Father Jacob at Kerau and Father Graham at Imoda, among the former, and Aletta Biersack, Jill Grant, and Marty Zelenietz, among the latter, were especially kind and helpful. Among other anthropologists and linguists whose assistance was invaluable, I would like to thank Achsah and James Carrier, Jane Fajans, Virginia Guilford, Iru Karkare, Francis Kettenis, Alice Logan, Pensa Roleasmalik, Tom Moylan, Geoff Smith, and Andrew Strathern. Mathematics education provided the instructional context for our work and among the mathematics educators who contributed to our success, Alan Bishop, Murray Britt, Ken Clements, Peter Jones, Glen Leon, Colin Meek, Brian Norris, Bob Roberts, Peter Stuckey, Brian Wilson, and Godfrey Yerua deserve special mention. To the extent that the Indigenous Mathematics Project was extremely ambitious, it depended heavily on the continued support of "angels" in the department to get us over the political and financial rough spots. Bernie Anderson, Vin McNamara, Beteul Peril, Paul Songo, Alkan Tololo, and Mali Voi were responsible for nurturing and guiding the project throughout its tortuous history and I do not think they have been disappointed by the results of their investment.

The several articles dealing with IMP as well as parts of this book have been read and reviewed prior to publication by nearly all of the individuals mentioned so far; to many I am therefore doubly grateful. Additional review was kindly provided by Harry Beilin, Charles Brainerd, Dan Freedman, Maurine Fry, Christopher Hallpike, Leslie Lancy, Bud Mehan, Louise Morauta, Robert Rueda, and Geoff Saxe.

I come at last to those individuals whose contribution to the project was as important as it was unobtrusive, the data analysts, graphic artists, and typists who translated my cobbled ideas and prose into a finished manuscript. This supporting cast was also very large but I would like to express my profound gratitude especially to Bill Andrews, Clyde Dent, Margaret Embury, Brad Hanson, Tim Koski, and Diane Smith.

1

Introduction

New Guinea, now Papua New Guinea (PNG), has for over 100 years served as a natural laboratory. The exotic flora and fauna have done much to stimulate comparative biology. In medicine, Carelton Gajdusek won the Nobel Prize largely on the strength of his discovery of *kuru*, a disease found only in Papua New Guinea. A portion of any introductory textbook in anthropology will be devoted to studies done in PNG. And this situation shows no signs of abating. The country is alive with basic research in many fields, which is aided and abetted by the modern government.

Since about 1960, however, a new theme has emerged. The Australian colonial administration, and later, the freely elected government of independent Papua New Guinea have sought to tame the exotic. The country has rapidly adjusted to the demands of participation in an international family of nations. International standards in law, economics, telecommunications, transportation, weights and measures, diplomacy, governance, and so on have been freely adopted. The diversity of customs associated with 3.5 million people speaking 700 different languages has been abridged in the process of nation-building.

In the short term, our research sought to capitalize on the natural-laboratory aspect of the country to address some important issues in the study of intellectual development, but the long-term goal remains. It is to improve educational policies and practices so that regardless of the child's cultural background, he or she will be able to master the skills necessary to operate under these various international systems. In concrete terms, we studied the varying responses to standardized, school-like tests as a first step toward standardizing the responses.

We operated under a number of political, practical, and theoretical assumptions. The principal political assumption has had to do with PNG's future as a nation and the implication of this role for the education of its citizens. Diplomatically, PNG's strong ties to the West, especially to Australia and the European community, are balanced by a developing relationship with Southeast Asia and Japan. In addition, Michael Somare, PNG's first prime minister, was the first foreign head of state to make an official visit to China following Mao's death. This emerging political neutrality masks a fundamental commitment to the products and processes associated with the multinational modern economy. Ties to foreign governments are overshadowed by ties to the IMF, World Bank, Lomé Convention, Law of the Seas Conference, various commodity cartels, and so forth. However, unlike Nauru and New Caledonia, for instance, the PNG government has been loath to permit the penetration of foreign technocrats along with the foreign institutions. Through a vigorous program of "localization," the government has attempted to train Papua New Guineans to fill newly created jobs in manufacturing, commerce, transportation, management, and in other areas.

A second political assumption was that the accidents of history should not be allowed to dictate the choice of people for training and employment. Coastal peoples, because of their more extensive contact with foreigners and foreign institutions, have had a head start, and as a consequence they tend to dominate the wage-employment sector of the economy, especially the civil service. The present government seeks to redress this imbalance. The third assumption was that cadres of English-speaking, technically skilled workers would be created by the education system, rather than through the gradual implementation of an employment pyramid. For example, the government has not sought to create a peasant–laborer class through the promotion of a plantation economy. The number of paid plantation laborers has steadily declined over the last 2 decades. There will be no gradual evolution from subsistence through peasant to manufacturing economies. Thus the education system must not only address itself to job preparation but to *enculturating* students in modern international languages, customs, and patterns of thought.

There are a number of ways that the government could have approached the problem of creating an educated elite. It might have concentrated its attention on educating the more Westernized coastal populations, especially those around Port Moresby and Rabaul. This option has been resisted in the interest of national unity. It might have used an examination-dominated selectionist model of education. In this model the early years of schooling are used primarily to separate out the intellectually most able students, who will be assured intensive training of very high quality. On the grounds of political expediency, this course has not been followed. Transition rates are high at every tier in the system, and gate-keeping mechanisms to insure that only very able candidates are admitted to the university, for example, are weakly maintained. Thus the PNG education system is closer, in many respects, to that found in the United States than to the European system and its descendants in former European colonies. Courses of study are adjusted to meet the abilities of students rather than rigorously selecting students on the basis of their fitness for a particular course of study. However, despite the various "gaps" that are bound to emerge in such a system, courses of study have not been notably *lengthened* to permit students to "catch-up." The mean years of schooling for various types of professionals (e.g., doctors, lawyers, teachers, engineers, etc.) is, in general, lower than in the United States, in some cases by several years. There has been little compensation made in the area of "teacher quality" either. Teachers, whether native or expatriate, are generally less well qualified than their counterparts in developed countries. Thus the major practical assumption under which we operated was that the only segment of the education system that was open to experimentation and improvement was the *curriculum*. As is indicated in Chapter 7, I now have grave doubts about the power of an improved curriculum per se to close this gap. Nevertheless the curriculum has been and continues to be the target of far greater attention in PNG than one typically finds in a developing country. In particular, the mathematics curriculum had received a great deal of attention prior to 1976 (see Chapter 7). There was such a degree of interest and momentum, as well as a cadre of trained individuals in the general area of mathematics education, that the suggestion of a major piece of basic research—designed ultimately to link up with curriculum development in mathematics—met with much enthusiasm. The original proposal for this research, entitled *The Indigenous Mathematics Project* (Lancy, 1979a), was scrutinized and subsequently endorsed by the highest echelons of the Department of Education, the National Planning Office, the prime minister and his cabinet, and UNESCO, all of whom committed funds toward it. This endorsement of the project also gave acquiescence to the view repeatedly stressed here that a wide gap existed between the goal of producing a large, technically sophisticated labor force and an education system designed to meet that goal as spelled out in the then-current education plan (see, for example, Grieve, 1979; Rogers, 1979).

A final practical assumption that had enormous weight in determining *how* the research was to be carried out related to staffing. Given the point made earlier concerning localization in addition to tight budget constraints, the research would have to be conducted almost wholly by temporary staff members who were nonprofessionals. Although the project began in mid-1976, a full-time director was not appointed until late in 1979. Two primary teachers without university-level training were the only other full-time staff members. The bulk of the research was carried out by volunteers—including myself—who took time out from teaching and administrative duties to contribute to the project. The "staff" was also augmented by a dozen graduate students in anthropology from universities in the United States, Australia, and Europe who interrupted their own fieldwork to assist with some phase of the project. Although the quality and intensity of the research may have suffered slightly from this reliance on volunteers, its relevance was greatly enhanced because it permitted a constant flow of communication between the theoretical milieu of the research project and the practical milieus of our teacher, administrator, and student participants.

There were also a number of theoretical assumptions that informed the initial research design. These are reexamined in Chapter 8 in the light of the subsequent findings in PNG as well as theoretical and empirical advances made elsewhere in the intervening period. The first assumption was that there existed a profound homology between the Papua New Guinean model of education and, by now, classic models of child development. Attention in educational practice and cognitive theory was not directed primarily toward the student's acquisition of discrete skills. Rather, the concern was to promote–account for the development of broad conceptual structures—structures that, as they became more complex, would permit the individual a greater facility in abstracting the essential elements from a situation leading to more rapid mastery of new situations and a more fluid transition from one situation to another.

Second, these structures were a joint product of the individual's biological and cultural heritage. Taking the genetic view led to two related concepts:

1. There were stages in an individual's cognitive development such that the patterns of thought associated with one stage would be qualitatively different from those associated with any other stage.
2. As a consequence, a child might not be in the appropriate stage to profit from a particular pattern of instruction.

Thus the failure of a child to learn particular concepts in a mathematics class might be related to the incompatibility between these concepts or the manner in which they were presented and the child's inherent cognitive makeup. The child suffers from a cognitive *deficit* vis-à-vis the curriculum.

Taking the environmental view also led to two related concepts:

1. The society in which the individual grew up played a role in shaping cognitive structures such that the preferred patterns of thought for one cultural group might be different from those of another group.
2. As a consequence, the patterns of thought acquired in the village might not be congruent with those associated with instruction in school.

The child's failure in mathematics class might be attributed to a *difference* between the cognitive structures the child brought to class and the cognitive structures that were imbedded in the lessons.

Our starting point, then, was the position that the locus of failure was not in any given math problem but in the cognitive structures that guided the child's initial attempts to make sense of the problem in his or her own terms. We proposed to study these structures through a *program of testing*, and to study their origins through a careful selection of subjects. The organic source would be probed by comparisons between children differing in age, gender, and nutritional status. The environmental source would be probed by comparisons among children from different societies. Additionally, we would try to analyze various aspects of those societies for their probable impact on cognition. Ethical and financial constraints precluded our opening up the genetic "black box," but we were more successful with the environment "black box."

As the reader will discover, there was a kind of creative tension between dogma and innovation throughout the course of the project. On the one hand, we had no brief whatsoever from the PNG government to use this study purely as a testing ground for essentially Western theories of cognitive development. Such a study might challenge the very under-pinnings of the curricula that rely heavily on these theories (see Chapter 7). On the other hand, we did not envision that the project would have a purely "applied" flavor either. Thus the theoretical assumptions guided the design and conduct of the study, but also, whenever it was possible to be reflexive, we turned our inquiry back upon itself and examined the assumptions themselves (see Chapter 6).

Ultimately our goal was to discover how children from Papua New Guinea developed intellectually in different geographical and cultural settings, in school in general and in mathematics classes in particular. In

the process we hoped to separate the factors that influenced this development from those that did not. We believed that once we had a better
understanding of these factors we could more intelligently intervene or
suggest interventions in the education system. Our best guess at the
outset was that confirmation of the deficit assumption would call for a
greater emphasis on conceptual development in the curriculum and the
provision of compensating educational services to reflect possibly wide
cross-cultural variation in the extent of such deficits. Confirmation of the
difference assumption would suggest efforts to establish a "bridging
curriculum" between the conceptual world of the village and the conceptual world of the school. A second, but obviously related, goal was to
carry out ethnographic research on indigenous mathematics systems.
Most of this research will be reported in other publications (e.g.,
Roleasmalik, 1979; Saxe, 1979b; Lancy & Strathern, 1981) and in
doctoral dissertations currently in progress.

Plan of the Book

Chapter 2 takes the reader on a tour in time and space. The Indigenous
Mathematics Project is first located in a historical context. An apprecia-
tion of this context is far more important here than in most studies of this
type. Most such projects are undertaken *despite* or completely beyond the
purview of the national government. The Indigenous Mathematics Project
was *sponsored*, however, by the Papua New Guinea government. A
knowledge of this history and of the contemporary struggle to resolve
some of the conflicts that it has engendered should help the reader
understand both the unique promise and limitations of the project. In the
second half of the chapter we pay a brief visit to each of the 10 IMP sites.
Here the reader is invited to dwell on the similarities and differences
among these sites and between them and the reader's own culture. A
minor theme is introduced that will reappear again and again—food-
getting. Food-getting is important because it is one of the few common
denominators in a survey of Papua New Guinea's rich cultural heritage
and because it may become a pivotal issue in our attempts to discover how
it is that culture influences cognition. Each site is located precisely on a
recent map of the region.[1] The maps are intended to convey more than
mere "color." An essential part of the replicability of a study of this type

[1] I am extremely grateful to Achsah Carrier for securing several maps that became
available only after my departure from Papua New Guinea.

is to be able to specify exactly the groups one has worked with. Names are a poor guide because these change continuously in Papua New Guinea.

The third chapter represents a review of the literature. This review has a special significance. The previously mentioned economic and staffing constraints meant that we had to "incorporate" the earlier, relevant research into the Indigenous Mathematics Project. We have accepted as given many of the earlier findings, theoretical assumptions, and methods. Even if we could have come up with viable alternatives—and I am not sure we could have—we were constrained by circumstances to make good use of this preexisting foundation. Max Kelly's work stands out in this regard, and the chapter thoroughly reviews his research as well as the theories of Jean Piaget and Jerome Bruner upon which he relied very heavily. Our thinking has taken at least one step forward, however, in the attempt to link theories of cognition to theories of culture. The means of achieving this link is found in a careful analysis of *category formation*. Theoretical strands from several disciplines are woven together to form a kind of backdrop for the description of research that follows. Category formation, then, is a second minor theme that is repeatedly invoked.

Chapter 4 presents what can be called the *core* study. Our basic objective was to "map" cognitive development in Papua New Guinea. I describe the six tests we developed, the selection of subject samples, and the procedure for administering these tests in the first half of the chapter; I describe the results in the second half. Although several different cognitive skills are probed, category formation remains the overarching issue. Testing was carried out in the 10 sites described in Chapter 2. At each site samples of younger–older, schooled–unschooled, and male–female children were selected. The most important finding is that culture accounts for the pattern of results obtained, while age and Western-style education are somewhat less important.

In Chapter 5 I recount our attempts to open the black box of culture. We systematically examine the impact of the indigenous counting system, classification system, game and tool inventories, urban residence, social class, and nutritional status on the results. The data reviewed are again based on the battery of six tests described in Chapter 4. The samples are those drawn in the original 10 sites as well as in sites added to test for urban-residence, social-class, and nutritional-status effects. We find that classification systems and possibly tool inventories as well may have an important influence on cognitive development. Social-class effects are also apparent, while urban-residence and nutritional-status effects are not.

I describe some digressions from the major survey in Chapter 6. These are in-depth studies undertaken in a few of the sites. After the first round of data collection a number of questions arose. We were concerned that our particular selection of tests and samples might have given us a faulty reading of the situation. In particular, our results had indicated that in some of our sites conservation—an important milestone in Piaget's theory of cognitive development—was not achieved. I describe how we extensively varied both the tasks used to measure conservation and the samples. The results confirmed the earlier impression that in some societies conservation is a product of experiences gained in school.

Our initial approach to culture and cognition highlighted the indigenous counting system as an important mediator in cognitive development. The first round of testing had led us to reject this hypothesis (see Chapter 5). However in the Oksapmin society the indigenous counting system, which deviated sharply in structure from the Western pattern, was still heavily relied upon. Geoffrey Saxe was able to exploit this situation in carrying out a series of studies on the acquisition of the indigenous counting system and the relationship between one's ability to use the system and facility with various logical operations, including conservation of number.

In each society we collected data on "folk" category systems. This is an important part of modern ethnography, but our initial results did not accord very well with existing theory. We found that these taxonomic systems varied greatly in depth and complexity from society to society. Working among the Melpa with anthropologist Andrew Strathern, we took an in-depth look at category formation, discovering in the process that the Melpa applied a binary rather than taxonomic structure in organizing items in their environment, and that this discrepancy probably helped to account for the Melpa child's poor performance on our tests, most of which required a taxonomic approach. A third minor theme is introduced in this chapter—namely the relationship between language and thought. An overview of these issues is presented at the beginning of the chapter, and referred to again in Chapters 7 and 8.

In Chapter 7, I review research that has been the primary concern of my colleagues Venina Kada, Rob Roberts, and Randall Souviney. There are four components in this research. First, there is a study of the history of education in Papua New Guinea—in particular, the history of efforts to develop a mathematics curriculum. Second, several national surveys of mathematics achievement were undertaken, and the results indicate some of the factors that might contribute to intranational variation in achievement. Third and fourth, the chapter reviews our attempts to examine in detail two of those factors—cognitive development and the quality of instruction. At the conclusion of the chapter, I list some of the conclusions and recommendations that our research has led to. Essentially we conclude that, whatever differences or deficits the child brings to school, these can be overcome. (The differences, especially, should not be a major concern in the future.) On the other hand, the curriculum is in all probability not the main stumbling block. Properly implemented by dedicated and well-trained teachers supported by an adequate range of materials, it requires only minor modification to enable it to close the gap.

The final chapter is an epilogue. It does not describe subsequent events in Papua New Guinea; this book is quite current on that score. Rather, it relates a number of theoretical developments that have taken place since about 1975 and that are germane to the research reported here. Perhaps the most important of these is *sociobiology*. What sociobiology has done is to give an incredible impetus to cross-species, cross-cultural, and historical comparisons of behavior. Two issues that emerged during the course of the Indigenous Mathematics Project are also beginning to appear in this renewed comparative research: the nature of the subsistence system and the nature of the information load in any society.

This review of recent developments also indicates how far we are from reaching consensus on the assumptions that are permissible in a study of this type. Piagetian theory has been "discovered" by primatologists (e.g., Parker & Gibson, 1979) and cultural anthropologists (e.g., Hallpike, 1979). Meanwhile, some cognitive psychologists have begun a concerted attack on fundamental aspects of Piagetian theory, including the stage (Brainerd, 1978b, 1978c) and structure (LCHC, in press) constructs. I attempt to find a middle ground that retains aspects of cognitive theory that seem to be supported by our data and rejects those that are not. The last chapter, then, begins to set an agenda for IMP–II.

Finally, I would like to alert the reader to what I feel is a major accomplishment of the Indigenous Mathematics Project, over and above the merits of the various studies in cognition and mathematics. I think we have been successful to an unprecedented degree in breaking down two formidable barriers that historically have compartmentalized social-science research—namely the barrier between "pure" and "applied" research and the barrier between anthropology and psychology.

2

The Digging Stick, the Steel Ax, and the Calculator

Papua New Guinea is a living manifestation of Wells's time machine. In half a day one can witness the application of the most advanced Space Age technology (in telecommunications, for example) and the application of a Neolithic technology that has remained unaltered for centuries. It is a nation in transition. The direction is clear, the pace uncertain. The motivating forces are partly international and partly local. Papua New Guineans are in no sense ashamed or rejecting of their roots; yet they are also enthusiastic about the products of the industrialized world.

The Department of Education that initiated, funded, and managed the project reported in this book must play parent to this transition process. It is charged with the responsibility of preparing an equitably selected minority of the nation's citizens to implement a comprehensive array of Western technologies and services, from bridges to art galleries to hospitals to airlines. But it must also prepare the majority of its citizens for life in the village. It must ensure that the lure of the modern does not become so overwhelming that indigenous religious, medical, political, and subsistence practices, which supported, unaided by outsiders, the creation of the "original affluent society" (Sahlins, 1972), are abandoned. The Indigenous Mathematics Project was created with these two conflicting and difficult responsibilities in mind.

The Indigenous Mathematics Project has two broad, complementary aims. First, to study and document the many traditional (or *native*) mathematics systems of Papua New Guinea. Second, to adapt the primary mathematics curriculum to the abilities and knowledge of entering pupils and to the demands placed on them for mathematics fluency in post-primary employment and schooling. Put more simply, the aim is to create a curriculum that *belongs naturally* to Papua New Guinea [Lancy, 1979a, p. 45; italics in original].

The purpose of this chapter is to provide the historical and cultural context for the IMP. The first part of the chapter covers the nation as a whole, and the latter half is devoted to the 10 individual societies in which we concentrated our research.

The wooden digging stick (or dibble) is the ubiquitous instrument of agriculture in Papua New Guinea. Once the forest has been cut and burned, the digging stick is employed in every phase of gardening, from soil preparation through weeding to harvesting. It is ancient and very simple and yet very effective (Golson & Hughes, 1977). It is used in the cultivation of a wide array of crops in an equally wide array of settings. It is symbolic of the incredible longevity and stability of the majority of Papua New Guinea's cultures.

The steel ax—and its cousin, the bush knife—symbolizes the pragmatism that pervades both the old and the new Papua New Guinea. The steel ax was the glue that first bound together the Papua New Guinean and the expatriate. Although warfare and murder were endemic in much of the country (and are still prevalent in some areas), the first Europeans were treated surprisingly well. This is due, at least in part, to their generous wholesaling of steel axes that rapidly replaced the indigenous stone varieties. (In many areas the steel axes *preceded* by decades the first European visitors.) However, as Hughes (see also Strathern, 1971) points out: "In parts of the Highlands, men at first and even second contact often preferred ornaments to steel [1977, p. 12]." With the exception of sago exploitation where stone axes are still used (Ohtsuka, 1977), the steel ax represented a quantum jump in efficiency, and dramatically increased the effectiveness of male woodcutters and warriors. Labor inputs to major subsistence activities involving woodcutting (e.g., felling trees to clear the forest for planting, cutting poles for buildings and stakes to fence gardens) could be substantially reduced. On the other hand, and unlike the situation in Australia (Sharp, 1952), the steel ax was not the opening wedge of vast cultural change in Papua New Guinea (Brookfield & Hart, 1971). Throughout many parts of the country, the steel ax, steel knife, and metal pots have been the only products of Western technology to be adopted and applied to traditional systems. The adoption of new cash and subsistence crops, irrigation, draft animals, sanitation facilities, soil conservation, more permanent housing materials, and so on, has been glacially slow,[1] despite widespread inducements from the government, the missions, and private concerns. The reason, I believe, lies in the fact that virtually all of these additional innovations would require a change in the nature or amount of labor "inputs." Thus at one level, change is occurring slowly, but at another level it is taking place at dizzying speed.

It may well be the case that students at the University of Technology in Lae are more familiar with the operation of scientific calculators than are their instructors: Many of the latter still cling stubbornly to the slide rule. The calculator is symbolic of much that is happening in Papua New Guinea. The use of very advanced technology in many areas is, in some respects, more disconcerting than the grass huts. There are no old cars in Papua New Guinea; the only architectural period represented is "modern." For some time it was easier to reach the United States by phone from PNG than from Australia; dozens of completely illiterate but wealthy coffee-growers from the Highlands have taken "round-the-world" tours. In villages hundreds of kilometers from the nearest road, one finds "trade stores" stocked with the latest cassette recordings of British and American pop music. One could go on and on.

All of this is very deceptive, however, because there is nothing resembling a permanent infrastructure to support it (Lancy, 1980a). The costs of modern goods and services are met by a huge Australian foreign-aid subsidy, the revenue from ultimately exhaustible natural resources (chiefly copper and gold), and the revenue from expatriate-owned plantations whose acreage and output have been declining for a decade. The implementation and maintenance of these high-technology systems have been almost entirely in the hands of expatriates, whose numbers, as a result of "localization" efforts, have been steadily declining. Meanwhile, the output of truly competent technocrats from the universities and technical colleges in Papua New Guinea is quite small, in large part because their foundation knowledge and skills are woefully incomplete (Bishop, 1978). Hence my use of the calculator as symbol of modernizing Papua New Guinea: It is so wonderfully efficient, but what happens when the batteries run down or when there is no function key corresponding to the problem you have to solve?

Prehistory

The majority of the people of Papua New Guinea are descended from migrants from Southeast Asia. (For the following discussion the reader

[1]Excepting, perhaps, coffee in the Highlands (A. J. Strathern, personal communication).

will want to refer to Figure 2.1, which is a map of Papua New Guinea. Figure 2.2 provides a key for this and all the subsequent maps presented in this volume.) During periods of glaciation sea levels fell, and large areas of the Sunda and Sahul shelves (Asia and Australia–New Guinea, respectively) lay exposed. Open-ocean journeys that now appear formidable would have been considerably easier to accomplish on foot and in relatively primitive watercraft. Birdsell (1977) sees the first wave of migrants arriving as early as 40,000 B.P. when the sea level would have been at least 50 m lower than it is today. The first migrants, who probably arrived in small bands over centuries, were Oceanic Negritos. They came from the Malaysian archipelago where relict populations still exist (e.g., the Andaman Islanders). Birdsell sees the New Guinea Highlanders as being very similar physically to these early migrants.

The earliest site so far uncovered in New Guinea (White, Crook, & Buxton, 1970) is at Kosipe, which is presently inhabited by the Tauade people.[2] This site dates from 26,000 B.P., and among the stone tools found there is a "waisted" blade, which is apparently lost from the tool inventory at some point. It does not show up in more recent levels. Since archaeological studies in New Guinea have just begun, earlier sites are expected to be found. Kosipe is located in an isolated, inland mountain valley.

The earliest site in central New Guinea is the Kafiavana Rockshelter near Mount Hagen (White, 1971). The earliest material from the rockshelter is dated at 11,000 B.P. Ax-adzes appear by 9000 B.P., and pig bones by 5000 B.P. Golson (1977) argues that agriculture may have been invented independently in the highlands. In another site in the Hagen vicinity, Golson has found signs of agriculture dating to 9000 B.P. He and his colleagues uncovered evidence that various land-management techniques were employed principally to channel water away from wet areas to render them suitable for planting. This type of land management waxed and waned between 9000 B.P. and 100 B.P. for reasons that are unclear. However, White (1977) makes the point that "from several sites in the Highlands we now have a technological tradition reaching back to the Pleistocene. Within this time span we find a stone technology, which, if anything becomes *less* complex over time [p. 23; italics in original]." One element that very clearly reduced the diversity, if not the complexity, of the subsistence picture was the introduction of the sweet potato (*ipomea* sp.) from South America by way of Polynesia about 400 years ago. The

[2]Very recent discoveries suggest that human beings were present in Papua New Guinea over 60,000 years ago (Groube, Tumbe, & Muke, 1981).

sweet potato is so superior to competing crops (chiefly yam and taro) that it has become the dominant cultivar throughout the Highlands (Powell, 1976).

Outside the Central Highlands, the situation is much more complicated. From about 5000 years ago new settlers began to arrive in small groups. These came also from Southeast Asia, but were Mongoloid rather than Australoid. The location of their settlements in modern PNG can be tentatively located in terms of linguistic criteria. That is, the languges of Papua New Guinea (Würm, 1972) are divided into two broad groups—the Austronesian languages associated with Mongoloid migrants and the non-Austronesian languages associated with the earlier settlers. Not surprisingly, the latter are far more diverse than are the former. Austronesian languages tend to be located in coastal areas. These Austronesian-speaking people, however, intermarried with the existing inhabitants and also with groups migrating west from other parts of Oceania, with the result that modern coastal citizens are impossible to typecast.

This second great migration to the area did bring with it many important new elements including in all probability pottery, several new plants, sailing canoes of an advanced design, and a propensity for trade. These people characteristically established large, permanent villages, in contrast to the small shifting hamlets found in the inland areas (Bellwood, 1979). At the present time the descendants of the Mongoloid migrants occupy one or another of two niches. The majority practice mixed cultivation, meaning that they exploit a variety of ground and tree crops. In many cases this cannot be strictly termed *agriculture*: That is, in the case of tree crops in particular, wild stands are "tended" but not cultivated per se. In some areas wild sago (*metroxlyon* sp.) accounts for up to 70% of the caloric intake (Ohtsuka, 1977). The second niche is occupied by a minority who make most of their living from trade, exchanging marine and manufactured products for starch with inland peoples. Finally, hunting, fishing, and gathering are present everywhere in Papua New Guinea in varying degrees. These activities contribute 10–80% of subsistence, depending on the area.

Although the evidence is scanty, there is nothing to contradict the view that all these subsistence systems have a considerable antiquity (see, for example, Allen, 1977; Kennedy, 1981). In the highlands, fairly minor adjustments to horticultural practices permitted population densities to rise to very high levels (Brown & Brookfield, 1963). In other parts of the country, warfare kept population levels low—much of coastal and lowland Papua New Guinea is uninhabited or sparsely settled. The only profund changes that have occurred in the last few hundred years appear to be the

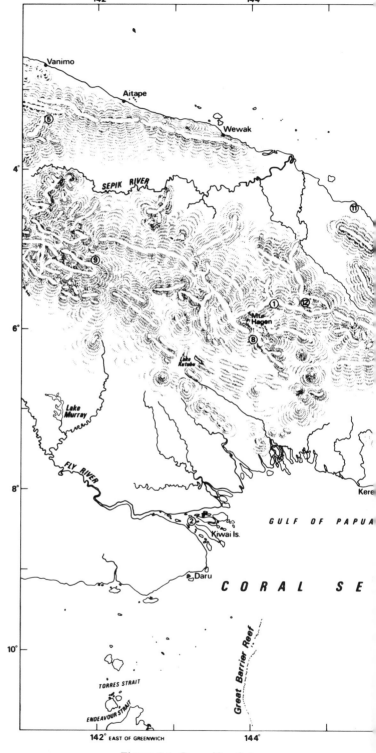

Figure 2.1. Papua New Guinea.

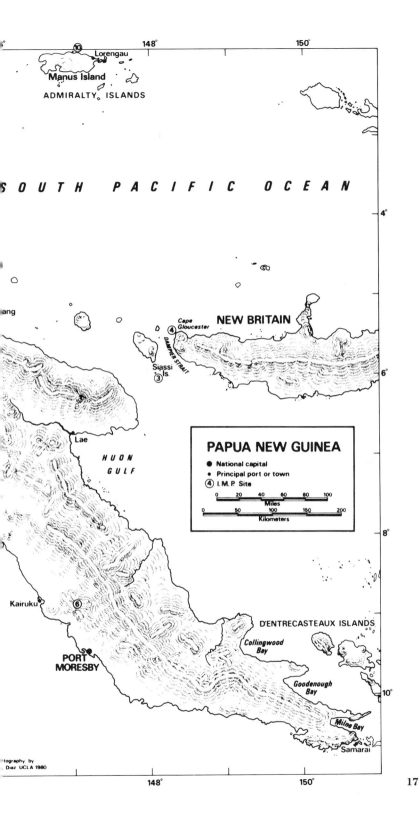

148°

150°

⑩ Lorengau

Manus Island

ADMIRALTY ISLANDS

S O U T H   P A C I F I C   O C E A N

4°

ang

Cape Gloucester

NEW BRITAIN

④

DAMPER STRAIT

Siassi Is. ③

6°

Lae

H U O N
G U L F

PAPUA NEW GUINEA

● National capital

• Principal port or town

④ I.M.P. Site

| 0 | 20 | 40 | 60 | 80 | 100 |
Miles

| 0 | 50 | 100 | 150 | 200 |
Kilometers

8°

Kairuku

⑥

D'ENTRECASTEAUX ISLANDS

Collingwood Bay

PORT MORESBY

Goodenough Bay

10°

Milne Bay

Samarai

148°

150°

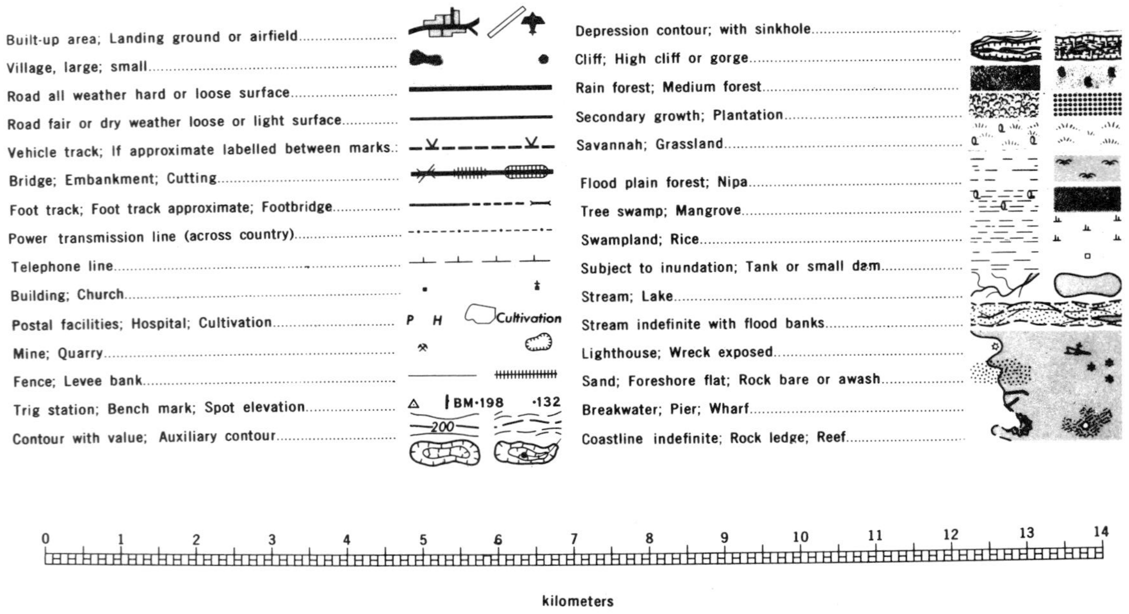

Built-up area; Landing ground or airfield..........
Village, large; small..........
Road all weather hard or loose surface..........
Road fair or dry weather loose or light surface..........
Vehicle track; If approximate labelled between marks.
Bridge; Embankment; Cutting..........
Foot track; Foot track approximate; Footbridge..........
Power transmission line (across country)..........
Telephone line..........
Building; Church..........
Postal facilities; Hospital; Cultivation..........
Mine; Quarry..........
Fence; Levee bank..........
Trig station; Bench mark; Spot elevation..........
Contour with value; Auxiliary contour..........

P   H   Cultivation

△   BM·198   ·132

200

Depression contour; with sinkhole..........
Cliff; High cliff or gorge..........
Rain forest; Medium forest..........
Secondary growth; Plantation..........
Savannah; Grassland..........
Flood plain forest; Nipa..........
Tree swamp; Mangrove..........
Swampland; Rice..........
Subject to inundation; Tank or small dam..........
Stream; Lake..........
Stream indefinite with flood banks..........
Lighthouse; Wreck exposed..........
Sand; Foreshore flat; Rock bare or awash..........
Breakwater; Pier; Wharf..........
Coastline indefinite; Rock ledge; Reef..........

0   1   2   3   4   5   6   7   8   9   10   11   12   13   14

kilometers

Figure 2.2. Legend for maps.

18

shift to wage employment in urban centers and cash-cropping.[3] In urban centers, imported foods substitute almost completely for locally grown or caught varieties, and in the village purchased foods supplement rather than substitute for staple foods. Subsistence systems have not been notably intensified to feed urban areas, nor have they been diversified in response to the introduction of new technologies.[4]

Recent History

New Guinea lay outside the orbits of all the high civilizations of Africa, Asia, Europe, and South America. Contact had to wait for the age of European exploration—a scant 300 years ago. Owing to geography and the hostility of indigenous people, the island presented formidable barriers to penetration by all but the most intrepid. The diaries of the early explorers are tales of incredible hardship and endurance (e.g., D'Albertis, 1880; Mikloucho-Maclay, 1975).

It was not until the 1880s that Germany and Great Britain established colonies in the northern and southern halves of present-day Papua New Guinea. These were established more as moves in the great colonial chess game than for any hope of gain. Papua New Guinea has almost certainly operated at a substantial loss—politically as well as economically—for all of its colonial overseers. The main objective of the early colonialists was pacification—to protect the lives of the handful of white gold miners, traders, missionaries, and planters. Their secondary objective was to suppress endemic intervillage warfare and raiding. Newly federated Australia inherited the Papuan colony from Great Britain in 1906, and attempts were made to establish plantations. However, these were not too successful, and the reason for this holds as well today as it did then: "Any products that could be grown in Papua could be produced more easily elsewhere and arrive at the main markets costing less [Griffen, Nelson, & Firth, 1979, p. 25]." Things did not go much better in German New Guinea: "After they had replaced their stone axes and obtained cloth and beads for decoration they began to lose interest in working for Europeans [p. 35]." Nevertheless, for most Papua New Guineans the first (and in many cases only) exposure to a wage economy, to people from other

[3]There are a few important exceptions like the Daribi, for example (Wagner, 1967), where basic subsistence patterns have changed in the last 100 years.

[4]The introduction of shotguns probably results in a brief intensification of hunting until the immediate area is denuded of fauna, leading to an ultimate decline in the contribution of hunting to subsistence.

regions, to European clothing, and other artifacts took place during brief periods of contract labor on coastal plantations.

Although contacts between the aboriginal inhabitants and white intruders were often violent, with the majority of casualties incurred by the former group, and although many natives were forced to work on roads and plantations at low wages, the colonial administration was quite benign. Hubert Murray was the first colonial administrator, and he set the tone for the entire region and for his successors. He was, by all accounts (West, 1968), extremely progressive, as was his German counterpart Albert Hahl. Circumstances also played a role. Missionaries had the upper hand in political affairs. The race to conscript souls by dozens of different sects began in the 1870s, and it continues to this day. Expropriation of land and forced labor were at odds with the overriding aim of pacifying the country so that missionaries could safely establish remote outposts and claim new territory. The original inhabitants, for their part, welcomed the missions because they purveyed two commodities that were in great demand—"cargo" (e.g., material goods) and strong magic to protect one from sorcery. Later of course, Papua New Guineans took matters into their own hands to increase the flow of cargo and the strength of the magic, and they created dozens of new sects (Worsley, 1968).

Following World War II, the pace of change increased somewhat, when Papua and New Guinea were united under Australian trusteeship. For the first time, truly national institutions began to emerge. However, the creation of a House of Assembly in 1964 with freely elected representatives (a majority of whom were native) only served to underscore the vast regional disparity in opportunities for wage-earning and *bisnis*. In particular, the inhabitants in and around the major towns of Port Moresby, Lae, Rabaul, and Madang were in a far better position to take advantage of the increased opportunities offered by the Australian administration than were other groups. Expatriates in the administration have worked very hard to rectify the accidents of history, but of the 29,000 civil servants in 1976, 46% were from the Papuan coast, which has 20% of the country's population, while 11% were from the highlands, which have 38% of the country's population.[5] Self-government arrived in 1973 and independence

---

[5]Secessionist movements have constantly threatened this fragile new nation. The most ironic, if not the most extreme, has been the Papua Besena Movement led by Josephine Abijah. The movement aims to secede the Papuan region (south coast of eastern New Guinea) on the grounds of exploitation by people from the rest of the country. However, the region has benefited most from the economic development of the country and contributed least. The region has no significant cash-earning exports—neither plantations nor mines, while the location of the capital in Port Moresby has meant that people from the region have gotten the lion's share of the white-collar jobs in the country.

in 1975. The first chief minister (later prime minister) was Michael Somare, whose plea to his countrymen was "accept our old traditional values but, at the same time, adapt easily to an alien electronic age of the twentieth century [quoted in Griffen, Nelson, & Firth, 1979, p. 275]."

Indigenous Mathematics Project Sites

I will defer to the next chapter a full discussion of the conceptual issues that guided the creation of the Indigenous Mathematics Project. Suffice it to say that previous research had indicated that cognitive development might be expected to vary from society to society, and this variation might, in turn, help to account for uneven performance in school mathematics. The overriding goal behind our selection of sites was to create a representative[6] sample of the main strands of cultural diversity in Papua New Guinea. A second goal was to sample from proponents of the four main counting systems operative in Papua New Guinea. I think we were successful at attaining both these goals, but in the final analysis pragmatic considerations played a large role. As I began to set up the project in 1976, two researchers sought me out and asked to be included. These were Hilary Pumuye from the Ialibu area, which became our first site, and Agnes Paliau from Ponam Island, which became our second site (Lancy, 1978a). Most of the other sites were added in a similar manner as researchers sought me out or vice versa.[7]

[6]Physical isolation and the absence of a money economy were also important criteria. Not one of the villages where we conducted our research is accessible by road. The villages can be reached only by a long arduous hike and/or a costly and uncertain trip by a single-engine plane and/or chartered boat. Any hardship this may have imposed on us was more than compensated for by the incredible generosity and kindness bestowed on us wherever we happened to "drop in."

[7]The brief descriptions that follow cannot be treated as primary data. It was not possible to undertake a full-scale ethnography in each of the IMP sites. Even where contemporaneous ethnography was undertaken, the aims of the ethnographer were usually quite distinct from the aims of the IMP (e.g., Zelenietz, 1980). My strategy, rather, was to involve ethnographers and linguists to as full an extent as possible in the design and execution of our more limited inquiries. Equally important, every IMP paper, report, and publication—including this book—has been sent to colleagues with a more complete knowledge of the languages and societies under study for their comments and corrections.

The Melpa

The Melpa represent in many ways the prototypical Highlands group. They occupy the very large Waghi Valley at altitudes of 1400–2800 m located in the central portion of the Highlands (see Figure 2.3). There are some 60,000 speakers of the Melpa language, which has many affinities with other languages in the area, including Imbonggu (Würm, 1964). They participated in prehistoric trade links to the northeast, east, south, and northwest (Hughes, 1977). Many prominent features of the Highland cultural complex are brought to a kind of apogee by the Melpa, including the big-man syndrome. Our study concentrated on groups in the northern Melpa area. These people have not suffered greatly from the impact of outsiders.

The Melpa have been gardeners for at least 6000 years, and they have raised pigs for nearly as long (Powell, Kulunga, Moge, Pono, Zimike, & Golson, 1975). Over that period of time they have learned to exploit many varieties of their principal staples—yam, taro, sugar cane, and bananas. About 400 years ago, or earlier, they adopted sweet-potato cultivation, which was relegated the other starchy cultivars to such marginal positions as "foods for special occasions," "famine foods," "medicinal foods," and so on. Gardens are located in the vicinity of dispersed hamlets of 3–10 houses, which are separated by gender. That is, there are men's and women's houses, with the latter being inhabited by children as well as pigs. Garden ground is prepared by men who must clear and fence the plot, often working in unison with other men. A large plot may then be subdivided into many individual gardens. These gardens are meticulously prepared and planted, and sweet-potato gardens in particular are usually bisected by shallow drainage ditches arranged in a rectilinear grid. Possibly only the Chimbu, who live to the east, garden as intensively as the Melpa. Mixed gardens are planted in soil that has fallowed for 5–20 years. After this initial garden has been harvested, sweet-potato gardens are planted in succession. As the soil weakens, mounds are made to concentrate the humus, and sweet potatoes are planted in these. The sweet potato is the main comestible for both pigs and humans (Powell *et al*, 1975).

The Melpa strive to produce a surplus that is converted by way of the *moka* into prestige (Strathern, 1971). *Moka* is the name given to the endless round of ceremonial exchanges between rival big-men over a wide area. The main outlines of the *moka* are that an aspiring big-man makes a prestation or gift to a big-man from another group. This man, then, must make a return gift that is larger than the initial gift at some later point in time. Otherwise, he loses prestige. The gifts are principally pigs and gold-

Figure 2.3. The Melpa.

lipped pearl shells (*Pinctada maxima*) set in an ocher-dyed hard-resin plaque. At a typical *moka*, pigs and shells both number in the hundreds. Because the big-man owns only so much property, he must augment his holdings by several orders of magnitude to make a gift. To do this he calls on his fellow clansmen, his affines, and other supporters for donations. The recipient of *moka*, on the other hand, distributes his gifts to those who have helped him make *moka* in the past. A successful *moka* brings prestige to the individual big-man and to the group that supported him.

Moka is accompanied by a "sing-sing" where further opportunities exist for the leaders and their groups to display their finery, wealth, fierceness, and numbers. (I shall discuss the sing-sing in some detail in the section on the Kewa; for the Melpa, the reader is referred to the 1971 publication by Strathern and Strathern.)

Exchange ceremonies similar to the *moka*, but usually on a smaller scale, take place in connection with the forging of alliances prior to warfare, compensation payments made following death in war, murder and sorcery, and bride-price payments preceding marriage. Here too are avenues to enhanced prestige for those who lead the negotiations and arrangements. Consequently, high-status Melpa men spend the greater part of their time in discussion and debate with their peers. These discussions, to a Westerner, are part business, part politics, part gossip, part religion, and part military tactics. Men, women, and, to a much lesser extent, children of lower status are the foundation on which the society rests. They carry primary responsibility for gardening, the provision of shelter, cooking, and pig husbandry. With reference to the latter, pigs are cooked and eaten en masse during the infrequent exchange ceremonies; hence the daily diet is quite low in protein (see Chapter 5).

The Melpa were first contacted in 1933 by the Leahy–Taylor expedition (Hughes, 1977). They found no items of European manufacture in evidence—the main symbols of wealth being then, as now, shells and pigs. The Melpa willingly traded for steel axes, but they preferred shells, especially baler (*Melo* sp.) and gold-lipped pearl shells. Strathern (1971) reports the remarks of one of his informants to the effect that the Melpa at first thought the explorers were the pale-faced cannibals of Melpa myth until they started trading shells for pigs. Then they knew they were human. The large influx of such shells during the succeeding 10 years caused severe inflation. During the World War II period, contact was broken off, and it was not resumed in earnest before the establishment of coffee plantations in the area, beginning in 1960. Coffee first became available in substantial amounts in the 1970s just when prices sky-rocketed worldwide. Hence, huge, unaccustomed amounts of cash flowed into the region—more so as royalty payments for expropriated clan lands than wages. This cash has been spent overwhelmingly on two commodities, beer and travel. Not much need be said about the former: It is a worldwide phenomenon, although Highlanders, more often than not, become aggressive rather than maudlin when they drink. Therefore violence has escalated beyond precontact levels in some areas. With respect to travel, the effects are bound to be more profound in the long run. Mount Hagen airport has become one of the busiest in the country, and the majority of the passengers are villagers on their way to visit the major towns of Port Moresby, Rabaul, Lae, and points farther afield. There are more vehicles per capita in the region than almost anywhere else in the nonindustrialized world, and they see heavy service since the Wahgi Valley is now crisscrossed by dirt tracks (and one major east–west road, much of which is paved), going in all directions.

Fortunately for the student of the Melpa, Ongka—one of the premier big-men—has produced a glowing autobiography, which was taped and edited by Andrew Strathern (1979). The work illustrates how effective the Melpa have been in turning aside and diffusing the thrusts of the modern world, as when Ongka, to cap his career, includes a fully licensed and paid-for Toyota Landcruiser with the more traditional wealth he gives away in a 1974 *moka*. It is as if the vast edifice of Western civilization, which Ongka has had ample opportunity to sample in visits to Port Moresby, amounts to no more than a supply of novel wealth objects, whose value is only realized in giving them away.

The Melpa response to *gaviman* (*Tok Pisin* = government) and mission inducements to change their way of life has been characterized by ambivalence. On the one hand, there have been entreaties to the government for more development. On the other hand, we heard a litany of complaints about the villagers' resistance to change from the principal and teachers at the Golke Community School, when we first visited the area to begin testing. The school is situated on a high narrow plateau, one of the few areas around that is level. The "sports field" is often taken over for community meetings: A murder-compensation conclave was in progress during one of our visits. The school was established in 1970; it was burned down in 1975 and has seen fitful service ever since. Attendance is poor, especially by females. One gets the impression that teachers and students alike come to some tacit agreement in the early grades as to who will get an education. The rest are just along for the ride; hence the de facto student body is small indeed. The government's policy of only admitting the top 30% of the Grade 6 class to high school probably contributes to this situation as well.

Whether or not to attend school is a difficult decision for all parties. Schooling is seen as a purely economic proposition (see Chapter 7).

Parents pay school fees, and children are sent to school only insofar as they can be expected to continue up the academic ladder far enough to land a white-collar job and then send part of their wages home. The odds are very long—especially for girls—and enrollment statistics bear out the parents' pragmatic inclinations. For children the choice is equally difficult. The drudgery of work in the garden is not much less than the drudgery of schoolwork. In fact many schools have gardens (Golke is not one of these) in which students are expected to work. If it rains, gardeners stay home; students trudge up to 5 km over mountain trails to school; and given the cool air, the scanty clothing, the heavy rainfall, and the unheated school buildings, one's motivation must be very powerful to press on with formal education. It is certainly the case that there are virtually no jobs available for anyone without postsecondary training. Hence a few years of schooling are of little use to the individual or his or her parents. There are no shops, offices, clinics, farms, or garages in Golke to utilize a supply of semiskilled labor.

Kiwai

Our study area in the Fly River region was the northwestern tip of 100-km-long Kiwai Island (see Figure 2.4). The island lies in the delta of the Fly River, and is the center of the Kiwaian language family, which has about 22,000 speakers. The island itself has a population of around 3000 who have their own distinctive dialect (Würm, 1973). Where the principal feature of the Melpa landscape is mountains, in Kiwai it is water. In addition to the river itself, Kiwai and other islands in the delta, as well as the surrounding plain, are flooded for much of the year. Single-hull dugouts are the dominant mode of transportation, and early accounts by explorers in small boats that met dozens of these canoes filled with painted and heavily armed warriors could have been written in Hollywood. Nevertheless, the area had an irresistable lure for adventurers of various kinds at the turn of the century. James Chalmers of the London Missionary Society succeeded in establishing a station on the island in 1892, but he was subsequently killed and eaten on nearby Goaribari Island. By 1920 the mother-of-pearl and bech-de-mer industries in the Torres Strait islands had declined completely, and the whole region, including Kiwai Island, lapsed into splendid isolation once again. Profound changes in the Kiwai way of life had already taken place, however, Kiwai society was effectively stripped of many of its more spectacular and characteristic customs. These included a highly ritualized pattern of warfare and murder, and high buildings (e.g., 154 m long × 9.5 m wide) that served

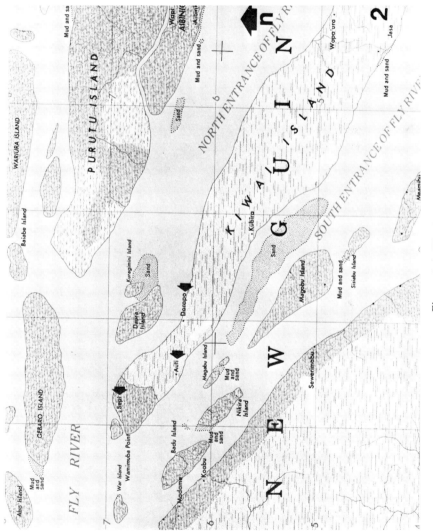

Figure 2.4. Kiwai.

27

simultaneously as a dwelling place and fort for the entire village (Landt-man, 1927). Each nuclear family had its own fireplace and eating and sleeping area within the communal long house (*moto*). These can be seen elsewhere in the region, but they have disappeared from Kiwai Island. One reason for their abandonment may be related to the custom whereby new long houses had to be consecrated with the blood and skulls of freshly slain enemies. At the turn of the century, the area was forcefully "pacified" by police patrols.

It is apparent, however, that the traditional technology of the Kiwai was fairly complex, and, excepting the realm of weapons, this is still true today. They have the most varied subsistence system of the IMP sites. Among their cultivars are the sweet potato (4 varieties), coconut (5), taro (1), banana (17), sago (14), sugar cane (1), and miscellaneous fruits and vegetables (24). Their exploitation of local fauna is equally varied; the area is a paradise for birds, and they have access to riverine, estuarial, and marine resources (Smith, 1978). The hunting of turtle and crocodile in particular require fairly elaborate technologies and complex social organizations. These resources are further augmented during frequent trading expeditions. This bounty is not utilized entirely for subsistence; prestation is practiced, however: "Among the Kiwai people there exists no difference of rank whatever [Landtman, 1927, p. 167]."

Villages are fairly large, each housing several hundred inhabitants. Houses are raised high on stilts to keep the contents dry, and raised beds are used for pathways and dry-land gardens. Schools are well built, having been established 10–15 years ago when government and mission support was more ample. The majority of teachers are Kiwai-speakers; hence the vernacular is regularly used in classes. There is no hostility toward education on the island, nor is there much enthusiasm either. Attendance in school beyond the second grade is largely a matter for the children themselves to decide. Children have a great deal of autonomy in general, and their stock of games is quite varied. We picked the Kiwai Island site because of Geoff Smith's knowledge of the language (Smith, 1978) and because they utilize a fairly rare Type II counting system (see Chapter 5). Unfortunately the ethnographic material that is available is quite dated.[8]

[8] Geoff Smith has sent me the following capsule summary of the current situation:

The present day village economy is still largely a subsistence one. Sago palms abound and this is the staple, together with bananas, taro, etc. There are plenty of barramundi and other fish around, but the absence of a freezer means that these too are only for subsistence needs. Some processed sago and crabs are sold in Daru market, but the journey from Kiwai Island, especially the northern tip is a long journey, often two days by canoe, and the sea is frequently too rough to make the journey, especially during the mid-year South-east trade winds. The villages are probably all now suffering from depopulation. Apart from the mud and mosquitoes, there are problems with erosion in many villages. The high mud banks are continually falling into the water due to the powerful,

Mandok Island

We have the opposite problem with Mandok: The ethnographic record is so fresh that it is still not published (see Figure 2.5). I am referring to the fieldwork undertaken by my colleague Alice Logan between 1979– 1981. Nevertheless, from her letters and field reports I can piece together at least a partial picture of life on Mandok. Seventeen hundred Mandok-speaking people live on six coral sand cays that lie just south and east of the high island of Umboi. The Mandok are opportunists. Occupying the barren "out" islands, they are situated at the center of a far-flung trading network (Harding, 1967; Sahlins, 1972). They utilize their manufacturing, seafaring, and trading skills to achieve an enviable standard of living. Specifically, men carve magnificient wood bowls, masks, drums, canoes, and paddles, which are in great demand in the region for use in bride-price exchanges, religious ceremonies, and for more utilitarian purposes (see Figure 2.6). Women make shell jewelry that is held in equally high regard. The Mandok are also accomplished fishermen, and they have, historically, traded part of their catch to the people of Umboi, who are gardeners. In more recent times (e.g., since 1920 when the area was pacified), the people on Mandok Island itself (population 435) have begun to make their own mixed gardens on Umboi and to exploit sago stands directly. By all accounts, they are indifferent gardeners.

In common with the Melpa, the Mandok do recognize the status of big-men, which is similarly enhanced by hosting, on a smaller scale, feasting and dancing. However, there is a wider array of avenues to success, in keeping with the increased division of labor on Mandok. There are roles for specialists in carving, the proper arrangement of rituals and cere-monies, and trading.

On Mandok Island houses are concentrated in a small area in the center. Other parts of the island are reserved for tree-crop cultivation and men's-society activities. An adjacent sand cay (*Por*) houses the Catholic mission and the community school. The surrounding area is entirely under Lutheran control, but Lutheran influence on Mandok was short lived. They threw out the missionaries rather than give up their customs. Much later, they observed from visits to Kilenge that the Catholics (a mission was

---

shifting currents with the loss of trees and houses. A considerable amount of time has been spent in Sepe village repeatedly rebuilding houses further from the shore. Many villagers have now settled in the "corners" on Daru Island and there is a large community in Port Moresby in the Kila Kila "horse camp." Life in these squatter settlements is frequently far from idyllic, with alcoholism, gambling and lack of food and hygiene facilities contributing to the problems. The Provincial Government does not seem to have done much for the area. The most important outside influence is probably the Catholic Mission at Samari in the south of the island.

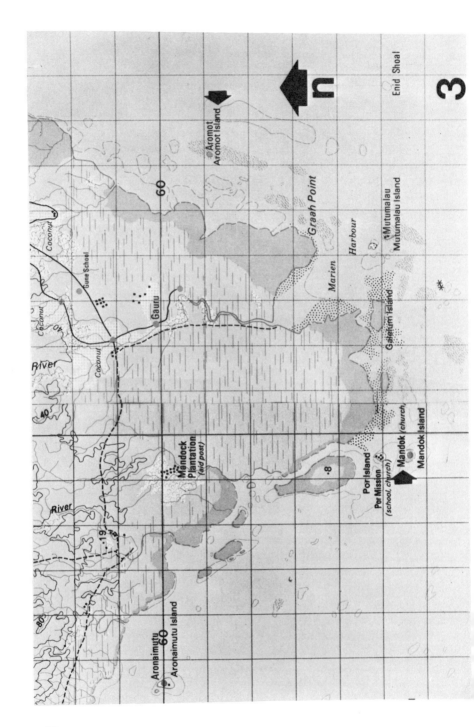

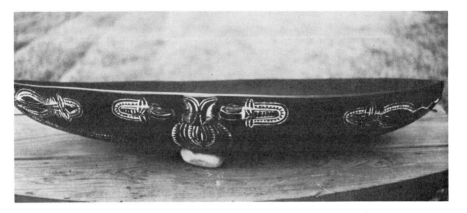

Figure 2.6. Mandok carved bowl.

first established there in 1929) made no attempt to destroy traditional practices. Therefore the Mandok invited the Catholics to establish a mission in their midst. Their faith was not misplaced. The Catholic priests (who tend to remain at their posts for decades in contrast to the relatively short terms of many other missionaries) have done much to aid the people in preserving their culture, especially in terms of their artwork and dances.

Relations with the central government in general and the education system in particular have been far less harmonious. As I will describe in Chapter 7, there was a brief period after Western-style schooling was first implemented in PNG when students could expect both a high-quality education and the guarantee of a high-paying permanent job upon completion of their studies. The Mandok fully exploited these opportunities, because commitment to formal schooling was very strong. When the first children went through the school system in the mid-1950s they did extremely well academically, and later, economically. Later the quality of schooling declined, jobs became scarce, fees were imposed, and interest in schooling plummeted. By 1974, few parents were sending their children away from the area to attend high schools or vocational schools. And those few students who did go away were not completing their studies. As a consequence of economy measures, since about 1977 boarding students have had to grow their own food. Therefore, many of the Mandok dropouts complained about having to work harder to earn their basic subsistence at school than at home.

The governments's hope that many of those who return to the village will be caught up in new business ventures is also unlikely to be fulfilled. Numerous "projects" have been started on Mandok, such as copra production, carving for tourists, operating a commercial trading vessel, etc. All have failed rapidly. People are unwilling to make a continued investment of either labor or capital in these projects. They cannot sustain anything like a 40-hour week without a weekly paycheck on the one hand, and on the other, when payment for goods or services arrives in a fairly large lump sum the individual recipient must quickly distribute it to avoid arousing the envy of kin and peers. This last aspect of life on Mandok is absolutely typical of all of our sites, and it helps to explain why, despite fairly long periods of Western contact in some cases (like Mandok), so little technological change has taken place.

Kilenge

The Kilenge are major trading partners of the Mandok (Harding, 1967), and the two partners have exchanged goods, food, brides, and ceremonies (Grant & Zelenietz, 1978; Zelenietz & Grant, 1980a). But their basic life-style is very different (see Figure 2.7).

The Kilenge number approximately 1000, and they live in three contiguous villages that stretch approximately 4 km along the coast (Zelenietz, 1980). Houses are laid out in two parallel rows set about 60–100 m back from the shoreline. Inland from the beach, the ground slopes gradually upward, then more markedly upward at the base of Mount Talawe. The range in altitude creating many microclimates and the frequent dusting with volcanic ash from Talawe affords the Kilenge a rich resource for their mixed slash-and-burn horticulture. Although taro is the staple, they exploit a great variety of tended and cultivated plants. During the long rains, they gather wild yams and cassavas. Thus, unlike Mandok, life in Kilenge revolves around gardening and pig husbandry rather than fishing and trade. They use the sea only to a limited extent for gathering on the reef at low tide. Net fishing has been introduced recently, but it is rarely practiced. A surplus of produce, pigs, and dogs are raised for trade for manufactured articles (e.g., bowls from Mandok, baskets from the Lolo people in the interior) and for consumption during ceremonies.

The Kilenge have a rich ceremonial life (Zelenietz & Grant, 1980a). These center on the men's house or *naulum*, but they are undertaken for specific purposes: for example, by a man wishing to enhance his prestige, or by a group of men wishing to have their children initiated. The ceremonies are usually named, and they may occur in cycles. The principal public manifestations of a ceremony are the appearance of costumed men wearing elaborate headdresses, beating drums, and singing and dancing. Other ceremonies may involve only one or two more

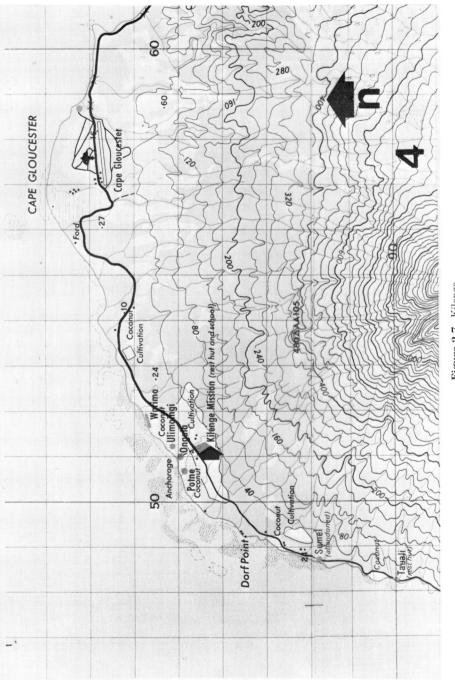

Figure 2.7. Kilenge.

elaborately "headdressed" or masked dancers. Dances are accompanied by huge feasts to which both near and far (e.g., non-Kilenge) neighboring groups are invited.[9]

The vigor with which the Kilenge maintain their ceremonies is at least partly due to the live-and-let-live attitude of the Catholic church. The mission is in fact somewhat removed from the villages, and interest in Christianity among the Kilenge apparently peaked many years ago and has been declining ever since (Zelenietz, 1980). A similar phenomenon must have occured vis-à-vis the school. Like the church, the community school is situated some distance from the villages. Of the 190 children who had shown up at the school long enough to have been "enrolled," only 90 were in attendance in June 1977, and this number had shrunk to 34 by the end of the school year in November (Zelenietz & Grant, 1980b).

Much Kilenge land is planted in coconut (*cocos nucifera* sp.) palms, ostensibly for the production of copra (dried coconut), but they find this type of work "inherently boring, if not blatantly anti-social [Grant, 1980, p. 14]." The Kilenge prefer to earn cash in the form of wages for working on the plantations or as unskilled laborers in East New Britain (Grant & Zelenietz, 1980). This pattern of short-term cyclical out-migration is practiced only by the Toaripi among the IMP sites. Wages earned are not remitted as cash; what is earned is consumed in subsistence and in the purchase of goods not available in the village. Ties between the town and village are strong, and the returnee is always welcome. Grant and Zelenietz (1980) have pointed out that "they pursue a rural oriented strategy in town. They judge their own and other people's actions in terms of village norms. They associate primarily with fellow Kilenge whose actions they can understand and predict [p. 232]."

Imonda

We tested Waris-speaking children at the Imonda site. However, the Waris people are virtually undocumented in Papua New Guinean ethnography (see Figure 2.8). Only quite recently has their language begun to be recorded by Bob Brown of the Summer Institute of Linguistics. Fortunately, however, the Waris appear to replicate the overall pattern and many details of Umeda society, which has been the subject of recent, thorough study (Gell, 1973, 1975). The Umedas are close neighbors (7.5 km apart), and the two groups speak mutually intelligible dialects. This was confirmed through my own observations and interviews with Father

---

[9]For an outstanding visual record of Kilenge art and dance, see Dark (1974).

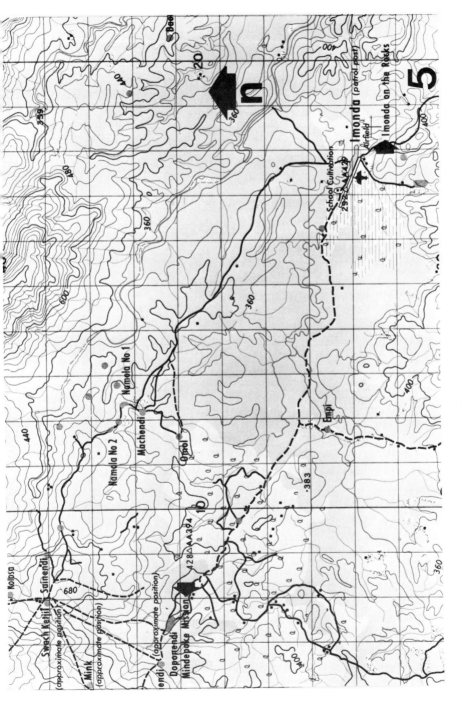

Figure 2.8. Imonda.

Graham and other long-term residents of Imonda. Henceforth I will speak, therefore, of *Imondas*, a term used locally that includes both these groups.

The Imondas are one of the few groups in Papua New Guinea that depend almost entirely on hunting and gathering for subsistence. They do grow a few crops in poorly developed gardens, but I suspected that this activity began recently. My hunch was confirmed by Brown that the only Waris garden-food term not borrowed from a neighboring language—presumably along with the food itself—would be *na* or sago. Women and children gather and process wild foodstuffs of various kinds, the principal starch being derived from the sago palm (see Townsend, 1974, for a description of the cultivation–gathering process that applies to Imonda very well). An important protein source is the larvae or grubs from several species of beetle (family Cerambyidae) that deposit their eggs in fallen sago trunks. The diet is augmented and enlivened by the occasional addition of wild pig. The Imonda have no domestic pigs as such, although they may raise an infant captured in the wild. Men hunt wild pig in the forests and swamps with well-made black-palm bows and arrows. Hunting, in fact, appears to be the major preoccupation of males.

There is ample evidence that the area was inundated by the sea until fairly recently—in geologic terms. Limestone outcroppings abound, and as one flies over the area, patches of brilliant white limestone appear like scars in the otherwise uniformly green swamp and forest. The terrain is very low in altitude, of course, with hillocks and the occasional mountain range. The Imondas live a dual existence. The Imonda village ("Imonda-on-the-rocks") itself is perched on a rocky outcrop that rises about 350 m from the plain. Houses are arranged to back onto the sheer precipice that marks the perimeter of their "island." The center is left largely open. Access is by a steep winding track that terminates abruptly in a staked palisade. The threat of attack from enemies must still be very strong. Houses are built very sturdily and are raised above the ground. The compact well-maintained village contrasts with the semipermanent camps that the Imonda construct in the bush. More time is actually spent in the latter, and Gell reports that the common response to threats of sorcery and murder are to retreat into the bush until the threat lessens. Sorcery is ubiquitous in PNG, but it plays a very large role in the lives of the Imonda people. This seems to be consistent with the acephalous nature of social organization; rank is absent, as are all forms of trade, exchange, blood payment, bride price, and other common Papua New Guinean institutions. Gell (1973) maintains that the only force that mitigates the perpetual atmosphere of antagonism between groups is the various rituals and ceremonies—a situation we find paralleled among the Tauade (Hallpike, 1977).

Life is precarious in Imonda. Aside from a generally poor diet (p. 134) and high incidence of disease, infanticide, sorcery, raiding, and open warfare take a heavy toll. Gell (1973) was unable to find a single case of three living generations in his genealogical studies. Life expectancy must be around 40 years.

The Imonda patrol post, on which is located the Imonda Community School, was one of our two testing centers, and was established in 1966. The other was at Wassengla (Mindepoke Mission Station). Some years later Imondas were first conscripted to work on coastal plantations, but they never went willingly, apparently. Many "escaped" before their contracts had expired. Mission schools were established about the same time, and Gell (1973) makes the observation that "it was the form rather than the substance of these skills which was transmitted . . . writing was a ritual activity . . . maths was still more of a performance [p. 26]." Government schools were erected in about 1973, and the situation has improved considerably. School buildings are more substantial, teachers are far better trained, and the supply of materials is more varied.

Tauade

Our site for research among Tauade-speaking people was the Kerau Mission, which opened in 1939 and is run by the Fathers of the Sacred Heart, two of whom have been in residence for nearly 25 years (see Figure 2.9). The mission and Community School occupy one of the few level areas of any size (an airstrip built in 1967 occupies another) in what is otherwise a vertical landscape. The Tauade make their livelihood from gardens and pigs. The former are strategically located at various elevations from 1000 (the Aibela River valley bottom) to 2500 m to take advantage of subtle shifts in climate with altitude. Yams, bananas, and taros are grown on the lower slopes, sweet potatoes on the middle and upper slopes, and pandanus stands are tended at the highest elevations. They achieve this varied and apparently adequate diet with a technology that is extremely primitive, according to Hallpike (1977); even their stone adze-heads were imported. Gardening and pig husbandry are largely the responsibility of women and children. Men are responsible for erecting large temporary villages, and for making other arrangements for periodic "sing-sings" and ceremonials. Their practice of tethering long lines of pigs to stakes for display purposes is also common to the Highlands, and

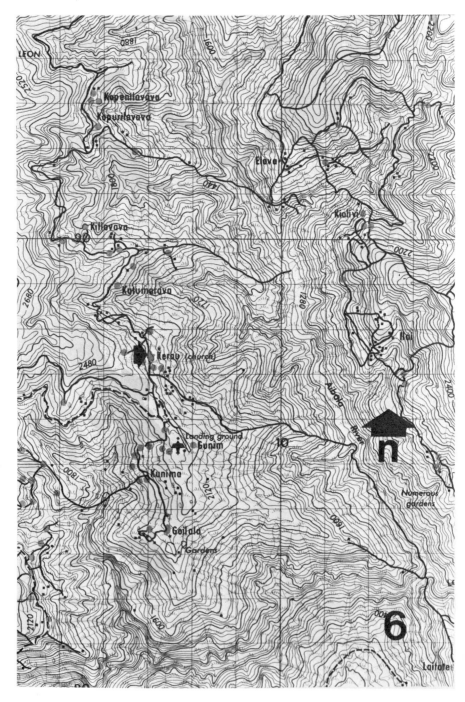

Figure 2.9. Tauade.

Hallpike sees more affinities—specifically based on blood-group analyses–to Highland societies in Tauade culture than to the more accessible Papuan coastal societies. My own admittedly cursory study of their language points, nevertheless, to coastal origins. Hallpike also says that Tauade leaders are hereditary chiefs rather than big-men. Therefore what we may have is a rich admixture of coastal and Highland characteristics.

The Tauade people are dispersed sparsely over a wide area. Hallpike found hamlet sizes varied from 3 to 42 individuals with a median of 12 (see Figure 2.10). There has been a significant degree of out-migration that is not cyclical, however. The Tauade constitute a recognizable (some say "notorious") subpopulation in Port Moresby. I use the term *notorious* because they are perceived (and crime statistics show this is an accurate perception) (Hallpike, 1977) as being extremely violent and dangerous. The theme of murder and retaliation pervades Hallpike's description of the Tauade, and it was my impression that the level of violence had, if anything, escalated in the 5 years intervening between Hallpike's study in 1972 and ours in 1977 (see also Madsen & Lancy, 1981).

Endemic violence may account in part for the inability of the Tauade—like the Kiwai—to capitalize on a period of early (circa 1911) and fairly intensive contact to propel themselves beyond their prehistoric technological and economic base. "Modernization" peaked about 15 years ago, and it has been declining steadily ever since. A sawmill, gardening for export to Port Moresby, and other money-making schemes, which were viable at one time, have completely ceased. Vehicle tracks, some dating from the 1940s, are no longer passable.

Government schools dot the area, and some have respectable histories. The existence of well-built and reasonably well-staffed and stocked classrooms must be considered in the context of a society that has almost no use for formal education. On the contrary, sending one's child to school may be positively dangerous; hence the "course" for Tauade students is arduous indeed:

> Primary schooling has been available to them for at least twenty years, a long time by PNG standards; furthermore they are allotted high school places equivalent to 50% of their graduating primary (grades 1–6) school classes, again, well above the average for the nation as a whole (30%) and one of the highest quotas for any region of the country. This allotment is made irrespective of children's actual level of achievement in primary school. And yet, only one Tauade has made it over the barriers that are erected in later years and matriculated at the University of Papua New Guinea [Lancy, 1978b, pp. 82–83].

Figure 2.10. Tauade hamlet near Kosipe Mission.

Toaripi

The Toaripi represent the most acculturated of the peoples we have studied. This can be attributed to three factors (see Figure 2.11). First, the Toaripi were involved in the Hiri trading circuit, exporting sagos, coconuts, and other foodstuffs, bows and arrows (which they get from the Orokolo to the west), and importing shell goods and pots (Allen, 1977). Thus they were far less insular at the period of first Western contact than most societies. Second, in their case this contact began very early with the arrival in 1881 of the peripatetic James Chalmers (Ryan, 1965). The third factor, amply documented by Ryan (1971), derives from the rather poor resource base upon which they may draw. This has meant that, in the absence of birth control and in order to survive, they have had to migrate in large numbers to Port Moresby. Like the Kilenge, however, they do not cease to be Toaripi, but instead inhabit several large "urban villages" in the city (see also pp. 123–124). Ryan calls this arrangement a *bilocal social system.*

In 1964 there were approximately 5300 Toaripi living in nine rural

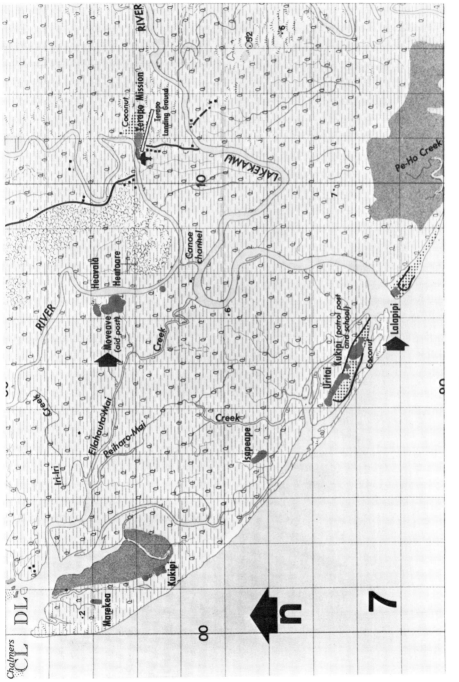

Figure 2.11. Toaripi.

villages, and 1300 Toaripi in Port Moresby.[10] These villages are large by Papua New Guinean standards. We carried out some of our studies in Uritai, for example, which had a population over 1000 by 1962 (Ryan, 1965). These villages are located on low-lying ground in what is largely an estuarine environment. Consequently garden land and whole villages are frequently washed away and "land disputes are endemic among the Toaripi [Ryan, 1965, p. 67]." Sago, carefully tended in the swamps, is the staple that is supplemented by garden products—yams, cassavas, and sweet potatoes. Arable land is found in scattered patches and can only be reached in most cases by traveling along the river in dugouts. Fishing is nearly as important as it is for the Kiwai. Women in particular make almost daily trips to the water to fish with small nets.

Cash-producing activities have been mooted for years, and although people earn some money from copra, they are heavily dependent on remittances. Cargo-cult activities have also held people's attention at various periods. One of the more notable of such movements was called the *Vailala Madness*. It was launched on the forsaken premise that the abandonment and destruction of traditional customs and artifacts and the adoption of Christianity would transport the Toaripi to a material level on a par with the European visitors. Despite the tragic consequences of their misplaced faith in the loss of much of their cultural integrity, the Toaripi enjoy a society that is yet rich and diversified, both technologically and socially. Toaripi villages continue to have a magnetic attraction for out-migrants (but see Morauta, 1979), even those who have been successful in the urban world. On the other hand, the opposing pull of the city may be less strong than it once was. Toaripi children are well aware that they can not hope to find a job in Port Moresby without schooling, and yet we found many (possibly even the majority) who were more than willing to forego life in the classroom for life in the village, on the river, in the gardens, and on the sea.

Kewa

Two groups of people inhabit the Ialibu area—the Kewa to the south and west and the Imboggu to the north and east (see Figure 2.12). Hilary Pumuye, who was eventually to become my close associate, was born in the border area between these groups. This, added to his status as the son of a big-man, meant that he was widely known throughout the area and was fluent in both languages (which are mutually intelligible). Our

---

[10]By 1972, over 50% of the Toaripi population was resident in Port Moresby (Morauta, personal communication).

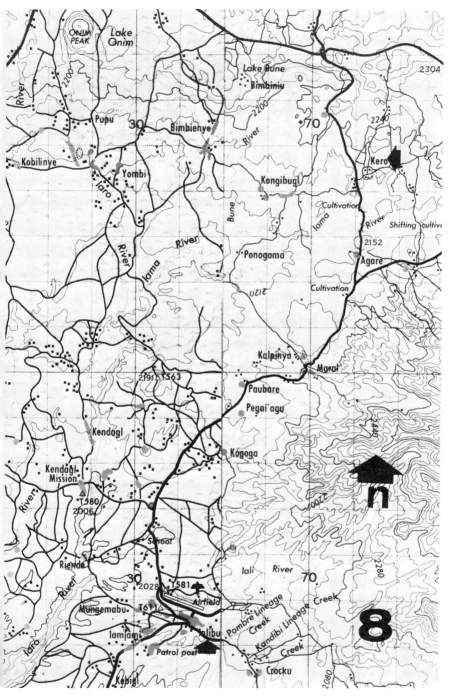

Figure 2.12. Kewa.

43

research has involved both Kewa and Imbonggu informants, but for the sake of simplicity I will henceforth refer only to the Kewa except where only Imbonggu were tested (see Chapter 6). I was able to obtain no evidence that these groups do not have nearly identical cultural practices in all the important areas.

The Kewa had their first glimpse of outsiders only a few years after the Melpa, but patrols into the area began only in the 1950s. Missions, schools, and roads followed during the 1960s. The principal difference between the Ialibu and Mount Hagen areas can be traced to the presence of coffee groves in the latter, their absence in the former, and the attendant differential impact on the local economy. Kewas have had to migrate to plantations on the coast and to more favored Highland sites to earn some cash. Their land—like that of the Toaripi—is far from lush, soils are thin, and the average elevation and rainfall is high. Their staple is the sweet potato, which is augmented—but to a lesser extent than elsewhere—by taros and yams (see Figure 2.13). Gardening is difficult but not all consuming: Men and women spend approximately 21% and 38%, respectively, of their time doing garden work (Leroy, 1975). Pandanus nuts are an important food source, and they are used in informal exchanges among friends and relatives. As Leroy (1975) points out, the Kewa view life as a constant struggle between opposing forces, e.g., the community versus the individual, domestic versus wild, cleared ground versus brush, male versus female, and so on. (A more complete discussion of binary opposition is provided in Chapter 6.)

This struggle is exemplified, while being temporarily resolved, in the *tawa*—a ceremonial exchange very similar to *moka*.[11] One such ceremony was held at the Imi village north of Ialibu in 1977. Several hundred people participated from three villages and four clans. The occasion was the gift of gold-lipped pearl shells[12] from one group to another. The gift was made only after a day-long dance in which the majority of people participated. Each group wore similar costumes. One group, for example, wore human-hair wigs, set off with the yellow crests of the sulphur-crested cockatoo and feathers from several other parrot species. Bark belts held cordryline-leaf bunches hanging in the rear, and bark cloth in the front. Faces were

---

[11]Leroy (1975), however, argues that "*Tawa* does not test managerial capacities and support networks the way *moka* does [p. 95]."

[12]Shells are more highly valued today among the Kewa than among the Melpa. Hilary's father accorded me the rare privilege (perhaps because I was accompanied by *my* father!) of seeing his extremely valuable collection. The shells were kept in a recess in his house, each individually wrapped in bark. As he unwrapped each shell, he pointed out its special features—its name, its value, and its provenance (e.g., previous owners). As much pride as he took in them he made it clear that he was merely the custodian for the shells that belonged, in reality, to his entire clan.

Figure 2.13. Kewa house and garden.

blackened with charcoal, and the bodies were covered with special oils leaving a glistening coating overall. Each man—there were 15 in this particular group—carried a ceremonial spear and a long thin drum. Standing in a line, this group chanted and danced in place, using drums and spears to emphasize the rhythm (see Figure 2.14). Other groups were dressed differently, but there was little variation within each group. The primary marks of differentiation were the choice of feathers (several bird-of-paradise species were represented, as well as parrots and the Nuigini eagle), and color and patterning in face and body paint. The line dance was employed by other groups, but the majority of individuals marched (see Figure 2.15) five abreast round and round an oval-shaped track (about 300 m in circumference) that had been worn into mud on the previously well-groomed ceremonial ground. It was rainy. With very little imagination, one could visualize an elaborate display of maneuvers by military marching units in the West, but with one tenth the panache. At last, the nearly 100 shells, each rubbed with red ocher and carefully placed in huge net bags, were carried around the track, with the bags suspended on poles. Full of shells, the bags noticeably bent the twin support saplings that were balanced on the shoulders of the carriers.

Figure 2.14. *Tawa* ceremony—line dance.

Oksapmin

The Oksapmin, although they live in one of the most isolated spots on the globe,[13] occupy a kind of crossroads (see Figure 2.16). Their tool inventory, for example, including black-palm bows, cassowary thigh-bone and bamboo knives, flint scrapers, and so on, is very similar to those used in societies to the north (e.g., the Imondas) and south (the Bimin). And like these societies, they rely to a considerable extent on hunting and gathering. Wild pig, hunted with bow and arrow, and cassowary, caught in snares, are major hunting objectives. The Oksapmin also participate in attenuated form in the very rich artistic and ritual practices of the plains of the Sepik and Fly rivers (Perey, 1973). At the same time, they are clearly linked to the Central Highlands culture complex, having much in common with groups to the east and west (P. Brown, 1978). Their staple is the sweet potato, which is planted in land cleared from secondary forest

[13]To the west, passage is blocked by the Victor Emanuel mountain range, to the north by the Ok Om River, and to the east and south by the Strickland Gorge—comparable in many respects to the Grand Canyon in the United States.

Figure 2.15. *Tawa* ceremony—marching groups.

(Weeks, personal communication). However, unlike the Melpa, garden plots are not neatly prepared grids, nor is there any tendency to built mounds. Taro is cultivated at the river's edge, and, depending on rainfall, in terraces just above the valley floor (Perey, 1973). There is a sharp division of labor by gender, and this too is a Highland trait. Men hunt, and women and children gather. Women tend sweet-potato and taro gardens, and men tend stands of pandanus.

Perey estimates that there are 6600 Oksapmin scattered in hamlets—which in turn form "village" clusters—over 250 km². He documents two periods during which the population suffered substantial declines—during a drought-induced famine in the 1940s and an epidemic brought on by introduced diseases (especially influenza) in the 1960s. The latter catastrophe was exacerbated by the extreme inaccessibility of the area. A mission station and air strip were established at Tekin in 1964, just two years after a patrol post and air strip were built 15 km away at Oksapmin. These strips can only handle light aircraft originating in Wewak and operating under VFR (visual flight rules). Another consequence of this remoteness is that the contract plantation-labor scheme completely by-passed the area until very recently. A few Oksapmin men have learned

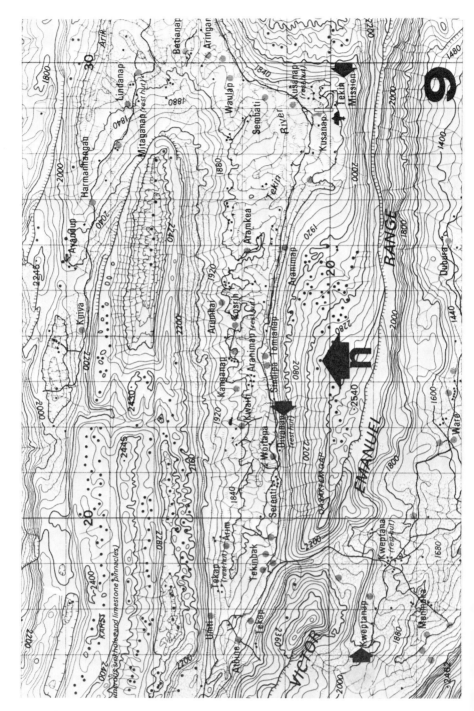

48

Tok Pisin while in prison for murder and doing odd jobs at the patrol post.

Oksapmin society is loosely organized. There is no big-man complex, nor are the systems of exchange as elaborate as one finds in the Central Highlands. There is some differential of wealth: Perey reports that a few men are able to accumulate enough of a surplus in pigs and sweet potatoes to "hire" the labor of less wealthy individuals. An incipient money economy based on the cowrie shell as the unit of exchange persisted until 1968.

Ponam

By contrast, Ponam society might be described as almost aggressively egalitarian (J. G. Carrier, 1980; Lancy & Madsen, 1981) (see Figure 2.17). Wealth is constantly dissipated through clan and kin-based exchange ceremonies that occur with striking frequency (perhaps as often as twice a week). Although I witnessed a number of these (and filmed one with Geoff Saxe), the intricacies were not readily decoded.[14] Nor is exchange the only occasion for ceremony: Other ceremonies are associated with important rites of passage such as marriage, childbirth, and death.

The second dominant fact of life on Ponam is the sea. The island is approximately 3 km long and up to 200 m wide. It is a sand cay built up over time on a limestone or coral base. It is one among half a dozen small islands punctuating the barrier reef that runs nearly the entire length of the north coast of Manus Island. There is open sea to the north and west of the island, a shallow lagoon (in fact the submerged reef) of about 25 km^2 in extent around the island, and an area of deep but protected water between the reef and Manus Island. Each of these major marine environments is further subdivided by the Ponams, and these divisions represent only one aspect of their intimate knowledge of and involvement with the sea that surrounds them. Aside from a few tree crops—coconut, breadfruit, citrus—they depend almost entirely on the sea for subsistence, trading fresh and smoked fish and other seafoods to Manus islanders for tubers, greens, bananas, and most importantly, sagos. Other items of trade include or included carved wooden bowls (imports) and shell money (exports). Their dependence on fishing and trade in turn have led to the development and elaboration of their outrigger canoes, which come in many sizes and configurations, each with its special purpose (see Figure 2.18).

[14]Achsah Carrier has touched on Ponam exchange in an unpublished paper (A. H. Carrier, 1979), and she is at work on her Ph.D. dissertation, which will provide an extensive report on the exchange system.

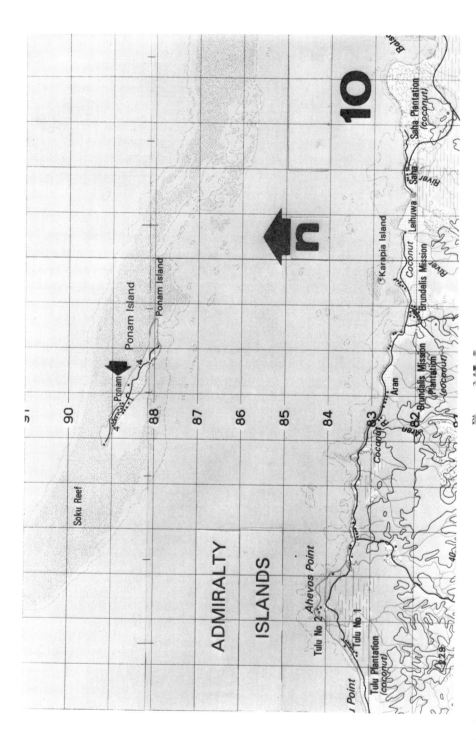

ADMIRALTY ISLANDS

Soku Reef

Ponam Island

Ponam Island

Ponam

Karapia Island

Coconut Leihuwa Saha

Brundalis Mission

Brundalis Mission
Plantation
(coconut)

Aran

Coconut R.

Saha Plantation
(coconut)

Saha

River

River

Bosui

Ahevos Point

Tulu No 2

Tulu No 1

Tulu Plantation
(coconut)

Point

N

10

90

88

87

86

85

84

83

82

Figure 2.18. Ponam fishing group returning with their catch.

Three hundred people live in one village in the center of the island in large houses that are raised off the sand on stilts. Corrugated iron and other flotsam from World War II have been put to ingenious uses in house construction and in the manufacture of tools and furnishings of various kinds. Some distance from the village is a community school and a church. The Catholic mission station proper is at Bundralis on the Manus coast: Ponam has never had a resident priest. Similarly, varied educational opportunities, although available since the 1920s, were confined to Bundralis and the government center—Lorengau. It has only been since 1973 that Ponam children could complete their elementary schooling on the island.

Nevertheless, Ponam children do extremely well in school, and provincial records indicate that this has been true for some time. Furthermore, Ponam students, unlike students on Mandok, continue to translate their facility with Western schooling into well-paid jobs. James Carrier has argued persuasively (1981a, 1981b) that Ponams realized quite some time ago that economic opportunities on the island are nil,[15] and that to acquire cash they must encourage their children to do well in school,[16] pay their school fees, despite the hardship this imposes, and remind them at every opportunity of the expectation that a substantial proportion of one's earnings should be remitted. And, again unlike Mandok, the system is working. Many Ponam students have finished school, gotten jobs, and are sending money home to the island.

Culture and Educational Development

As our work progressed we were to document how successful Ponam children and children from some other societies were in adapting to the demands of Western-style schooling, and on the other hand, how unsuccessful the Kilenge and others had been in taking the same challenges. But this was common knowledge in 1976, at least in the sense that the Department of Education was aware at a low level of differential success rates as a function of the student's "home background." How widely these rates varied was not known, nor did anyone have a very good guess as to what caused this variation. The term *culture* was in the wind, but it was far too global a concept upon which to base a program of research, let alone policy initiatives. The task, then, was to try and "unpackage" both culture and success—a process already well underway by 1976.

---

[15]In 1978 the island purchased a kerosene-powered freezer and two ice chests with a loan and technical assistance from the government. They quickly caught enough fish to fill the freezer. These were loaded into the ice chests and taken to Lorengau where they were sold to a government purchasing agent. This all took place within a week after the freezer was installed; within 2 weeks the freezer had stopped working. Six months later they had still not gotten anyone to come out from Lorengau to repair it, but had to continue monthly payments on their loan. This is a fairly typical story in Papua New Guinea. What was unusual was the absolutely fatalistic response of the people. They were not surprised at how it had turned out. In the other sites similar failure of development schemes inevitably brought forth a torrent of anger against the government or the local out-group that had "sabotaged" the project.

[16]Ponam was the only IMP site with virtually 100% enrollment in Grades 1 to 6.

3

Cognitive Testing
in Papua New Guinea

Margaret Mead must be credited with the first application of cognitive-development theory in Papua New Guinea in her 1932 study of childhood animism on Manus Island. Her primary purpose was to test the universality of axioms of cognitive development postulated by a Western psychologist (in this case Jean Piaget) and developed from research with Western children. The universality question dominates much cross-cultural psychology to this day, and it was Kelly's and Philp's primary concern in their research during the late 1960s and early 1970s in Papua New Guinea. If we take the theories of Bruner and Piaget as representative, the support for universalism has not been impressive. For example, Dasen, in a review of cross-cultural tests of Piagetian theory, finds "more and more evidence accumulating to show that concrete operational thought is not necessarily attained [1972, p. 31]."

The three cornerstones of cognitive-development theory are that patterns of cognitive-processing change with increasing age, that most important changes are qualitative in nature, and that each such change results in more efficient (less context-dependent, less egocentric, more flexible) strategies for processing information, especially new information. Deviations from this pattern uncovered in cross-cultural research have been accounted for by either deficit or difference models (Cole & Bruner, 1971).

Deficit models are extremely compelling because even the casual observer will notice that there are many "things" present in the environment of Swiss schoolchildren that are not present in, say, the environment of desert aboriginals. Attempts to discover which of the many "missing ingredients" are crucial have not, however, been terribly successful (Deutsch and Associates, 1967). The weight of evidence to date (Cole, Sharp, & Lave, 1976; Sharp, Cole, & Lave, 1979) implicates formal schooling as one crucial difference.

Undoubtedly the most comprehensive study of variation in cognitive development influenced by environmental deficits has been undertaken with Australian aboriginals. The authors (Seagrim & Lendon, 1980) and their colleagues used a Piagetian framework to study cognitive development among various groups of aboriginal children. Their most consistent finding is that the closer the *home* environment approaches the Western model, the more closely does performance approach the Western standard. Nutritional and health status, urban residence, and specific training had no impact on the depressed performance of children from impoverished families. On the other hand, "Aboriginal children who had been adopted into, or fostered early in their lives by white families, outperformed the Hermansburg children on our tests to such an extent that they approached or sometimes equalled white norms [p. 121]."

Speculations about qualitative *differences* in cognitive processes as a function of culture or environment frequently are found in the writings of comparative anthropologists. Frazer's 1922 analysis of medicine in non-Western societies carries the suggestion that "primitive" man tends to reason analogically (e.g., sorcerer burns the nail clippings of an intended victim who will subsequently contract a fever), to the exclusion of other, presumably more rational, processes. Lévy-Bruhl (1926), another comparativist, described the "mythical bonds" that primitives create between objects or events that are otherwise distinct on logical, scientific, or evidential grounds. Moreover, these bonds are impervious to dissolution on the basis of contradictory evidence, or more generally, the primitive belief system is "closed" because individuals lack an "awareness of alternatives to the established body of theoretical tenets [Horton, 1967, p. 155]." The most prominent modern theoretician in this area is, of course, Lévi-Strauss (1966). However, these writers have not seriously challenged the universalist position because, as Piaget (1970) points out, their evidence is based entirely on "collective representations" like kin systems, language, myth, etc., and "the logic or pre-logic of the members of a given society cannot be adequately gauged by already crystallized cultural products; . . . what we want to know about is *individual* inventions [p. 117; italics added]." To sharpen this point, consider the reaction of social scientists to a scholar who made generalizations about Americans' musical skills and sensibilities based on an analysis of "The Star-Spangled Banner."

There are, then, problems associated with both deficit and difference theories in accounting for deviations in cognitive development. In both cases, there is the absence of adequate evidence, insufficient or undifferentiated ethnographic evidence in deficit accounts, and unconvincing (e.g., absence of cognitive-test data) evidence in the difference accounts. As we shall see, cross-cultural researchers in Papua New Guinea have gradually come to recognize the need to collect the necessary evidence, and in the process a rapprochement between these opposed views seems likely.

The theories of Jean Piaget (especially Inhelder & Piaget, 1958) and Jerome Bruner (especially 1964) have thoroughly dominated cross-cultural research in Papua New Guinea. Attention has focused on the transition from Piaget's preoperational to concrete-operational stages. There are several reasons for this. The theory has received overwhelming empirical support in the West and considerable support from research in developing countries as well (see especially Price-Williams, 1961). That is, the cognitive processes of children aged 7–11 do seem to be qualitatively different from those of 3–6-year-olds in ways predicted by the theory. Second, the various tests of conservation developed by Piaget and his colleagues to chart this transition are extremely flexible and adaptable to a variety of situations and subject populations (e.g., Furth, 1966; Lancy & Goldstein, in press). In short, conservation has proven to be an extremely congenial vehicle for universality tests. The basic paradigm involves the initial establishment of identity between two substances. The experimenter then transforms one substance without changing its amount and questions the child to see whether he appreciates that "*certain attributes* . . . remain invariant in the wake of substantive changes in *other attributes* [Flavell, 1963, p. 299; italics in original]." For example, in the conservation-of-number task, the child aligns two rows of five identical plastic beads, so that a one-to-one correspondence is established. Then the experimenter spreads one row apart so that it is now longer than the comparison row. The child who can conserve number will appreciate that this transformation has not changed the fundamental identity of the two rows; they still have an equal number of beads. The preoperational child, however, will claim that the longer row has "more."

Bruner's theory and methods offer complementary features. Unlike conservation tasks, Bruner's procedures provide the investigator much more than "succeeds" or "fails" to work with in the data. His tasks permit a number of different solutions, each reflecting different underlying processes. Second, much more than Piaget, Bruner has addressed himself (1960, 1966a, 1966b, 1971) to the application of cognitive processes in educational settings and the relationship between patterns of instruction and patterns of cognitive growth. Hence, his ideas have had a special relevance to a nation in the process of building an education system, training teachers, developing curricula, establishing standards, etc.

Piagetian Research

The first study of conservation (Prince, 1968, 1969) in Papua New Guinea was also the largest (in terms of sample size = 3520). In this study schoolchildren were group tested for conservation of length, quantity, weight, area, and volume. Subsequently, there have been 11 further conservation studies. All of the investigators (for recent reviews, see Price, 1978; Shea, 1978a) find a delay—with reference to Western norms—in the age of acquisition for the various conservation skills from about 4 years for the "earliest" task (number) to 8 years or more for the later tasks (e.g., area). Shea (1978b) and Shea and Yerua (1980), using a large sample drawn from many areas of the country, found that 50% of children aged 10 or older and/or in Grade 5 or higher conserved number. By contrast, fewer than 20% of children in the same age–grade range achieve area. In other studies with high-school students (Jones, 1974; Price & Nidue, 1974), it was found that the 50% level for area is reached in Grades 9–10.

Several of the investigators have singled out aspects of Papua New Guinean languages as accounting for the observed deficit (Prince, 1969; Rawlinson, 1974; Kelly & Philp, 1975). Prince (1969), for example, compared the rate of conservation achievement for two groups of same-age Teachers-College students. In one school (Rintebe), the language of instruction was *Tok Pisin*, and the vernacular (tested in *Pisin*); and at the second (*Awabe*) the language of instruction was English (tested in English). The former group performed at a level comparable to Grade 4 subjects Prince had previously tested, whereas the latter performed at a level comparable to Grade 7 subjects. Kelly and Philp (1975) find a small but consistent advantage accruing to subjects tested in English as against same-age–grade pupils tested in the vernacular for conservation of length. Kelly and Philp point to a specific aspect of the language of their subjects (Melpa)—namely, the difficulty of expressing reversibility. The other writers suggest or hypothesize more general language differences to account for the superior performance of those tested in English.

In common with research done in Europe and America, the majority of subjects tested in Papua New Guinea have been schoolchildren. However, age and grade are not perfectly correlated, and where this factor has been capitalized on (Shea, 1978b), grade effects have been stronger than age effects. Contrary to Piagetian theory, formal schooling appears to make a significant contribution to the achievement of concrete operations. Kelly (1971a) tested 432 children from three different societies; half had attended school for 1 to 6 years; an age-matched group had not attended school. He found that the proportion of subjects achieving conservation of quantity and length was higher among the unschooled at lower ages (7–12), but the advantage shifts to the schooled children after age 12. This would seem to suggest that education effects are found only in the *later years* of primary school. In fact, age effects were very weak for all groups, and the proportion conserving length *steadily declined* over age for the unschooled children. In a later study with Melpa children only, it was found (Kelly & Philp, 1975) that more than three times as many school children conserved length, compared to a sample of their unschooled counterparts. These findings are consistent with studies done in many other developing countries that also show a marked effect of schooling on the attainment of conservation (e.g., Greenfield, 1966).

Few investigators have taken advantage of the enormous cultural diversity that exists in Papua New Guinea to conduct intranational research in cognitive development. Most have explicitly or implicitly compared Papua New Guinean subjects with same-age–grade Western children. The projects of John Shea and Max Kelly are exceptions to this trend. Shea (1978b) compared groups from five different regions of Papua New Guinea: coastal Madang, central Morobe, the Ialibu area, Jimi Valley, and Milne Bay. Children ranged in age from 9 to 16 and were in Grades 3 to 6. Sample sizes varied from 98 to 339. The results are shown in Table 3.1.

Regional differences are apparent here, and such differences tend to be greater as the tasks become more demanding. The range over regions for the proportion conserving number is 38–68%; that for area, 13–77%. Kelly compared children from three language groups: Avatip (Middle Sepik), Melpa (Central Highlands), and Goilala (Papuan Highlands). Kelly's "language groups" were more carefully matched on level of acculturation (all low) than were Shea's "regions." Language group makes a significant contribution to performance on conservation of quantity but not length (Kelly, 1977). One reason for the failure to find significance in the conservation-of-length comparison is that levels of success are universally low for all language groups. Kelly offers no prior reason for selecting these three groups based on a specific hypothesis concerning possible

TABLE 3.1
More Than Forty Percent of Sample Achieving Conservation by Task and Region

	Task			
Region	Number	Length	Quantity	Area
Madang	+	+	+	+
Milne Bay	+	−	+	+
Ialibu	+	+	−	−
Jimi	+	+	−	−
Morobe	−	+	−	−

language–cognition effects. He does offer an intriguing post hoc hypothesis, however: "The order of achievement of the subjects in language groups was in inverse proportion to the number of counting words used in that language as revealed by the interpreters [Kelly, 1971a, p. 57]."

There is a clear indication in the conservation literature of a developmental lag of several years for Papua New Guinean schoolchildren. Further, there is evidence that this period of delay is greater in some language groups than in others. Finally, there is the strong suggestion that, in the absence of formal schooling, many individuals—perhaps most—do not make the transition to patterns of cognitive-processing that according to Piaget, characterize the concrete-operational period.

Brunerian Studies

Like Piaget, Bruner (1964) has proposed several stages through which the child passes during the period of cognitive development. Investigations in Papua New Guinea have concentrated on the transition from Bruner's *ikonic* to *symbolic* stages: Language replaces imagery as the prime source of rules, structures, and concepts for the child to represent and organize his world.

Several of Bruner's procedures have been employed in Papua New Guinea; the first to be described is the double-classification matrix (Bruner & Kenney, 1966). Nine plastic cylinders varying incrementally in height and diameter are arranged in a 3 × 3 matrix. After viewing the complete matrix, the child must replace varying numbers of the beakers in their correct position. In one of these tasks, the child must replace a row of beakers. He or she can do this by attending to either of the two stimulus dimensions (single classification). In another task he or she must replace items on the diagonal; hence he or she must attend to both dimensions simultaneously (double classification). Finally, one task re-quires that he or she replace all of the beakers with the matrix reversed by a 180° rotation. This requires a verbal formulation of the rules by which the beakers are ordered. The authors identified two problems that younger children confronted in these tasks. First, they have a great deal of difficulty seeing similarities or relationships among the beakers, tending to see each as unique. Second, they rely too much on their image of how the matrix looked when it was complete, which causes them increasing difficulty as the task becomes more complex. For American subjects, they find that children younger than 5 do not succeed on any of the tasks: 80% of the 5-year-olds succeed on the single-classification task; 60% of the 5-year-olds and 75% of the 6-year-olds succeed on the double-classification task ; and 20% of the 6-year-olds and 80% of the 7-year-olds succeed on the reversal task.

Kelly (1971b) used this procedure (squared-off wooden blocks replac-ing the plastic cylinders) with his Avatip–Melpa–Goilala subjects. Sev-enty-five percent of his 6–9-year-olds achieve success on the single-classification task. Again we see a 3–4-year developmental lag. The gap with the more difficult tasks is greater. Only 50% of children aged 10–12 and 13–20 succeed in the double-classification and reversal tasks, respec-tively. The order of difficulty is substantially the same as it is for Bruner's subjects, however, and steady improvement over age occurs on all the tasks, even for unschooled children (unlike conservation). The school-children do better on every task at every age level. In a replication of this study with Anglo and European Australians, Philp and Kelly (1974) find developmental patterns parallel to those found in Papua New Guinea. International differences are significant on all the tasks favoring the Australians, but intranational differences are not (again, unlike conserva-tion).

The second Brunerian task to be discussed is the "bulb-board" task developed by Olson (1966). This task also records the transition from ikonic to symbolic thought.

Most studies of problem solving in children characterize the behavior of the pre-school child as receptive or respondent to stimuli, while the behavior of the older child appears to be determined far more by the plans or hypotheses the child generates, rather than by immediate stimuli. The transition, we have urged, depends upon the development of representational systems. And one of the important aspects of such development is the shift to symbolic or linguistically mediated representation . . . as symbolic representation comes to be handled more competently by the child we should expect that information would be less tied to specific instances or images, that a "conceptual space" would replace (or augment) the earlier "image space," and that encounters with new instances would be used to decide among alternative hypotheses rather than to check the "correctness" of a single image [pp. 135–136].

The child is confronted with two to four patterns represented by lit and unlit bulbs arranged in symmetrical matrices. Directly in front of him or her the child has his or her own bulb matrix. These bulbs may light up when pressed. Programmed into the child's board is one of the patterns displayed on the stimulus-pattern matrices. The child's task is to determine which of these patterns is "hidden" in his or her board by testing to see which of his or her bulbs light and in what arrangement, thereby forming a match with one of the stimulus patterns. Three possible strategies emerged, all of which could be used to solve the problem but with varying degrees of efficiency. In the most efficient strategy, the child compares the stimulus patterns and focuses on those bulbs that are maximally informative (e.g., a bulb that is lit in one pattern but not the other). The child then presses the corresponding bulb on his or her matrix, thereby reaching a solution after only one or two presses. In a less efficient strategy, the child attempts to test each pattern successively; that is, he or she presses the same bulbs on the board that are lit up in one particular pattern that he or she has focused on. This strategy has elements of both "conceptual" and "image" space. Finally, the least efficient children press virtually all the bulbs as if they were trying to extract the entire pattern from their matrix, and *then* they attempt to match this with one of the stimulus patterns. Since the child is permitted to press only a single bulb at a time and the light goes on only when the bulb is pressed, the memory demands on a child using such a strategy are enormous. Olson found that 100% of his 3-year-olds used the least efficient strategy, and this drops to 0% among 9-year-olds. The midlevel strategy is first used by the 5-year-olds. Eighty percent of them used this strategy, and this figure remains constant through age 9. Twenty percent of the 9-year-olds use the most efficient strategy; none of the younger children do so. Overall, older children are more likely to solve the problem, and they press fewer bulbs in doing so than younger children.

The bulb board that Kelly (1971c) used in Papua New Guinea was in most respects identical, but on the face of it, the problems would seem to have been more difficult. For example, in one problem the pattern in the child's matrix incorporated *two* of the four stimulus patterns, and the child had to determine which two were represented (Kelly, 1970). Again the subjects are from the Avatip–Melpa–Goilala study. Only 3% of the sample used the most efficient strategy, and they were much less likely to use a midlevel strategy and much more likely to use the least efficient strategy than 7-year-old and 9-year-old American children. Age, grade, and language group had no apparent effect on strategy (Kelly, 1971d). However, age and language group are shown to contribute significantly to success at *solving* the problems (Kelly, 1971c).

It might well be argued that at least part of the failure of Papua New Guinean children to use symbolic strategies to the same degree as Western children can be explained by their unfamiliarity with the stimuli used in the experiments described thus far. With the last experiment of the series, this problem does not arise. Philp, Kelly, and their colleagues also utilized the "picture-sorting" task developed by Olver and Hornsby (1966). In the original task, 42 drawings of objects were presented in a random array to children aged 6 to 11. The drawings depicted common objects potentially "groupable" in a variety of ways. The child was asked to make a group. After he had done so, he was asked how the pictures in the group were alike. Then the drawings were returned to the array, and the child was asked to make another group, and so on, for a total of 10 trials. (For comparable Genevan research, see Inhelder and Piaget [1969].)

The youngest children tended to form pairs; groups got progressively larger with age; only 25% of the 11-year-olds' groups were pairs. In looking at the children's explanations, the investigators were interested in whether or not the child had formed a group in which the items could be exhaustively described or labeled by a single word or phrase (superordinate), as against a variety of alternatives where the items were dealt with singly (collections) or serially (complexes). Thirty-four percent of the 6-year-olds' groups met the superordination criterion, while 69% of the 8-year-olds' and 85% of the 11-year-olds groups did so. They were interested also in the basis for the grouping—whether perceptible (shared perceptual attribute), functional (shared function or functionally interrelated), or nominal (shared label or name). The use of a perceptible basis steadily declines from 47% at age 6. Functional bases increase to 48% at age 8 and do not increase thereafter. Nominal bases occur for 6% of 6-year-olds groups, and this increases to 32% for 11-year-olds. Ikonic thought is implicated by complexive structure (contrasted with collections) and perceptible bases; symbolic thought by superordinate structure and nominal bases.

Although the published details are scanty (Huntsman, 1973), it appears that the Papua New Guinean replication followed the original study closely. The objects used as stimuli varied from location to location (e.g., Avatip, Melpa, Goilala), and the investigator used drawings and photographs as well as actual objects, since he was uncertain as to whether or not the children would recognize the items from photographs. (They did, but drawings gave them some difficulty, however.) In terms of structure, subjects who were in school showed a developmental progression comparable to the subjects tested in Cambridge. Twenty-five percent of the first-graders' groups met the criterion for superordination, and this figure rose to 65% for sixth graders. The same sort of 4-year developmental lag that we have seen in some of the other experiments is evident here as well.

The basis for the subjects' groups shows a somewhat different trend. In Cambridge, the perceptible base declines; functional increases, then levels off; and nominal steadily increases over the age range tested. In Papua New Guinea *all three* bases show a steady gain from the first through the sixth grade. However, perceptible and nominal bases are less often relied upon by the children, while functional bases are more heavily relied upon. Huntsman (1973) comments:

> The results suggest that the children's preoccupation is with the appropriate uses of things; equivalence is bound up with the concerns of the communities: It reflects the orderliness and regularities of a working relationship with the environment. It is little wonder then that functional bases are the most common ones used in all age groups. Unlike the North American children the young New Guinea subjects do not use arbitrary functional attributes for grouping items together; their responses in fact tend to resemble those of the older children. They show a keen interest in the items as individual things. Village children particularly seem less concerned with abstraction or with a theoretical approach to things. The impact of schooling possibly encourages a more rapid development of semantic hierarchies that will permit more flexibility with respect to the bases used in making equivalence judgments [p. 7].

The pattern for children who have not attended school is quite different (see Table 3.2). On structure, older children are no more likely than younger children to use the superordinate, which never exceeds 16% of the total. Similarly with base, the perceptible is rarely used (it does not exceed 8%), and the nominal is *never* used. Function is overwhelmingly the preferred basis, increasing to 74% for the oldest children's groups. Kelly (1970) reports a significant language-group effect on these results, but he fails to indicate the exact nature of such effects. He suggests, however, in reference to variation in the use of nominal bases, that the relative frequency of grouping (category) terms in the respective languages may be a contributing factor. Interestingly, unschooled subjects tested in Senegal show yet another pattern (Greenfield, Reich, & Olver, 1966) of responding on this task. The Senegalese children increase their use of the superordinate as they grow older. However, while American children seem to show increased preference for the nominal base with increasing age and Papua New Guinean children prefer the functional base, for Senegalese children the preferred base is perceptible (specifically, color). As we might expect, then, in an experiment where the stimuli are indigenous, language and culture effects appear to be maximized.

TABLE 3.2
Grouping Bases for Photographs (Expressed as Percentages)

	Base		
Grade	Perceptible	Functional	Nominal
1	11	47	1
4	14	60	8
6	21	65	14

Implications for a Theory of Culture and Cognition

I would like to try and summarize the major implications of the research that preceded the Indigenous Mathematics Project. By and large the theoretical positions of both Piaget and Bruner have received qualified support. The qualifications are very straightforward, and the theories hold up reasonably well as long as the children tested are undergoing formal schooling. Second, there is a substantial developmental lag in the age at which Papua New Guinean children—as compared to Western children— experience the various qualitative shifts in cognitive processes. These two factors help to account for the few findings that deviate from the theory. In several studies, no qualitative shift (e.g., no development) occurred. However, this can be attributed to the fact that no subjects older than 15 were tested. In two studies (Jones, 1974; Lewis & Mulford, 1974) of conservation in which high-school students served as subjects, development continued throughout adolescence. Jones (1974), for example, found that 51% of Grade 10 students achieve conservation of area, and this proportion increases to 88% for Grade 12 students. Most authors, when they have addressed the developmental lag issue at all, have offered "deficit" explanations. These hypotheses have not been tested systematically except in a single study carried out by Kelly (Kelly & Philp, 1975), which will be described in Chapter 6.

Two further qualifications for the theories can be noted. First, subjects who have not attended school exhibit something other than a mere "lag" in development. There is some evidence to suggest that the "normal" shifts in processing strategies do not take place at all, and also some evidence to suggest an "alternate" pattern of development not accounted for by the major theories. Second, it appears that the developmental lag is not uniform across cultures within Papua New Guinea. It is more pronounced for children from some language groups–regions. These two factors taken together imply that a "difference" account for the divergence in patterns of cognitive development might be fruitful. Developing a difference account requires some investment in rethinking theories of culture and cognition.

Cognitive psychology and cultural anthropology do have at least one common concern that can serve as both the link between the two modes of inquiry and as a basis for pursuing the questions raised in the beginning of this chapter. This concern is with the kinds of categories people make and the processes underlying category formation. Human beings are universally confronted with a paradox, namely "the existence of discrimination capacities which, if fully used, would make us slaves to the particular . . . ," which is resolved by "man's capacity to categorize [Bruner, Goodnow, & Austin, 1956, p. 1]." Grouping, categorizing, generalizing, etc., represent a fundamental human need every bit as basic as the need to eat, to drink, or to socialize. Categorizing has attracted the attention of psychologists (notably, Anglin, 1970, 1977; Bruner, Olver, & Greenfield, 1966; Inhelder & Piaget, 1969; Rosch 1977, 1978) and anthropologists (notably, Goodenough, 1956; Metzger & Williams, 1966; Frake, 1969; Berlin & Kay, 1969; C. H. Brown, 1979). What then are the issues?

First, there are two broad types of categories (Elkind, 1969). We have those in which various manifestations of the same thing are judged to be *identical*, such as the phases of the moon. Conservation is the experimental paradigm par excellence for the study of identity categorization. The young child fails to appreciate that once the two rows of beads have been rendered identical by matching to achieve one-to-one correspondence, they remain identical despite changes in the relative length of the two rows. The half moon is still the same moon even though part of it is obscured. As we have seen, the formation of identity categories, which seems to occur routinely with maturity in Western children, may in fact be a consequence of the kinds of experiences that Western industrialized society provides for them.

Then there are categories in which things that are demonstrably different are judged to be *equivalent*. Human beings create a bewildering array of equivalence categories. Following Bruner and his colleagues (Bruner *et al.*, 1966), we can distinguish between the basis for an equivalence category and the structure. Some of the varying bases that have been studied are the affective, functional, and formal (Bruner *et al.*, 1956); the prototype or image (Rosch & Mervis, 1975; Posner, 1976); the theme (Bruner *et al.*, 1966) or script (Schank & Abelson, 1977); and the analogy or metaphor (Levinson & Carpenter, 1974; Brooks, 1978).

Each of these bases, in turn, has been singled out as critical in differentiating the cognitive processes of Western and non-Western peoples. Lévy-Bruhl (1926) noted the extent to which emotion (*affect*) entered into the thinking (categorizing) of "prelogical" man. Luria (1976) carried out research on equivalence categories among the Uzbeks— seminomads living in the Russian steppes. Their thinking appeared to be dominated by *functional* considerations.

E: We go back to the original series: hammer-saw-log-hatchet.

SI: It's the hammer that doesn't fit! You can always work with a saw, but a hammer doesn't always suit the job, there's only a little you can do with it.

SII: You can throw out the hammer, because when you saw a log, you have to drive a wedge into it.

Same tendency as before

E: Yet one fellow threw out the log. He said the hammer, saw, and hatchet were all alike in some way, but the log is different.

SIII: If he wants to make planks, he won't need the log.

SI: If we're getting firewood for the stove, we could get rid of the hammer, but if it's planks we're fixing, we can do without the hatchet.

Grouping varies with situation depicted

E: If you had to put these in some kind of order, could you take the log out of the group?

SI: No, if you get rid of the log, what good would the others be?

E: But these three things are tools—right?

SI: Yes, they're tools.

E: What about the log?

S: All three subjects: It belongs here too. You can make all sorts of things out of it—handles, doors, even the handles of tools are made out of wood!

E: Still, aren't these three things alike in some way?

SII: No, what's missing here is a man, a worker. Without him, there's nothing alike about these things.

SIII: You've got to have the wood here! There's nothing alike about these things unless the log's here. If you keep the log, they're all needed, but if you don't, what good are they? [Luria, 1976, pp. 61–62].[1]

The unusually large number of Africans capable of eidetic imagery (Doob, 1965), the ability of Australian aboriginals to track accurately the featureless desert (Kearins, 1975; Lewis, 1976), or of Pacific islanders to navigate without the aid of charts (Gladwin, 1970; Lewis, 1972)—all suggest the importance of visual *imagery* in the thinking of these people. Recall also the Senegalese study mentioned previously. Cole and his colleagues (Cole, Gay, Glick, & Sharp, 1971) found that the Kpelle of Liberia had enormous difficulty in recalling 20 words presented in a variety of formats, until they tried embedding the words in a story that dramatically assisted their recall (see also Mandler, Scribner, Cole, &

---

[1]Reprinted by permission of Harvard University Press.

DeForest, 1980). Perhaps a *thematic* basis for forming associations or categories predominates in the thought of the Kpelle and other non-Western people. Murphy (1976), however, sees the *metaphor* as an important vehicle for Kpelle thought, especially in terms of how they categorize individuals. And, of course, metaphor and analogy are overwhelmingly seen in the areas studied by symbolic anthropologists (see especially Lévi-Strauss, 1966; Turner, 1974). The widespread practice of totemism in non-Western societies, where individuals, clans, tribes, etc., take on the attributes of various nonhuman entities, illustrates this phenomenon.

Formal categories can be set against the other types in terms of their relative reliance on language (more) and context (less). In formal categorization, language becomes "an instrument of analysis and synthesis in problem solving wherein the analytic power of language aids in abstraction or feature extraction, and . . . in reorganizing and synthesizing the features thus abstracted." Categorization can also be accomplished "without dependence on shared percepts or actions. . . . Decontextualization permits information to be conceived as independent of the speaker's vantage point; it permits communication with those who do not share one's daily experience or actions [Bruner, 1971, p. 149]."

Formal categories are those in which certain critical attributes are extracted from the to-be-compared items. An equivalence judgment depends on the items sharing a relatively large (as compared with other items not judged to be equivalent) number of attributes. In the United States, very young children form concepts on the basis of the function that items share (Nelson, 1973). However, the growing individual tends more often to form formal as opposed to other kinds of categories. He or she shows greater facility in attending to attributes that are relevant to the discrimination at hand (e.g., Are the items the same or different?). He or she can work effectively with a greater and greater number of attributes together and in succession, and he or she can, when called on, ever more easily attend to attributes that are now relevant but that previously were not. This trend has been observed consistently only for Western children. However, the cross-cultural literature on the topic of the various bases for equivalence grouping is scanty and contradictory. One very strong possibility that is suggested by a review of this literature is that all such bases are available to all human beings—even very young children—but that various aspects of culture selectively reinforce the use of one or the other of them so that (*a*) none tends to dominate; or (*b*) one or more tend to dominate. The predominance of formal equivalence in Western society most likely reflects a series of historical events—the extreme division of labor (Horton & Finnegan, 1973; Munroe & Munroe, 1980), the invention of writing (Olson, 1976; Goody, 1977) and formal schooling (Rogoff, 1981).

The number of available *structures* is even greater than the number of available bases, and the preceding remarks apply here as well. A very long list, which is probably not exhaustive, has been compiled by Tyler (1978). He gives 15 different structures for the organization of items (pp. 255–289). We begin, however, with no structure at all—an array of elements that our hypothetical subject sees as being completely unrelated to each other. A great deal of research shows that, all other things being equal, the Westerner sees similarities where the non-Westerner sees differences (Olson, 1976). If the latter are "slaves to the particular," then the former, clearly, are "slaves to the general."

The most basic category is a pair, and pairs can be structured in a variety of ways. Pairs can be linked in a series or chainlike fashion (Olver & Hornsby, 1966). Frequently, pairs are formed on the basis of binary opposition (C. H. Brown, 1979), and these can be combined to form a hierarchy (Sahlins, 1976). Equivalence can also be determined through a multidimensional grid (Bobrow, 1975; Hunn, 1976), where each axis of the grid represents a bipolar attribute. Finally, trees and taxonomies are created when attributes are mapped onto hierarchies (Tyler, 1969).

As with bases, there is overwhelming evidence that the various structures are universally available to all individuals. Western children tend to use a variety of structures for forming equivalence when they are younger (Olver & Hornsby, 1966), but the taxonomy comes to dominate and gets more and more complex with age. Anglin (1977, pp. 200–221) shows this progression very nicely in data from children (ages 2.75 to 6) and adults. The list of attributes that subjects give as relevant to the category *dog* increases from 6 to 40. Subordinate terms (e.g., *guard, poodle*) increase from 0 to 17, and superordinate terms (e.g., *pet, animal*) increase from 0 to 4. The data would seem to indicate that this is a very gradual process, and that there is no qualitative shift from totally nontaxonomic to taxonomic structures.

Also like bases, the dominance of taxonomic structures may be a Western phenomenon. In the area of the identification and arranging of plants and animals, the taxonomy seems to be universally employed (Berlin, 1978). However, languages differ in the degree of complexity inherent in "folk taxonomies" of the plant (C. H. Brown, 1977) and animal (C. H. Brown, 1979) domains. Brown and his colleagues (Brown, Kolar, Torrey, Truong-Quang, & Volkman, 1976) have found that taxonomic structuring principles are used in several "nonbiological" domains as well, although this exercise has not gone uncriticized (Van Esterik, 1978, 1979; Durrenberger & Morrison, 1979).

The attribute grid—componential analysis—is widely implicated in studies of kinship structure (Goodenough, 1956). However, societies in the New Guinea Highlands may represent a significant exception to this trend (Strathern, 1972). The chain structure is uncommon or unnoticed in research on non-Western thought, although it has been implicated in at least one study in Papua New Guinea (Lancy, 1978a). Pairing (especially binary opposition) is ubiquitous in the cognitive makeup of societies, especially in terms of the formation of symbols marking various distinctions in religious and social life (e.g., *clean* versus *unclean* [Douglas, 1966]; *left* versus *right* [Needham, 1973]; *raw* versus *cooked, hot* versus *cold* [Lévi-Strauss, 1969]).

With some exceptions to be discussed in a later chapter, anthropologists have assumed that the structures of these various domains (plants, animals, kinsmen, religious systems) do not vary in any systematic way across cultures, but rather it is content or particular features of structure that vary. Hence this literature has not been useful for generating hypotheses about the possible causes of differences in cognitive processes. There are two areas however where scholars have made extensive comparisons of structure—counting (e.g., Zaslavsky, 1973) and the naming of colors (Berlin & Kay, 1969). A discussion of research on the structure of counting systems in Papua New Guinea will be deferred until Chapter 5, but a single, relevant study of color-naming structure will be reviewed here.

The nice thing about color terms from my point of view is that the total color nomenclature of a language can be represented as reflecting various degrees of structure, and there appears to be a clear evolution from simple to complex as one considers languages with color nomenclatures of varying sizes. At the most basic level—Berlin and Kay's Level 1—are languages that have only a pair of color terms (usually light and dark). At the other extreme, English color nomenclature clearly is represented as a hierarchy, with *color* as the head term. Then several named primary colors (hues), are at the next level (e.g., *red, blue, yellow*). At the next lower level we might find a distinction based on saturation (e.g., *pea green* ["real green"] versus *aqua* ["sort of green"]). One level lower might be a distinction based on value (e.g., *pea green* ["light green"] versus *emerald green* ["dark green"]). And at the lowest level the distinction is between individual colors (e.g., *pea green* versus *olive drab*)—altogether a five-level taxonomy (see C. H. Brown *et al.*, 1976).

The study (Rosch, 1972) to be described involved a comparison of subjects at the extremes of this continuum—the Dani from the Central Highlands of western New Guinea and American adults. The subject is shown a color chip by the experimenter for a few seconds; then it is put away, and the subject must now pick the identical chip from an array of 160 different colors. Not surprisingly, the Americans were much more successful at this task. In a series of experiments that extended Rosch's research, Lucy and Shweder (1979) tried to uncover why it was that the American subjects did so well at this task. First, they found that the subjects used self-generated verbal descriptions to aid them in the task. Second, many of these were shared; that is, several chips elicited the same color name from most of the subjects. These names are part of the common lexicon. Third, many subjects appeared to be using a kind of taxonomic strategy in making a verbal differentiation among the colors. For example, when they forgot the Level 2 term—the primary color name—they were completely lost. Distinctions at this level were the most critical. Primary color terms were often supplemented with terms that distinguished saturation and value, and their verbal descriptions became more detailed if the test chip had to be located among many very similar chips—that is, they used as many features of the taxonomy as the situation called for.

The authors see their work as vindicating Whorf's 1956 theory that patterns of thought are reflected in patterns of language—in particular, in the way people create categories and in the kinds of things they choose to keep together in their categories. For the Dani, color as an abstraction appears to be largely irrelevant. A single binary opposition suffices to categorize all the colors. For Americans, color is apparently much more important; for them hundreds of distinctive color, or color-related, lexemes organized into a five-level taxonomy are required to categorize the colors. Witkowski and Brown (1981) reviewed the processes whereby languages added color terms and related this to "increasing technological control over color in the form of dyeing, painting and other activities [p. 15]."

Taken together, the Dani study and the picture-sorting study of equivalence formation illustrate the way in which the issues discussed in this chapter can begin to become focused. The Dani research shows that a relatively deficient color nomenclature and taxonomy leads to a relative *deficit* in performance on a cognitive task. The equivalence study shows that differences in the preferred (e.g., function) basis for grouping items leads to *differences* in performance on a cognitive task. In the "worldview" of various peoples, items are located in a kind of two-dimensional space. One dimension represents a continuum in which, at one end, the item (action, object, person) is embedded in a field of contexts (images, actions, functions, metaphors), and at the other end the item is embedded in a field of words (names, attributes). On the second dimension, the continuum represents the extent to which any item can be "connected" in a hierarchy with levels of abstraction and degrees of inclusion. Although the evidence reviewed thus far would seem to suggest that the location of a society's worldview in this two-dimensional space is predictable from a knowledge of its "development" in Western terms, research among the Tiv of Nigeria (Price-Williams, 1962) in particular would urge extreme caution in drawing such a conclusion.

Implications for a Program of Research

I have cited educational issues in Chapter 1 as a basis for the study of culture and cognitive development in Papua New Guinea. Here I have sketched out the kinds of theoretical issues that such a study must address. It remains only to indicate the kinds of evidence that these issues, both practical and theoretical, would seem to demand. In terms of dependent variables, we wanted to use cognitive (as opposed to sensori-motor, IQ, or whatever) tests. Several constraints were apparent. We could not use any of the hundreds of tests in which either the stimuli or the responses involved drawings or written material. Such materials–skills were unavailable to the majority of our potential subjects. Ideally, the tests would be derived from the work of Piaget and/or Bruner to provide continuity with earlier research and to capitalize on the potential of these theories for instructional design. In particular, the tests should tap "category formation." Since we would be comparing children, tests that had been shown to discriminate poorly in this age range (e.g., conservation of area in which the majority failed) would be passed over. The tests that we chose to use had been previously used in PNG—namely conservation-of-length, the two-classification matrix, the bulb-board, and the picture-sorting tests. We added two further tests—counting and words free recall. A full description of the tests and the rationale for our choices will be found in the next chapter.

In one sense, however, the tests themselves are the least important aspect of design. In a major research effort spanning nearly a decade (Gay & Cole, 1967; Cole et al., 1971; Lancy, 1972; Ciborowski & Cole, 1973; Scribner, 1974), a score of investigators, including myself, had sought to study culture and cognition by endlessly varying the cognitive tests while holding the "culture" (Kpelle versus American) constant. In the Papua New Guinean study the tests were to be held constant, while the "cultures" were to be varied as widely as possible. The selection of sites (cultures) was governed in part by an initial examination of data from a parallel comparative study of classification systems.

Several promising areas for the study of classification have already been mentioned. Color nomenclature presented one serious obstacle. What evidence we were able to garner at the outset indicated little variation intranationally in the structure of the color lexicon for various languages. Kinship presented another kind of problem—too much *intracultural* variability (Langness, 1964; Sankoff, 1972). Although a great deal of progress has been made in recent years, the overall linguistic picture in Papua New Guinea is still very cloudy. Comparative studies have almost exclusively involved lexicostatistical analyses of shared or cognate vocabularies. We found no "starting points" here.

Counting systems appeared ideal for our purpose, since the earlier collections–reviews gave evidence of interesting and systematic intranational variation. Ultimately we were to collect and classify over 200 different counting systems. Folk taxonomies also looked promising. There had been a substantial amount of previous research (Glick, 1964; Diamond, 1966; Bulmer & Tyler, 1968; Bulmer & Menzies, 1972, 1973; Dwyer, 1976a, 1976b; Hays, 1979), although it was confined largely to the New Guinea Highlands. We were to collect folk taxonomies from 14 societies, in 11 of which we simultaneously conducted cognitive testing with children. Our procedures and results for the comparative studies of counting and classification systems are reported in Chapter 5.

Our goal was to "mesh" the two types of cognitive data (e.g., ethnographic and experimental) as far as possible. We elicited counting systems and tested children's counting skills; we elicited classification systems and tested children's ability to classify (in the picture-sorting and free-recall experiments). In both cases the "responses" to the ethnographic research were to become the "stimuli" in the experimental research. Given Piaget's criticism of Lévi-Strauss, it is clear that collective products (e.g., counting, classification systems) could not be used directly to infer individual cognitive processes; hence the need for context-free tests. At the same time, any attempt to link cultural variability to cognitive variability is pure speculation unless this can be done explicity—by showing that variation in the pattern of the collective products is predictive of variation in patterns of cognitive-test performance.

Aside from culture, four further independent variables were to be included. Age was recorded because we were ultimately concerned with cognitive *development*. For most of the research to be reported, age ranged from 6 to 13 years. Grade was recorded because we were concerned secondarily with the interaction of formal schooling and cognitive development. In most of the research, grade ranges from 0 to 6; on two occasions we included high-school students as subjects. Gender was also of interest because the life-styles of males and females in some Papua New Guinean societies are reported as being radically divergent. These three variables were systematically sampled in each society. Eight females and eight males were selected from each of two age levels (6–9, 10–13) with less than 3 years of schooling, and from one age level (10–13) with more than 4 years of schooling. Finally, a Mid-Upper-Arm-Circumference measure (MUAC)—a normed indicator of nutritional status—was taken from each child.

I would like to indicate here some of our "expectations." We expected to confirm earlier research that had shown a developmental lag for Papua New Guinean schoolchidren when compared with Western children. The principal implication of this finding would be that, given comparable goals, the task facing Papua New Guinean educators would be recognized as being more difficult than that facing their counterparts from developed nations: They would have to "move" their charges much further in the same period of time. We expected to confirm Kelly's finding that the extent of deficit varied intranationally. We hoped to go further, however, and ultimately tie in cognition closely enough to culture so that a "diagnosis" could be made without resorting in each instance to cognitive testing. Specifically, we hoped to be eventually able—from very limited information—to pinpoint societies whose children were at the greatest risk of failure in formal schooling due to probably great cognitive deficits. Such children could then be targeted for various remediation efforts. If we became very lucky, we hoped to be able to isolate those cognitive processes that were most divergent from the Western norm and thereby help to focus this remediation effort. Finally, we expected that the ethnographic data might serve as a rich source of ideas for the construction of "bridging" curricula that linked the world view of the child's society with the Western view of the school.

Intercultural Variation
in Cognitive Development

Procedure

As we saw in the previous chapter, Papua New Guinea had already received a considerable amount of attention from cross-cultural psychologists prior to the beginning of the Indigenous Mathematics Project. Our fundamental concern was to extend and replicate this earlier research. The tasks that Kelly had used had all yielded interesting results. Each evoked a different pattern of influences from culture, school, and development. Further, all tapped one form or another of category formation—the theoretical construct found most helpful in uniting cognitive-test and ethnographic data. We would use these tasks, with some modifications that will be described later, and two other tasks not previously administered in Papua New Guinea—counting and free-recall.

It followed that if the nature of the counting system had a discernible effect on cognitive patterns (see Chapter 5) generally, it should have a very direct effect on counting behavior. If children showed equal facility at counting a relatively large array regardless of the type of counting system used, this would greatly weaken any hypothetical counting–cognition link. The child would also be asked to count the same array (23 matchsticks) in *Pisin* or English. Here we wanted to assess the relative ease with which schoolchildren from the various sites acquired a "foreign" cognitive system, again with the view that children, from societies where Type I and Type II counting systems especially were used (see Chapter 5), might have inordinate difficulty in learning a new and very different enumeration system.

The free-recall procedure was, like the Olver and Hornsby (1966) picture-sorting task, an indirect test of the child's proficiency at forming equivalence categories. In typical use of the paradigm, some number of items (12–20) drawn equally from a set of categories (4–5) are read aloud to the child in a random order, and the child is asked to recall them. Older children and adults unconsciously order the random lists—either in storage or retrieval—by category, so that their recall is "clustered"; words from the same category are recalled in clusters. Young children do not reorganize the words to the same degree unless they are prompted to do so. Kpelle children, however, do not show this same sort of shift to category clustering as they get older (Cole et al., 1971). This test, then, is also susceptible to age and cultural influences.

The tasks we employed were therefore "tried and true." Where we hoped to innovate was in terms of our selection of samples and in the collection of ancillary ethnographic data. Most cross-cultural cognitive research has compared only two societies: developed versus under-developed. This type of design has been criticized on many grounds (Campbell, 1961); for example, differences in the "cultures" are so many and varied that interpretations of the variation in cognitive-test performance in terms of the culture "variable" are untenable. Berry (Berry & Annis, 1974), for example, has carried out a long-term program of cross-cultural research in perceptual and personality predispositions in *several* societies that were all at the same level of development in Western terms, but his work and that of Dasen (1975) is exceptional. We intended, then, to work in several societies, all of which were relatively unacculturated. Given Papua New Guinea's state of development, this stricture still leaves a wide-open field. Two further constraints were imposed. First, we hoped to choose sites where anthropologists or linguists had recently conducted or were currently conducting fieldwork. We anticipated having to rely on their assistance and/or on their data to flesh-in the "culture" variable. The sites finally chosen for the initial round of testing were Ialibu (Kewa language, Type I counting), Tekin (Oksapmin, I), Golke (Melpa, I and II), Imonda (Waris, II), Lalavaipi (Toaripi, II), Kiwai Island (Kiwai, II), Kerau (Tauade, II), Gloucester (Kilenge, III), Siassi Islands (Mandok, III), and Ponam Island (Ponam, IV).

The first two sites to be investigated were Ialibu (see Figure 2.12) and

Ponam Island (see Figure 2.17) where Hilary Pumuye and Agnes Paliau had done ethnographic studies of the indigenous mathematics system and subsequently served as hosts–interpreters for our research. These sites were used to pilot our instruments and ideas. Consistent with a counting-system theory (Lancy, 1978a), Ponam, with a Type IV (base 10) counting system, yielded higher levels of performance on the tasks than Kewa (Type I, body counting). Testing was carried out in these two sites in late 1976; the remaining sites were visited during 1977.

In general, our program in any given site went as follows. Our first task on arrival was to find an individual to serve as interpreter and experimenter. Typically, he was a teacher or an ex-teacher. These individuals spoke the vernacular as well as English, were native to the village, had considerable experience working with children, and easily understood the aims of our tasks. In addition to the experimenters, our team consisted of a recorder (one of two Papua New Guinea research assistants on the project), whose job it was to train and assist the experimenter and to record the subjects' responses, and a supervisor (myself in most cases), whose job it was to conduct the ethnographic research and to set up and oversee the experimental research.

Once the aims of our research were explained to the experimenter, the three of us proceeded to the school and the village to explain our mission and to solicit assistance and cooperation, including the provision of accommodations. At the beginning of our stay, we would usually address the entire population assembled for council day or *dey bilong gavaman*, and at the end we would discuss our findings and their implications with the assembled Community-School teachers.

Several days were given over to the collection of vernacular names for common items and categories. Stimuli for the cognitive tasks were drawn from this inventory. With the stimuli complete, we began a training–pilot-testing phase. The experimental sessions were held in a spare room in the school or in someone's house. Here we tested children who would not be involved in the experiment proper—usually third or fourth graders. This pilot phase served to train the experimenter and to test-out the stimuli. If it turned out that our "common items" were not recognized by these children, they were discarded and replaced. Next, we drew up our samples. These were random samples of eight boys and eight girls from the sixth grade (the fifth grade in schools that had no sixth grade). This was the "10–13 school" group. The experimenter was asked to find children of the same age who had never attended school. Aside from screening out handicapped children, and children who were obviously older than 13 or younger than 10, we took the first eight boys and eight girls from this population as our "10–13 unschooled" group. The "never-attended" rule had to be bent slightly in a few cases to a "not-yet-progressed-beyond-Grade 3" rule because the rate of attendance varied from less than 50% (Toaripi) to nearly 100% (Ponam). The same procedure was employed to create the "6–9" group. Some of these children were in Grade 1; others were not. Grade is not perfectly correlated with age in Papua New Guinea; hence, where we had to make a choice we did so on the basis of grade rather than age. Thus, some samples are older than others (e.g., because children from these areas start and finish school at a later age). In most cases, exact ages are not known, so ages are recorded as estimates (see Table 4.1). In addition to the age of each child, we also recorded the mid-upper-arm-circumference measure (MUAC). This measure is associated with past and present nutritional status and is normed for age. We had every reason to believe that the extent of undernutrition varied among the 10 sites.

The Tests

Children were tested individually in the presence of an experimenter, a recorder, and a supervisor, with the subject seated across the table (or school desk) from the experimenter. The recorder and supervisor re-

TABLE 4.1
Breakdown of Samples by Age and Education

Group	Overall Age	Overall Grade	Group 1 Age	Group 1 Grade	Group 2 Age	Group 2 Grade	Group 3 Age	Group 3 Grade
Ponam	10.31	2.75	7.44	0.75	11.56	3.44	11.94	5.00
Mandok	10.54	2.33	8.00	1.75	11.75	0.31	11.88	5.06
Toaripi	9.52	1.96	7.25	0.5	10.5	0	10.81	5.38
Kiwai	10.02	2.50	7.06	0	11.19	1.88	11.81	5.63
Oksapmin	11.44	2.02	7.56	0.88	12.81	0	12.13	5.19
Kilenge	9.65	2.50	6.5	0	11.06	1.63	11.38	6.00
Kewa	9.96	1.94	7.06	0	11.25	0	11.56	5.81
Tauade	11.50	2.17	7.81	1.0	12.75	0.06	13.94	5.44
Melpa	10.54	2.06	7.25	1.0	12.25	0.06	12.13	5.13
Imonda	10.63	2.10	7.44	0.94	12.38	0	12.06	5.38
Grand Means	10.41	2.27	7.33	.68	11.38	.74	12.13	5.38

mained unobtrusively in the background. The experimenter began the procedure by talking to the child about common acquaintances and mundane affairs to set him or her at ease. Then the tests were administered, the "instructions" (in all cases in the vernacular) having been worked out and rehearsed during the pilot period. In point of fact, as will become obvious from a description of the tests, they—excepting free recall—were administered in a clinical manner. The subjects were encouraged to ask questions, to try out something and then change their minds, incorrect responses were corrected, etc. The experimenter appreciated that the subjects were being tested and was encouraged to guide the children as fully as possible, short of displaying the "correct" response. Furthermore, neither the experimenter nor the recorder was aware of our hypotheses concerning the possible effects of age, schooling, and culture on performance. Girls in particular were shy in the presence of male testers and had to be handled delicately. Administration took longer (total time varied from 40 to 90 minutes). As we shall see, there is no evidence from the results that girls performed more poorly than boys. However, they might have performed at a superior level had we been able to provide same-sex experimenters and recorders. In all, 480 subjects were tested. All completed the battery, but a few of the youngest (fewer than 2%) were unable to complete parts of it. The use of three individuals to administer these tasks may seem like overkill, but it proved necessary because often only one of the three of us would notice that the subject did not fully understand what was required. Experimenters attended to the child's speech, the recorder to responses, and the supervisor to nonverbal cues given off by the experimenter and subject. Between us, I think we caught all the doubtful cases, and we were able to repeat or rephrase the instructions or the training until the child understood the requirements.

The first test administered to the subject is conservation of length. The experimenter locates two lengths of stick—the species varying with locale—and cuts these so that they are equal and approximately 40 cm in length. The sticks are placed parallel to each other collinearly about 5 cm apart. Their placement is horizontal from the subject's perspective. The subject is asked to determine if the two sticks are the same length. Invariably, subjects push the two sticks together and "eyeball" the two ends. If unsatisfied at that point or if uncertain, they are encouraged to grasp the sticks and hold them vertically with one end of each resting on the table. They can then look across the top of the pair. If they are still not satisfied that the sticks are equal, they are handed a knife (Papua New Guinean children learn to handle knives with ease at a very early age) and told to make them even. This they proceed to do, and they are encouraged to whittle away until they are quite certain that the sticks are the same length.

The sticks are then returned to their original configuration. The experimenter displaces the stick that is closer to the subject by about one third to the right. The subject is then asked whether they are the same. If he or she says that they are, he or she is scored as "conserving," and is then asked for an explanation. If he or she gives an explanation that implicates the essential identity of the sticks, he or she is scored as "conserving with reason." If the subject says they are not the same, he or she is asked which one is now longer. The majority of subjects unhesitantly point to or touch the stick that they feel is longer, and then we repeat the procedure from the beginning (the only difference is that the farther stick is displaced to the left). If the subject persists in claiming that one is longer, he or she is scored as "nonconserving." If he or she changes his judgment, a "tie-breaker" procedure is used whereby the two sticks are placed perpendicular to each other to form a "T" (from the subject's perspective). This provokes a common optical illusion: The horizontal segment looks longer. If the subject now persists in claiming they are the same, he or she is scored as "conserving," and an explanation is sought. If the subject reverts to a nonconserving judgment, he or she is scored accordingly. As it turned out, we had to use the tie breaker with only 4 of our 480 subjects.

The second procedure is the double-classification task, which is modified slightly from the original. The materials consist of a matrix board divided off by partitions into 3 × 3 slots, and nine blocks painted a uniform shade of blue. The largest block is 4 cm on a side and 20 cm tall. The remaining blocks decrease in size by 20% increments. From the subject's perspective, the blocks decrease in height along the columns from farthest to nearest, and in thickness along the rows from left to right. There are five problems, which are presented in an invariant order. The subject is first encouraged to look carefully at the blocks. Then he or she is told to look away while the experimenter removes the shortest row of three blocks. The subject is then told to put these blocks back in their proper places. If he or she fails, the experimenter corrects the arrangement. The procedure is repeated, but this time the middle-thickness column of blocks is removed. For the third problem, all blocks except the largest are removed; in the fourth problem, all are removed. In the last problem, the subject does not look away; instead he or she watches as the experimenter removes all the blocks; then the experimenter rotates the matrix board clockwise 180° on its center axis. The subject is told to replace the blocks so that when the board is rotated back again (mimed by the experimenter), it will look as it did originally. The subject is given one point for successfully rebuilding the matrix and an additional point for successfully mastering the altered perspective.

In the first two problems, the child must extract only one attribute (single classification) from the array, either height or thickness, and use this information to mediate the solution. In the remaining problems, he or she must simultaneously coordinate both attributes (double classification) and for the last problem the subject must reverse the transformation that the experimenter has effected. As with all the tasks, there were no time constraints. The subjects were encouraged to rearrange the blocks if they were not satisfied with their initial efforts, and errors were corrected before proceeding to the next problem.

The third test we have called the *flap board*. It is an extensively modified (Jones, 1974) version of Olson's (1966) bulb-board test. Kelly's (1971b) use of the bulb-board test showed that it had considerable potential. But in its original form, it was too strange and difficult, and it required electricity to operate, which would not be available in our target sites. The flap-board test is entirely analogous to the bulb-board test, but it represents a less drastically unfamiliar task and does not require electricity.

There are three kinds of materials—model patterns, test patterns, and a flap board. The patterns each have 25 black and white circles arranged in a 5×5 symmetrical array. The pattern is achieved by the arrangement of black and white circles. Similarly, the flap board has 25 holes, each of which is covered by a "flap." The board is placed near the subject, flat on the table. The model patterns are placed side by side just above the board, also flat on the table. One test pattern is placed inside the board. It is identical to one of the model patterns, and its circles are in register with the holes in the board. The overall objective is for the subject to determine which of the model patterns the test pattern is identical to by "looking at" the test pattern, one circle at a time.

The test phase is preceded by a practice phase in which two model patterns are used (Z versus T). The child is encouraged to trace these respective patterns with his or her fingers. Then the matching test patterns are placed just beneath the model patterns. Again the subject is encouraged to trace the patterns and to verify that they are identical to the corresponding model patterns. With all the flaps up, one test pattern is placed in the board. The experimenter asks the subject to point to the model pattern that is in the board. The experimenter then closes the flaps and again asks the subject to point to the model pattern. The experimenter opens a few flaps, one at a time, and shows the subject the correspondence between the location of individual black and white circles on the model pattern and under the flaps. The experimenter takes out the test pattern. They are again laid under the model patterns, and the experimenter explains that while the subject is looking away, he will put one of these inside the board, with the other face down on the table, and the subject will have to determine which one is inside. This done, the experimenter tells the subject to open the flaps ("doors" in the actual instructions) one at a time and look at the test pattern. As soon as he or she knows which pattern is inside, the subject should point to the appropriate model pattern. The practice phase continues, randomly alternating the test patterns until the subject makes three correct matches in a row.

Four problems are presented during the test phase. There are in every case four model patterns in two sets, an easier set (proportion of black to white circles is less than .5) used in the first two problems, and a harder set (proportion of black to white dots is greater than .5) in the last two problems (see Figure 4.1). In addition, just before beginning the second problem, the experimenter exhorts the subject to try and guess the pattern by opening only a few flaps. Otherwise, subjects are not restricted in the number of flaps they open (a flap must be closed, however, before another may be opened), nor in the time they may take to solve the problem. Nor are they penalized for wrong guesses: They are merely told to keep on trying.

Three distinctive patterns of responding were identified and served as a basis for scoring. The subject who uses the *minimum* strategy, for example, will notice that the lower left circle is black in two of the model patterns and white in the other two. He or she opens that flap and finds a white circle. He or she next opens the middle flap in the row farthest to the left and finds a white circle. He or she correctly identifies the second-from-left model pattern after opening only two flaps. The subject who uses a *partial-pattern* strategy typically stares at one particular model pattern for a while, and, continuing to keep an eye on it, he or she begins to open a set of flaps. If the subject is considering the second-from-left pattern, he or she will probably open all the flaps in the farthest right column, and, having found all the circles to be black, he or she will point to this model pattern. If told that he or she is wrong (assume that the test pattern matches the third-from-left model pattern), the subject scans the

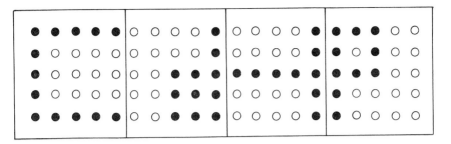

Figure 4.1. Flap-board model patterns.

remaining patterns and settles on the third pattern from the left. He or she then opens all the flaps in the second column from the right and then makes a correct match by pointing to the third-from-left pattern. As a practical matter, if the subject has opened from 4 to 12 flaps before arriving at the correct match, he or she is scored as using a "partial pattern." The third strategy is again quite different. The *total-pattern* subject pays almost no attention to the model patterns initially, but instead methodically looks under each flap row by row or column by column. After opening about half of the flaps, he or she begins to scan the model patterns very briefly while opening more flaps. The subject may make a correct choice before he or she has opened all the flaps, or the subject may in fact have to go back and take a second and third look under some or all of the flaps. Clearly, he or she is trying to see the whole test pattern rather than decompose it into its critical elements. These subjects have to be repeatedly reminded not to leave the flaps open and not to open several at a time.

The fourth test is picture-sorting. Working with several adult informants, we elicit the individual and category names for a variety of common items that can be located in or around the village. From this information, we select 5–7 categories to use in the experiment. No category may have more than five exemplars, nor less than three. We endeavor to use items that can be categorized relatively easily on a perceptible, functional, or nominal basis. We try, wherever possible, to make these categories comparable across societies, so that each set contains, for example, items of Western clothing (*kolos* in Pidgin), people (a man, woman, boy, and girl), food, tools, and body ornaments (*bilas* in Pidgin). Note that— excepting *bilas*—these are also prominent categories in American children's vocabularies (Rinsland, 1945). Less frequently used are the categories of weapons, pigs, traditional buildings, containers, hunting implements, cooking implements, tree fruits, and body parts.

The choice of a category depends on finding a name or phrase in the language that informants agree is the appropriate name for the category. (As we shall see in the next chapter, this severely constrained our choices in several societies.) The choice of an item depends on its being easily and unambiguously photographed, and on complete agreement among informants that the item belongs to the category in question. The total number of items eventually used varied from 24 to 28. Items are gathered together, and Polaroid color photographs are taken of each against a neutral background. During the pilot phase, subjects are asked to name each picture. On the very few occasions when a picture is not identified by two or more of these subjects, it is eliminated from the array.

During testing, subjects are first asked to name each picture, and they are corrected if necessary. The experimenter shuffles the photos and then lays them out in four to five parallel rows in front of the subject. He or she is asked to pick some of the items that go together and make a "line." In Papua New Guinea, *line* has a broader meaning than its English gloss. Usually translated as *clan*, the term invariably is used by extension to refer to arrays of various kinds. Having made the line, the subject is asked why the items go together. The recorder notes the number of items in the line, as well as the grouping basis and structure (p. 61), from the subject's explanation. The photographs are returned to the array, and this *free-sorting* procedure is repeated two more times, followed by three trials of a *forced-sorting* procedure. Taking items not used previously by the subject if possible, the experimenter forms a line that conforms to a native category and asks the subject why the items go together. Base and structure are again noted. This task yields three pieces of information for the first three trials—number in the group, whether the subject used a nominal or some other base, and whether the subject used a superordinate or some other structure—and the latter two pieces of information for the second set of three trials.

Next the subject is asked to count 23 matchsticks in his vernacular and then the same 23 matchsticks in English or *Pisin*. The experimenter records the highest number attained without error in both cases. Finally, the experimenter administers the free-recall procedure. Four items from each of four named native categories are used. For these items, we draw on those categories and items that met all the criteria for inclusion in the picture-sorting task, except that it was considered they could not be photographed. In the free-recall task, for example, we have used house parts, birds, trees, fish, dances, etc. The subject is then asked to recall the items in any order. The recorder writes down the words recalled by the subject. When the subject indicates he or she is finished, the procedure is repeated.

There are three free-recall trials altogether. Scoring is based on the number recalled (repetitions and intrusions are not scored) and on "clustering." In examining the recall protocols, each pair of items from the same category recalled together earns a 4, each trio a 9, and each quadruplet a 16. These figures are summed and divided by the total recalled on that trial to yield a clustering score (0–4).

Results

Conservation-of-Length Task

The administration of this task presented few problems. Children seemed eager to "study" the sticks and had no trouble in taking our directives and questions seriously. On the basis of previous research in Papua New Guinea, we had been led to expect relatively poor performance on this task. In Kelly's study (1977), success exceeds 10% only in the case of the oldest (12+) "schooled" group. Hence, we were pleasantly surprised to find that success exceeded 50% in 3 of our 10 societies for the sample as a whole, and in 5 of the societies when only the performance of 10–13-year-old schoolchildren is considered. In a similar study done with urban French-speaking Canadians, the 50% level is reached around age 8, and by 11.5 years all children successfully conserve length (Pinard & Lavoie, 1974). To be sure, we also replicated Kelly's findings in that in several of our sites success did not exceed 10%—notably among Taude- and Melpa-speakers, two of Kelly's three language groups. Culture effects are, therefore, highly significant.

As Table 4.2 indicates, when children conserved successfully, they were usually able to give a satisfactory explanation for their response. Schooling has a significant impact on these results. Kelly (1971a) had initially found no effect of schooling, but in a later replication with Melpa-speakers (1977) a school effect ($p < .01$) did emerge. As we shall see under the discussion of education effects, they do not take place in every site. From

TABLE 4.2
Conservation of Length (Percentage Success)

	Conserve	Conserve with reason
Overall (480)	4.6	25.9
6– 9 years (160)	5.0	17.5
10–13 years (160)	3.8	20.8
10–13 school (160)	5.0	40.3
High (Ponam)	16.7	68.8
Low (Melpa)	0	4.2
Age effects		NS
School effects		***
Culture effects		***

$*p < .05.$
$**p < .005.$
$***p < .0005.$

my interpretation[1] of Piaget's formulation, neither culture nor schooling is expected to have much impact on conservation of length, while age or developmental effects are expected to be large. Our findings show the reverse of this expectation. Developmental effects are not significant over all 10 sites and are significant in only 1 individual site (Ponam), which can be discounted because the older Ponam group has significantly more education (see Table 4.1) than the younger group. Thus, while Kelly's (1977) study offers qualified support for the theory in finding a weak developmental effect ($p < .05$), and neither education nor culture effects, our broader sampling of sites indicates that the effects of education and culture appear to be stronger than age. The relationship between age and grade are shown clearly in Table 4.3. The only reversal to the trend of improved performance at each higher level of schooling is found in the youngest group. But Kelly (1971a) also reports a finding of "precocity" among the youngest unschooled children—a phenomenon noted elsewhere (Bovet, 1974) with conservation of quantity. The failure to find an advantage accruing to children in the first few years of school actually strengthens the case for education effects overall, because it indicates that the superior performance of the older educated children is not accounted for by a "selection" factor.

[1] An interpretation that two reviewers of this manuscript, Harry Beilin and Christopher Hallpike, have taken exception to.

TABLE 4.3
Conservation of Length (Percentage Success) by Age and Grade

	Grade		
Age level	0	1–3	4–6
5–8	27.4 (84)[a]	16.2 (117)	—
9–11	17.7 (79)	38.0 (21)	63.3 (120)
12+	16.2 (99)	21.4 (14)	42.8 (166)

[a]N is in parentheses.

The Matrix Problems

The nine-block matrix was, in many ways, our most satisfactory task. Like the flap-board task, it is almost totally a nonverbal task (for both the experimenter and the subject), but unlike the flap-board task, children had little difficulty in understanding the requirements. Another source of satisfaction is the degree to which the pattern of results conformed to results obtained in the original use of the design (Bruner & Kenney, 1966). The problems are of three types. "Thickness" and "height" are single-classification problems; the child can solve the problem by attending to only a single attribute. "One-left," "all-1," and "all-2" are double-classification problems. The child must attend to two dimensions simultaneously; "reversal" requires the child to reconstruct the matrix after a 180° rotation. Success on these three types was 88%, 72%, and 23.2%, respectively. This trend is highly significant (Pearson chi-square $=$ 639.69, 2 df, $p < .0005$). A Gutmann-scale analysis was applied to three of the problems: height, all-1, and reversal. The *coefficient of reproducibility* of .97 indicates a near-perfect score. What this means is that children who were successful on the reversal problem also succeeded on the two easier problems, and children who were successful on the double-classification problem also succeeded on the single-classification problem.

Consistent with the American (Bruner & Kenney, 1966) and earlier PNG (Kelly, 1971b) studies, developmental effects are significant for every problem (see Table 4.4). The farthest-to-the-right column of the table shows a "total" that is obtained by assigning the subject a score of 1 for each of the six problems solved and summing. On average, the older group solved about one more problem than the younger group. However, this advance comes from improved performance on all the problems. The evidence for an ikonic-to-symbolic shift is not strong. Anecdotally, we can report that young children tended to make more errors, which they later corrected by looking at the resultant "pattern" and detecting the irregu-

TABLE 4.4
Matrix Problems (Percentage Success)

	Thickness	Height	One left	All-1	All-2	Reverse	Total
Overall (479)	85.4	90.2	70.8	74.6	70.0	23.1	4.14
6– 9 years (160)	76.3	80.6	52.5	58.1	54.4	11.9	3.33
10–13 (160)	86.9	94.4	75.0	78.8	72.5	25.6	4.33
10–13 school (159)	93.7	96.2	85.5	87.4	83.6	32.1	4.75
High (Mandok)	95.8	97.9	85.4	91.7	83.3	47.9	4.69
Low (Melpa)	70.8	81.3	52.1	58.3	56.3	6.3	3.29
Age effects	*	***	***	***	***	**	***
School effects	NS	NS	*	NS	*	NS	*
Culture effects	*	*	**	**	*	***	***

$*p < .05.$
$**p < .005.$
$***p < .0005.$

larities. All of the children tended to reconstruct the matrix row by row or column by column. They did not use an "interrupted" strategy based on either an image of the complete matrix in memory or a thoroughly symbolized representation to replace the blocks (for a discussion of this issue, see Greenfield & Schneider [1977]).

Comparing the age trends with the earlier research, we find a virtually perfect replication of the Kelly (1971b) findings, although children from only three of our sites approach the success rate of his subjects on the reversal problem. In comparison with the North American children that Kelly (1971b) studied, the deficit of 3 years in the achievement of single and double classification is also replicated here. In a study done with Canadian children (Brainerd, 1979), 80% of 6-year-olds and 8-year-olds succeed on single and double classification, respectively. The reversal test is considerably more difficult for the Papua New Guinea children than it is for American children. Eighty percent of American 7-year-olds succeed on this test (Bruner & Kenney, 1966), whereas in PNG success never exceeds 50% at any age or grade level in any society. The reversal test may represent an extreme test of Bruner's symbolic-processing mode—a mode that is not as often exercised in PNG.

Like Kelly, we find that the contribution of schooling to performance on the matrix problem is only marginally significant. However, this is probably due to a ceiling effect. The unschooled 10–13-year-olds are successful about 80% of the time (on all but reversal); therefore, there is not much room for additional improvement as a result of formal education. Culture effects are again marked, and this is especially true as the problems become progressively more difficult. The range between the society with the best success rate ("high") and ("low") steadily increases as we consider single classification, double classification, and reversal.

Flap-board Task

The flap-board test was the most difficult task to administer because the majority of subjects did not initially apply a systematic strategy toward a solution. The practice phase lasted up to five trials in some cases, and it was clear that a great deal of learning was going on. Children employed what Olson (1966) identified as a *search strategy*. The child searches almost randomly for bulbs that light or, in our case, for black circles, all the while paying very little attention to the model patterns. The extensive use of a search strategy in pilot work that does not lead to solution convinced us that a success measure based on a correct match of test and model patterns would not be very meaningful. The practice phase, then, was designed to bring the child to the point (reached in all but two cases) where he or she could systematically apply a strategy that would lead to correct matches. These strategies were not taught per se. Practice tended to lead to the application of the "total-pattern" strategy. The exhortation on the first problem to "try and get it by opening only a few flaps" led to a large number of children shifting "up" to the more efficient "partial-pattern" strategy. Results for these strategy choices are shown in Table 4.5. The strategy of the majority very clearly is "total pattern," which is used by 69% of the children in the first problem and by 48% of them in the second. The use of the "minimum" strategy is very low, exceeding 10% only on the second problem—where the prompt is given. There was a tendency for children to use the "total-pattern" strategy less often following the prompt (Olson's "constrained" condition), and this tendency carried over in the remaining three problems (Pearson chi-square = 78.74, 6 df, $p < .0005$). This effect wipes out any impact of the shift from easier (1, 2) to harder (3, 4) problems (Pearson chi-square = 5.66, 2 df, NS). However, children use the "minimum" strategy only about half as often on the harder problems as they do on the easy problem that is preceded by the prompt.

The use of more efficient strategies in Papua New Guinea would seem to fall behind comparable development in American children. Recall that Olson's (1966) 9-year-olds never used the total strategy; partial and minimum strategies are consistently used by 80% and 20% of his subjects, respectively. Comparable figures from our sample of 478 subjects, whose mean age is around 10, are 38%, 15%, and 0%, respectively. These figures

TABLE 4.5
Strategies for Flap-board Problems (Percentage)

	PB #1		PB #2		PB #3		PB #4		Total ($\bar{X}$)
	Partial	Minimum	Partial	Minimum	Partial	Minimum	Partial	Minimum	
Overall (478)	30.2	0.8	41.2	10.8	43.5	5.8	28.5	4.8	1.78
6– 9 years (160)	18.1	1.3	30.0	1.9	28.8	1.9	25.0	2.5	1.13
10–13 years (159)	27.0	0	42.1	13.2	47.2	5.0	36.5	3.8	1.74
10–13 school (159)	45.9	1.3	52.2	17.6	55.3	10.7	54.7	8.2	2.47
High (Ponam)	54.2	8.4	66.7	45.8	58.3	16.7	56.3	10.4	2.44
Low (Kilenge)	8.3	0	12.5	0	12.5	0	12.8	0	0.79
Age effects	NS		***		***		NS		***
School effects	**		*		†		***		***
Culture effects	***		***		***		***		***

*$p < .05$.
**$p < .005$.
***$p < .0005$.

represent the proportion of children who used a particular strategy on three out of four of the problems. Although Kelly has reported on his results with the Olson procedure on three separate occasions (1970, 1971c, 1971d), they are far from clear. It appears likely that our modifications yielded improved performance, and this, combined with our broader sample selection, led to age, education, and culture effects that he did not find. In the farthest to the right column in Table 4.5, a "total" is shown. This figure is arrived at by assigning a value of 1 to each problem in which the subject used either the partial or minimum strategy and summing. The highly significant age, education, and culture effects are clear from this composite measure. The procedure is extremely sensitive to slight shifts in cognitive-processing brought about by environmental and developmental factors.

Picture- Sorting Task

Setting up this task took a great deal of effort, although the actual administration went very smoothly. Unlike previous studies, we chose items to photograph that were drawn from categories that were highly salient for the children being tested. In the original study (Olver & Hornsby, 1966), the selection of items was virtually random. In the Kelly study (Philp & Kelly, 1974), items were chosen to represent several specific categories, but the categories did not change from site to site. (Items changed minimally.) Our design is aimed more at testing whether the child can use his or her own symbol system rather than a test of symbolic thinking per se. While some categories were used in several sites, others were selected because of their relevance to the peculiar lifeways of each site: For example, in Golke where warfare is endemic, *weapons* was a category; on Ponam where subsistence is based entirely on the exploitation of marine resources, *fishing gear* was a category; and in Imonda where hunting contributes substantially to the diet, *hunting things* was a category.

The ideal set size is 3–5. This ideal is a function of an "objective" sorting of the stimuli based on the taxonomy elicited from adults. For every category, there are at least three members and no more than five. Three fourths of the subjects' sets met this criterion (e.g., "number" columns 1, 3, 7). Children made the groups we expected them to make. To a lesser extent, the description they provided for each set reflected hierarchical organization. Their expressions tended, at least two thirds of the time, to cover all of the items in the set (e.g., "superordinate" columns 2, 5, 8, 10, 12, 14). Finally, they were somewhat less likely to supply an all-

TABLE 4.6
Strategies for Picture-Sorting (Percentage)

	Free Sort-1			Free Sort-2			Free Sort	
	Number (3–5)	Structure (superordinal)	Base (nominal)	Number	Structure	Base	Number	Structure
Overall (473)	77.8	67.3	67.9	76.8	71.0	61.0	74.6	69.6
6– 9 years (155)	79.2	55.2	69.5	76.6	61.7	52.9	69.5	61.7
10–13 years (160)	74.8	75.6	66.9	72.6	78.8	63.1	78.0	76.1
10–13 school (158)	79.5	73.6	70.4	81.1	75.5	69.8	76.1	74.2
High (Toaripi)	97.9	92.9	95.8	91.77	89.6	100.0	91.7	93.6
Low (Kewa)	50.0	41.7	8.3	50.0	45.8	14.9	41.7	41.7
Age effects	NS	***	NS	NS	***	NS	NS	*
School effects	NS	NS	NS	NS	NS	NS	NS	NS
Culture effects	***	***	***	***	***	***	***	***

*$p < .05$.
**$p < .005$.
***$p < .0005$.

encompassing label ("nominal" columns 3, 6, 9, 11, 13, 15) for each set. Note that columns 16–19 present means over the the sorting trials for four dependent measures. Column 16 shows the mean number of sets of size 3–5 that subjects made on the three free-sorting trials. Column 17 shows the mean number of times the superordinate structure was employed over all six trials; column 18 the mean for nominal base; and column 19 the mean number of responses that employed superordinate structure *and* nominal base. (See Table 4.6.)

It is difficult to compare these results directly with the earlier North American and Papua New Guinean research. As Rosch has shown (1978), whether the individual responds categorically in a given situation depends on what categories are made available. In particular, there are basic-level categories that are far easier to recognize than categories higher or lower in the taxonomy. We took pains to use these basic-level categories in constructing our picture set and therefore found a much greater use of the superordinate structure than did Kelly (1970) and Huntsman (1973). It was still less than among North American children (Olver & Hornsby, 1966). We found developmental effects, as did the earlier investigators. A higher proportion of our subjects used a nominal base than did those in either of the two previous studies. The use of basic-level categories accounts for part of this difference, but we were very liberal also with

.se	Forced Sort-1		Forced Sort-2		Forced Sort-3		Totals			
	Struc-ture	Base	Struc-ture	Base	Struc-ture	Base	Total number	Total superordinate	Total nominal	Total S.N.
.9	72.3	65.0	67.3	64.0	73.3	61.7	2.29	4.26	3.89	2.91
.4	64.5	66.5	53.5	61.9	63.9	60.6	2.25	3.60	3.73	2.33
.3	72.5	60.6	73.1	65.0	78.1	59.4	2.27	4.53	3.76	2.91
.1	82.4	70.4	77.4	67.3	80.5	67.3	2.32	4.64	4.16	3.48
.9	97.7	100.0	93.0	100.0	95.8	93.8	2.81	5.43	5.88	5.17
.7	50.0	16.7	41.7	12.5	54.2	8.3	1.46	2.85	0.79	0.50
S	NS	NS	***	NS	*	NS	NS	***	NS	*
S	*	NS	NS	NS	NS	NS	NS	NS	NS	*
**	***	***	***	***	***	***	***	***	***	***

respect to what was permissible as a "nominal label." We accepted any response that matched that of adult informants confronted with the same set of items. In practice, this meant that many "names" were in fact "phrases." For example, *beb to urat* ("things for work") was accepted as "tools" on Mandok. Also, although the previous studies do not report on the degree of correlation between structures and bases, I suspect these are high; that is, nominal bases are associated with superordinate structures. Nevertheless, we find a very low correlation ($r = .06$) between the two. In general, correlations between *total nominal* and all the other variables in the battery are very low.

North American children supply a variety of structures and bases to account for their groups in their experiment, and this very nicely fits Bruner's three modes of representation: *enactive, ikonic,* and *symbolic.* Our results show far less variation. We find only collective (items dealt with singly) or superordinate structures and either nominal or functional bases. For a set of "large digging stick," "small digging stock," "bush knife," and "ax," four prototypical responses would be: "gardening things" (superordinate–nominal); "These are things we work with in the garden" (superordinate–functional); "Women use this to dig the ground," "We use this to get out the sweet potato," "We use this for cleaning the garden," and "Men use this to clear out the trees" (collective–functional);

and "digging stick-large," "digging stick-small," "bush knife," and "ax" (collective–nominal). This last occurred infrequently. Taken together with Kelly and Huntsman's study, it appears that the ikonic mode is not employed by Papua New Guinean children on this particular task. Furthermore, there is some support in these results for Potter's claim (see also Nelson, 1974) that "concepts, not appearances or names, are the enduring mental representation of reality [1979, p. 56]." Children are more likely to make a concept-based group than they are to use either a name or an ikonic code to link members of the group.

As Table 4.6 shows, there is substantial intracultural variation in these patterns. An examination of four deviant cases will be instructive. Among Kilenge and Melpa children, there is a marked tendency to group items as *pairs*. Of their sets, 23% and 31%, respectively, are pairs, and this compares with a figure of 8% in the other eight societies. Having made their pairs, these children then describe an interdependent—usually functional—relationship between the individual members of the pair. Therefore they are far below the norm in the use of the superordinate nominal structure–base combination. (In Chapter 6 I will review additional research that we conducted on pairing in Melpa.) Kewa- and Kiwai-speaking children, on the other hand, tend to make very large sets. Forty-two percent and 31%, respectively, of their sets are larger than 5, and this compares with a figure of 4% in the other eight societies. These children tended to use superordinate structure, but at a very gross level. On Kiwai, for example, children grouped three distinct four-item categories (people, body parts, dancing apparel) into a single set that they described as "things having to do with people." Hence, Kewa and Kiwai children did not often use the approprite nominal.

Unlike identity categories, which are virtually absent in several societies (as reflected by performance on the conservation-of-length task), equivalence categories are found in all 10 societies. Second, age or developmental effects are very weak for identity but quite strong for equivalence-category formation. The older children are more likely to use the nominal base (column 18), subordinate structure (column 17), and these in combination (column 19). While the trends are significant for only the latter two measures overall within the individual societies, developmental effects are significant on all three measures in at least 5 societies (see Table 4.10). Just the opposite is true for education effects that are pronounced for identity categorization but are virtually absent in equivalence categorization. However, this may be due to the same sort of ceiling effect as the one that occurred with the matrix problems.

Although counting is the next task in the battery, I shall defer a discussion of the results to the next chapter. Here I will mention only that counting does not seem to fit into the equation very well. Success at counting and counting-system type neither predict cognitive-skill attainment nor vice versa.

Free-Recall Task

The free-recall task was specifically designed to tap the same underlying processes as did the picture-sorting task—namely, equivalence-category formation. It is therefore not surprising that the pattern of results should be quite similar.

In North America, studies have shown (see review by Tulving, 1968) that after about the age of 6, children make a steady improvement over trials in their recall and organization of randomly presented words. Furthermore, it has been argued that clustering reflects the child's attempt to locate categories in the list, to code or name them, and then to use the category names to organize the individual items (Cohen, 1963). Given the stimuli used in our study, for example, the child will improve his or her recall if he or she notices that there are 4 named categories. These 4 names are relatively easy to recall, and the child uses them to aid his recall of the more difficult individual names of which there are 16. In general, then, older children should increase their clustering over trials, and thereby increase their recall. Younger children may not show this trend, because as enactive or ikonic thinkers they fail to appreciate the symbolic aspects of the task and fail to take advantage of the built-in mnemonic of categories (see Table 4.7).

By and large, this is what we have found. Performance over trials improves for both recall and clustering, although this is significant only for recall (column 10). Recall and clustering (column 9) are positively correlated, however. Older children recall more items and cluster more of their recall than younger children, and they show marginally greater improvement over trials. Although these trends are not as pronounced as those one finds with North American subjects, the typical study employs more trials (e.g., further opportunity for improvement) and a wider range of ages (e.g., greater likelihood of an age effect) than we utilized.

As with picture-sorting, schooling effects are nil, while culture effects are large indeed. In some societies children use the category structure inherent in the list of words to organize and thereby increase their recall (cf. Rundus, 1973). In other societies, this tendency—while not absent—is much weaker. The continuum between strong and weak "taxonomizers" parallels a similar continuum obtained in the picture-sorting experiment. The correlation, for example, between the number recalled over three

TABLE 4.7
Free-Recall Task (Means)

	Trial 1		Trial 2		Trial 3		Over 3 Trials				
	Recall	Clustering	Recall	Clustering	Recall	Clustering	$\bar{X}$ Recall	$\bar{X}$ Clustering	Recall clustering correlation	Recall trials effect	Clustering trials effects
Overall (478)	6.15	0.89	6.96	1.02	7.78	1.05	6.96	0.99	***	***	NS
6– 9 years (158)	5.44	0.88	6.42	0.92	6.76	0.95	6.21	0.91			
10–13 years	6.49	0.97	6.83	1.06	7.86	1.15	7.06	1.06			
10–13 school	6.51	0.84	7.61	1.07	8.72	1.04	7.61	0.98			
High (Ponam)	10.98	1.64	10.58	1.62	11.71	1.56	11.09	1.52	***		
Low (Tauade)	3.25	0.46	3.65	0.38	4.29	0.51	3.73	0.61	NS[a]		
Age effects	***	NS	NS	NS	**	*	*	*	***	*	
School effects	NS	NS	*	NS	*	NS	NS	NS	***	NS	NS
Culture effects	***	***	***	***	***	***	***	***		**	NS

[a]Nine of 10 sites correlation that are significant at 5% level or better.

 *$p < .05$.
 **$p < .005$.
 ***$p < .0005$.

trials and superordinate structures over six trials is +.275. The parallel is not perfect because the free-recall results are influenced by a memory factor that does not obtain in the picture-sorting experiment.

Overview

The five tasks were subjected to a principal components factor analysis without rotation. Two factors had eigenvalues exceeding 1.5. Together they account for 52% of the variance and are easily interpreted. Table 4.8 shows the factor loadings and intercorrelations for the five summary variables. Factor 1 is a Cognitive factor, while Factor 2 is a Memory factor. All of the measures load on the Cognitive factor, while only the conservation-of-length and free-recall tasks load on the Memory factor. It has been established (Pascual-Leone, 1970; Lawson, 1976; Case, 1977) that conservation involves a memory component. Unlike the Cognitive factor, the Memory factor does not interact in any meaningful way with the independent variables. However, in follow-up research to the original study, a direct memory measure (M-space) has been included in a revised battery (see Chapter 7).

We have no evidence that the battery draws on any underlying processes besides memory and cognition. The application of these processes seems quite uniform over age, grade, sex, and culture. Several alternatives were examined. If memory skills were differentially distributed relative to cognitive skills, we would expect that groups might do well on memory tasks (conservation, free recall), and poorly on the others or vice versa. This does not happen. Another possibility is that groups might do well on identity categorization (conservation, flap board) and poorly on equivalence categorization (picture-sorting, free recall) or vice versa. This does not happen either. Groups might do well on tasks that employ familiar

TABLE 4.8
Correlation Matrix–Factor Loadings

	Matrix	Flap board	Superordinate	Free recall	Factor 1	Factor 2
Conserve length	0.15	0.11	0.20	0.34	0.31	0.19
Matrix total		0.40	0.29	0.24	0.42	0
Flap-board total			0.23	0.19	0.36	−0.03
Superordinate total				0.27	0.86	−0.24
Free-recall average					0.56	0.53

stimuli (conservation, picture-sorting, free recall), and poorly on the others or vice versa. Ten percent of children in school (16 out of 160) do *better* on tasks with *unfamiliar* materials than on those with familiar materials. The same pattern holds for 27% (13 out of 48) of Tauade-speakers and 21% (10 out of 48) of Melpa-speakers. Fewer than 5% of children in any age–grade group or society show the reverse tendency. It could be that children attending school gradually lose fluency in their mother tongue, which could handicap them on the tasks with familiar stimuli. But this explanation fails when applied to the Tauade and Melpa results because here, even children who have not attended school seem to be at a disadvantage with the familiar stimuli. (In Chapter 6 I go into some detail on the issue of familiar-versus-unfamiliar material without, however, entirely resolving the matter.)

This is a minor deviation from what is otherwise a very clear trend— namely, that all the tests tap the same underlying processes. Figure 4.2 shows the distribution of a "total score." This total score is a composite of scores on the conservation-of-length tests (values of 0, 2, 4), matrix height (0, 1), one-left (0, 1), all-1 (0, 1), reversal (0, 1), flap-board partial and minimum strategies (0–4), total superordinate structures (0–6), and free-recall average split into thirds (average recalled less than 5.67 = 0; 5.68−8.33 = 1; 8.34+ = 2). This composite yields a possible range of 0– 21. The actual range is from 2 to 21, and the scores are normally distributed as shown in Figure 4.2.

Table 4.9 presents an overview of the interaction of independent and dependent variables. Sex or gender has no predictive power whatso- ever. Although it was pointed out that the life-styles of men and women differ considerably in some Papua New Guinean societies, these differ- ences have no discernible effect on cognitive development. Educa- tion effects are generally significant, but they are uneven. That is, on some tasks the effect is not significant (free recall) or only marginally significant (matrix, picture-sort). Culture effects are extreme. We had thought that, by using familiar materials and testing for the child's application of his or her own society's classification system, these effects might be muted. This has not happened. In the next chapter the basis for such culture effects will be explored. However, I would like to note that there is every evidence of a continuum, from societies where children employ "symbolic media- tion" in a manner consistent with and at only a slightly later age than children from the industrialized societies, to societies where symbolic mediation, while employed far less frequently, is nevertheless present. Specifically, in all 10 societies, at least some children conserve length, solve all or most of the matrix problems, use at least a partial-pattern strategy to solve the flap-board problems, and arrange, describe, and

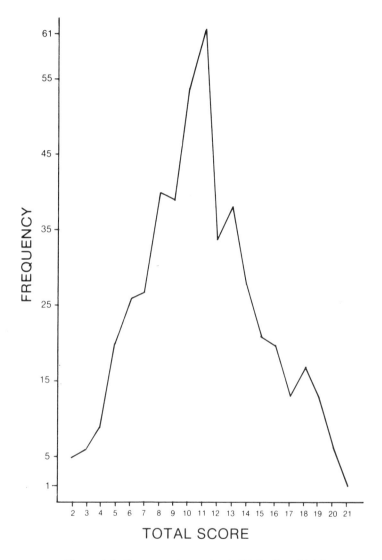

Figure 4.2. Frequency (percentage) distribution of total score.

TABLE 4.9
Age, Education, Sex, and Culture Effects

				Dependent variable		
Independent variable	Conservation of length	Matrix (total)	Flap board (total PP,M)	Picture-sort (superordinate nominal)	Free recall (recall average)	Total score
Age	Chi-square(2) = .569, NS	$F_{(1,318)} = 32.435$ $p < .0001$	$F_{(1,317)} = 17.118$ $p < .0001$	$P_{(1,313)} = 7.546$ $p < .0064$	$F_{(1,316)} = 6.802$ $p < .0095$	$F_{(1,318)} = 31.977$ $p < .0001$
Education	Chi-square(2) = 16.811 $p < .0002$	$F_{(1,317)} = 7.492$ $p < .0065$	$F_{(1,317)} = 21.603$ $p < .0001$	$F_{(1,317)} = 6.86$ $p < .0092$	$F_{(1,317)} = 2.672$, NS	$F_{(1,318)} = 17.107$ $p < .0001$
Sex	Chi-square (4) = 4.59, NS	$F_{(1,474)} = .022$, NS	$F_{(1,473)} = .001$, NS	$F_{(1,469)} = 1.179$, NS	$F_{(1,473)} = 2.658$, NS	$F_{(1,475)} = 2.103$, NS
Culture	Chi-square(18) = 143.883 $p < .0001$	$F_{(9,467)} = 4.495$ $p < .0001$	$F_{(9,466)} = 9.519$ $p < .0001$	$F_{(9,462)} = 59.771$ $p < .0001$	$F_{(9,466)} = 57.876$ $p < .0001$	$F_{(9,468)} = 13.028$ $p < .0001$

[a]Note: Age and education effects tested via analysis of variance; sex and culture via analysis of co-variance (age, grade, covariates).

TABLE 4.10
Within-Culture Age Effects[a]

Group	Conservation of length	Matrix	Flap board	Tasks Picture-sorting Structure	Base	Superordinate nominal	Free recall Recall	Clustering
Ponam	**	**	*	***	*	***	*	*
Mandok	NS	NS	NS	NS	NS	NS	**	NS
Kiwai	NS	***	***	**	***	***	*	*
Toaripi	NS	NS	NS	NS	**		NS	*
Kilenge	NS	*	*	NS	NS	NS	*	NS
Kewa	NS	***	*	NS	*	NS	NS	NS
Oksapmin	NS	***	*	**	NS	**	*	NS
Imonda	NS	*	**	*	NS	*	NS	NS
Tauade	NS	NS	NS	NS	NS	*	*	NS
Melpa	NS	NS	NS	*	**	*	NS	NS

[a]*Note*: Tests were chi-square for conservation of length. Otherwise, they were one-tailed *t*- tests.

$*p < .05.$
$**p < .005.$
$***p < .0005.$

recall groups of items indicative of their ability to form equivalence categories.

Developmental or age effects present a very complex picture. While these effects reach significance for every task except conservation of length, within individual societies the pattern is less clear. As Table 4.10 shows, only on Ponam are developmental effects found across the board.[2] Three explanations are probable. First, it is possible that the cognitive skills under examination depend for their development on environmental inputs that are characteristic of more complex societies and do not unfold in any linear—let alone stagelike—fashion as a function of maturity. Second, an explicit assumption of cognitive-development theories is that hierarchical organization and the formation of identity and equivalence categories is a cultural universal. This assumption may be unwarranted, leaving open the distinct possibility of alternative *end points* to cognitive development. Third, it may be that the age span we have selected is too narrow to capture the full range of development. This last possibility seems quite likely in several cases. The younger groups of Mandok- and Toaripi-speakers performed at very high levels, suggesting that they were not young enough, whereas developmental effects for Imonda, Tauade, and Melpa subjects might have been much more pronounced had we sampled an older population.

[2]My colleague Maurine Fry reminded me of the fact that in most studies in which the impact of heredity versus environment (nature versus nurture) is probed, the range of environments sampled is far narrower (because they are done in the United States and Europe) than one finds in Papua New Guinea. Hence heredity appears to make the major contribution.

5

Cultural Complexity

Aside from the important and extensive work done by descriptive linguists, comparative research is rare in Papua New Guinea. One volume (Rubel & Rosman, 1978) on exchange ceremonies in 13 societies indicates a direction such research might take. The authors show that by building on a common core of principles, the 13 societies have evolved to varying levels of complexity in terms of social structure. The ethnographic work done in the Indigenous Mathematics Project shares this orientation—the search for common principles followed by a comparison that seeks to discover the extent to which variation is compatible with a rough "levels-of-complexity" model.

Implicitly we accept Goodenough's (1957) definition of culture as consisting "of whatever it is one has to know or believe in order to operate in a manner acceptable [p. 167]" to members of the society. Or as Roberts has stated succinctly: "It is possible to regard all culture as information [J. M. Roberts, 1964, p. 438]." By focusing on culture as an information-processing system, once can more easily link up with the activities of schools and tests. All three areas involve the application of cognitive skills. We first looked in detail at counting systems: How do the societies we chose to work with deal with numerosity?

Counting Systems

There were several signposts that pointed us toward an early encounter with Papua New Guinea's indigenous counting systems. First, several authors had discussed links between counting-system complexity and overall cultural complexity (Menninger, 1969; Zaslavsky, 1973; Brainerd, 1979). Second, a preliminary survey had indicated the existence of an interesting and varied array of counting systems in use in the country (Wolfers, 1972). Third, cognitive psychologists have suggested that counting forms the basis for the later development of cognitive skills (e.g., Klahr & Wallace, 1976). Fourth, research designed to uncover the strategies that children use to solve arithmetic problems shows that most children rely heavily on counting even in the seventh grade, despite the fact that they have been taught numerous facts and algorithms that, supposedly, eliminate the need to count (Lankford, 1972; Ginsburg, 1977). Thus, counting skill may be a good predictor of skill in arithmetic. Finally, we had Max Kelly's work (reviewed in Chapter 3) that indicated that intercultural variation in cognitive development might in some way be mediated by the complexity inherent in indigenous counting systems.

Drawing on sources provided by colleagues at the University of Papua New Guinea and the University of Technology at Lae,[1] we assembled reasonably complete data on the counting systems from 225 languages or 30% of the total. These fell neatly into four types. Type I is a body-parts tally system. Parts of the body above the waist are enumerated, beginning with the fingers on one hand and going up one side of the body and down the other. The Kewa use a body-parts counting system (see Figure 5.1) that has a modulus of 68. The Oksapmin system, while very similar, goes only as high as 29 (see Figure 5.2). The number of body parts employed varies from 12 to 68, and the particular parts chosen vary, but the fingers are always used. It has been reported that on those occasions where the number of items to be counted exceeds the modulus, the sum is expressed as so many wholes ("men"), in addition to a remainder. At pig exchanges, every effort is made to have the total be "even" so that it will be more easily remembered in subsequent negotiations. Type I systems are found in the Southern Highlands, West Sepik, and Madang provinces, and they make up 12% of the total.

The Type II counting system is also a tally system, where counters like sticks stand for the objects being counted. The base is usually some number between 2 and 5. The basic number words are primary lexemes

[1] I am particularly grateful to Ann Deibler, Max McKay, and Glen Lean for access to their counting-system data.

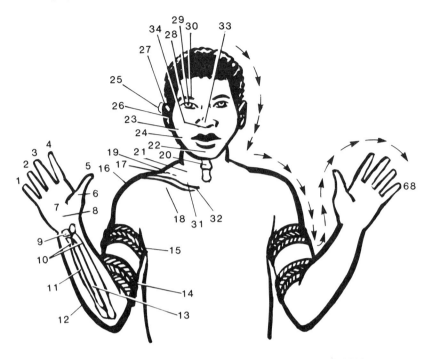

Figure 5.1. The Kewa counting system. (From Pumuye, 1978.)

and do not name parts of the body. The Kiwai employ the Type II system (see Figure 5.3), which is, in fact, binary. However, they may have used a body-parts counting system in the past (Landtman, 1927). Type II systems are found in the Western, Gulf, and West Sepik provinces, and they represent 15% of the total. They are probably more widespread than this, however, since societies that employ predominantly Types I, III, and IV counting also use Type II for special purposes (e.g., Kilenge) (Kettenis, 1978). In fact, our ethnographic studies suggest that there is some interinformant and situational variation in the use of counting. Apparently not one of the Papua New Guinean counting systems has the sort of rigid characteristics associated in our minds with number and counting.

Type III systems usually have a mixed base of 5 and 20. Some have borrowed the Austronesian word for "10" (*sang*), and thus have become 5–10–20 systems. An example is Kilenge (see Figure 5.4). The word for "5" is usually *hand*; for "10," *two hands* or *sang*. "Fifteen" is *three hands* or *two hands and one foot*, and "20" is *one man*. Only the lexemes for "1" to "4" are unanalyzable. The Type III system appears to be rooted in some combination of the other systems, but it is very widespread in Papua

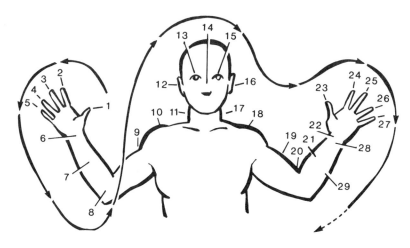

Figure 5.2. The Oksapmin counting system. (From Saxe, 1979c.)

New Guinea, making up nearly 40% of the sample. Type III counting is characteristic of languages in the Morobe, Eastern Highlands, Western Highlands, East Sepik, Northern, Milne Bay, and West New Britain provinces.

The Ponam utilize the Type IV system (see Figure 5.5)—a base-10 system in which no body parts are indicated. Discrete, as opposed to compound, number words are found for the numbers 1–6, 10, and sometimes for 1–10. Most striking are the readily recognized terms for 100 and 1000. These constitute what Salzman (1950) calls the "frame pattern." Type IV systems seem to be extremely economical in terms of number-word construction; they are flexible and appear to be used in a variety of applications. These systems are generally found in the southeastern part of Papua New Guinea and in the New Guinea islands region. There is far less variation in structure and in number names among Type IV systems than among the other three systems, the implication being that they have a common and relatively recent origin. This notion is reinforced

> *na'u* = 1
> *netowa* = 2
> *netowa na'u bi* (*bi* is a trial suffix) = 3
> *netowa netowa* = 4
> *netowa netowa na'u* = 5

Figure 5.3. The Kiwai counting system. (From Smith, 1978.)

teia = 1   *sangaul* = 10
lua = 2   *sangaul teiaviolim* = 11 (*violim* = only)
tol = 3   *sangaul lua* = 12
punge = 4   *tamta* = 20
massa = 5   *tamta teiaviolim* = 21
massateia = 6   *tamta teiasangaul* = 30
massa lua = 7   *tamta tol gegeiia massa tol* = 68 (*gegeiia* = over)

Figure 5.4. The Kilenge counting system. (From Kettenis, 1978.)

by evidence that some societies with Type IV systems still use Type I systems for special purposes. The Buin (Laycock, 1977) have a Type IV system, but they use a Type I system for counting shell money. A Type II system is used for counting coconuts on Petats Island (Corner, personal communication); otherwise, a Type IV system is employed. Both of these examples are taken from Bougainville.

Virtually all the languages with Type IV systems are Austronesian. Exceptions tend to occur as a result of borrowing between non-Austronesian and Austronesian neighbors. Type III counting is associated mainly with the non-Austronesian languages, although a few Austronesian languages have Type III systems. Type I systems are associated with the Trans-Fly phylum. Considering the way counting is accomplished as well as the structure of the tally systems in particular, a legitimate question can be raised concerning the extent to which number is treated as a concept.

> Before number can begin its evolution as a *concept*, however, an apparently simple assumption must be made. Explicitly, it is necessary to assume that *number is a property that is independent of sensible objects*. In other words, number refers to the sensible world but it is somehow more than this; this is what will be called the abstract attitude towards number. The importance of the abstract attitude is very great because it permits us to use numbers and to invent computational systems such as arithmetic and algebra without having to ground what we do in direct experience or observation [Brainerd, 1979, p. 4; italics in original].

si = 1   *sanguff ne' si* = 11
luoff = 2   *lunguff* = 20
taloff = 3   *lunguff ne' si* = 21
faff = 4   *tulunguff ne' taloff* = 33
limeff = 5   *limenguff ne' limeff* = 55
wonoff = 6   *sangat* = 100
hataloff = 7   *sapao* = 1000
haluoff = 8
hase' = 9
sanguff = 10

Figure 5.5. The Ponam counting system. (From Lancy, 1978a.)

Contrast this statement with the following: "Thus Umeda lack an overall number system . . . but supply the deficiency by creating a new series whenever a particular set must be specified [Gell, 1975, p. 162]." Not unreasonably, we considered that the tally systems do not treat number as a concept, whereas the true counting systems do, especially Type IV. Therefore we wished to know whether the apparent absence of the number concept intervened in the cognitive development of children and in their acquisition of modern mathematics.

For this series of analyses, data from 7 of the 10 sites will be employed. The Tauade were eliminated because, according to Hallpike (1977), they do not count at all, having number words for "one" and "two" only, with larger sums being expressed as "many." Our own test of counting ability confirmed that Tauade children had considerable difficulty counting beyond 2 in the vernacular. The Melpa were eliminated because their counting system does not clearly belong to one of the types (Strathern, 1977). The Melpa count up to 4 on the fingers on one hand; then 4 more on the opposite hand. Then they bring their two fists together to make a "whole." From there they count in multiples of 8 or sometimes 10. Kiwai was eliminated because, according to the linguist Geoffrey Smith (personal communication), children are rarely observed using the indigenous counting system. This left Kewa and Oksapmin representing Type I systems, Toaripi and Waris, Type II, Kilenge and Mandok, Type III, and Ponam, Type IV. There is some justification for dividing the types on the basis of modulus—Type I systems have a modulus; the others do not—or on the basis of tally properties that are notably present in Types I and II. Both of these possibilities are considered later.

Table 5.1 arranges performance on several of the cognitive tasks as a function of counting-system "type." Type would seem to discriminate best on the conservation-of-length test but poorly on the other tests. The trend that is apparent is heavily influenced by the generally outstanding performances of children from Mandok and Ponam—performances that may be better accounted for by other factors that will be discussed later. Table 5.2 arranges performance on a mathematics test as a function of counting-system type. (This will be fully described in Chapter 7.) The test was constructed in such a way that grade-level equivalents could be established. These are ordered into the five categories that are shown on the left of the table. Ponam performance again creates a relationship that is more apparent than real. In retrospect, we might well have included a second society with Type IV counting, but these are scarce, and the majority lie in the pathway of over 100 years of extensive Western contact.

These results cannot withstand intensive scrutiny for another and more important reason. The next-to-last tests that were administered to our

TABLE 5.1

Cognitive-Test Performance as a Function of Counting-System Type (Expressed as Percentage)

	Type			
	I	II	III	IV
Conserve length	15.6	24.2	53.1	70.8
Matrix height	84.4	87.4	94.8	97.9
Matrix all - 1	69.8	78.9	81.3	85.4
Matrix reversal	33.3	20.0	12.5	39.6
Partial or minimum on second flap-board problem	46.9	38.9	47.9	79.2
N	(96)	(96)	(96)	(48)

subjects were counting in the vernacular and counting in English. The experimenter spreads out 23 matchsticks in front of the subject and asks him or her to count them. The child is scored as correct for the highest number reached prior to the first error. This is done first with the instruction to count in *Tok-ples*, then with the instruction to count in English or *Pisin*.

When using the vernacular, 6–8-year-olds counted on average to 8 and to 20 in English or *Pisin*. For 10–13-year-old children not in school, the figures are 9.5 and 22, and for schoolchildren, 10.5 and 23. Age and education effects are not significant ($F = 2.79$, .62, respectively) for the vernacular, but they are for English–*Pisin* ($F = 10.32, p < .01; F = 9.30, p < .01$). The most striking finding here is the enormous gap that exists between counting in the vernacular and counting in English. In every society, children were much better able to count in English (*Pisin* was in fact rarely used), even in those cases (Type I, Type III) where the

TABLE 5.2

Mathematics Achievement as a Function of Counting-System Type (Expressed as Percentage)

	Type			
	I	II	III	IV
Three or more below grade level	4.6	10.8	11.3	1.2
Two below	18.0	27.5	15.9	9.6
One below	35.1	27.9	35.1	22.2
At grade level	30.4	20.8	22.5	31.2
One or more above	11.9	12.9	15.2	35.7
N	(194)	(240)	(151)	(157)

indigenous counting system ought to accomodate the sum of 23 with ease. The only exception took place with Ponam children who counted to 19 in the vernacular and to 22 in English. Significantly, Ponam's Type IV system is structurally the closest to a metric system. All of the children counted well in English, including those who had never been to school, thus undermining any attempt to link counting-system type directly with cognitive development. There is also little evidence that the indigenous counting system mediates the acquisition of the metric counting system. All but two of the societies were clustered together on the English counting test. The two exceptions were Kilenge children who did significantly worse than the others and Oksapmin children who did significantly better (Duncan Multiple Range Test, $p < .01$, in both cases). Kilenge employ Type III counting and Oksapmin Type I. If anything, we might expect the reverse of these findings, because the Type III system is much "closer" to the metric system than is the Type I system. Perhaps it is not the structure of the counting system per se but the *pattern of use* that is crucial:

> One of the major differences, for example, between a more or less technical society may well be familiarity with such basic operations as counting and measuring and many differences on specific [cognitive] tasks may stem from a differential use of these basic techniques [Goodnow, 1969, pp. 458–459].

We were able to carry out only a limited ethnographic study of number use in practice. However, we found evidence that number is intimately linked with objects. On Kiwai, "one" is indicated by a suffix; "two" and "three" most often by adjectives. There are singular, dual, trial, and plural pronouns. Number is also expressed by means of suffixes to verb stems (Smith, 1978). On Ponam, numerical classifiers are widely employed. For example, the set of classifiers *sahun, lohun, tuluhn*, etc., is used when referring to things that occur in collections, such as a pile of coconuts, a school of fish, or a deck of cards. The set of classifiers *solel, lolel, tululel*, etc., is used when referring to things that are long and limp—e.g., a rope, a fishing line, an octopus arm, or a belt of dogs' teeth. They have a well-developed system of ordinals for naming successively born children in a family (see Chapter 6), but no general system of ordinals beyond *first, middle,* and *last*. There are no widely employed measures, but things that are frequently traded (e.g., sago, smoked fish) have "sizes" (A. H. Carrier, 1979; Paliau, personal communication).

In Kewa, number names, which are also parts of the body, are used metaphorically to signify various units of time, including the phases in the preparation for a pig-killing festival (Pumuye, 1978). In Kilenge, various items are grouped into named sets of fixed sizes. Taros are grouped by twos in sets called *ronge*; breadfruits are grouped by fours as *ale*; coconuts also by fours as *mol*; tobacco leaves by fives as *gomoa*; and so on (Kettenis, 1978).

The consensus of my colleagues is that people are indifferent to quantitative aspects of things beyond "one," "two," and "many." This is true even of the Ponam who, although they have a robust counting system and ample opportunities to count (since they are constantly engaged in intra-island and off-island trade and exchange), remain unimpressed by "mere numbers" (A. H. Carrier, 1979). Similarly, the Loboda have a Type III system and are frequently caught up in exchanges of immanently countable foodstuffs, but they do not see it that way:

> Things for the Loboda people are either qualitatively different from one another (e.g., yams and tobacco) in which case they are not sufficiently similar to allow their being counted into a simple total. Or, they are qualitatively comparable (as all the yams making up a pile of yams) in which case the total sum is not subdivided into individual . . . units . . . rather it is treated as a single whole [Thune, 1978, p. 76].

The Loboda express no fear of counting nor an inability to do so, but rather there is a tendency throughout the culture to eschew the level of abstraction of which a finite number system is a part—other things are more important.

A somewhat different picture emerges from a study of the Melpa and other Highland societies that practice the large-scale exchange of valuables. They too are indifferent to counting in general, and number is far less pervasive in the language than it is in Kiwai, for example. In their routine activities, they count very little and seem to pay little attention to quantitative aspects of their world. However, in the context of *moka* (see Chapter 2)—the exchange system—the important men go to extremes in counting the one or two (pigs, shells) types of goods to be exchanged. They count things often; they count in the absence of actual referents (the items need not be present); they add, subtract, and multiply; and they have evolved procedures for counting to very large numbers by using two or more counters. One man keeps track of the ones, a second keeps track of the eights or tens (Strathern, 1977).

The available evidence would suggest, then, that counting has little practical merit in the traditional cultures of Papua New Guinea, nor do extraordinary exchange ceremonies inevitably call forth an orgy of counting. As new activities are introduced (e.g., trade stores, copra production and sale, etc.), Western numerical tools are used to cope with them or the indigenous system is modified. Saxe (1981a) found that in order to add 14 shillings and 7 shillings, Oksapmin trade-store owners count to the nose for 14, call the left eye 15, the right thumb 1, the left ear 16, the first finger

2, and so on, until they reach the left forearm, which they call 21. This lack of numeracy may not have very drastic consequences either. It is important to point out that, even in the West, widespread numeracy is a recent phenomenon. The average man in the Middle Ages at least had almost no understanding of arithmetic, even though the foundations of mathematics as a science were laid then and earlier by "learned men" (Dantzig, 1954). Furthermore, Shweder (1977) has raised questions about the extent to which individuals with apparently good grounding in mathematics and logic (e.g., nurses) make full use of this knowledge in routine aspects of their work (see also Churchill, 1966). In Papua New Guinea, I frequently found post-office clerks (with a Grade 8 education or better) solving the problem of how much to charge for a 450-g packet, when the rate was 30 t per 50 g, by repeated addition rather than by division and multiplication.

Undoubtedly, there is some point in the acquisition and practice of mathematics when understanding number as an abstraction becomes necessary. It is still not clear where that point lies, nor the extent to which growing up in a nonnumerically oriented society (Thune, 1978) hinders the attainment of this level of abstraction.

Classification Systems

Writing some years ago, I reflected on our failure to make much headway in developing a theory of culture and thought despite extensive effort:

> All too frequently, cross-cultural studies show differences in performance for some test by people from two or more cultures without being able to satisfactorily account for these differences. For this reason no theory of the relationship between culture and thought has emerged with any credibility. The remedy appears to be to redo, wherever possible, the ethnographies of primitive or traditional societies with an eye for the kinds of situations that will have an impact on cognition. We must have the kind of cultural accounts which will allow us to predict with some confidence the presence or absence of particular cognitive traits on the part of all members or some specified sub-group of the society under investigation. In other words, cross-cultural psychology must be preceded by within-culture psychology [Lancy, 1977, p. 298].

Very few ethnographies of this type have in fact been published, and only one such study has been carried out in Papua New Guinea (Hutchins, 1980). Instead, anthropologists have attempted to single out certain domains for study that were especially amenable to analysis in cognitive terms. Kinship is a favored topic, as are medicine and "emic" or "folk" versions of botany and zoology. Aside from the cognitive orientation, these studies are characterized by a concern for members' knowledge (á la Goodenough) and by a common set of methods. These methods have been described by Frake (1969) and others (see especially Metzger & Williams, 1966; Lounsbury, 1969) and grouped under the heading *ethnoscience* (Sturtevant, 1964).

We had two purposes to serve in conducting ethnoscientific research in each of the Indigenous Mathematics Project sites. First, for several of our cognitive tasks we wanted to use local stimuli. These stimuli had to have certain properties: They had to be familiar, and they had to form sets derived from native conceptions of how the universe is ordered, rather than our own. This requirement led us to employ ethnoscientific methods. A second objective was related to our desire to conduct ethnography with "an eye for the kinds of situations that will have an impact on cognition [Lancy, 1977, p. 298]." It was felt that it might be possible to find direct links between native category systems and children's processing strategies for categories that were probed in the cognitive tests. In proposing to collect and *compare* native category systems, we were also, in effect, testing the hypothesis that these would differ in important respects. Much of the research on category systems has, in fact, tested or operated under the opposite assumption. Bulmer (1968; Bulmer & Tyler, 1968; Bulmer, Menzies, & Parker, 1975), for example, argues that, except for minor details, Kalam (a PNG society) classification principles are indistinguishable from scientific (Western, Linnaean) principles. The extensive study of native classification systems for flora and fauna in the natural world has been undertaken by Brent Berlin and his colleagues. Based largely on research with Mayans, they conclude that they are best represented as a taxonomy with five levels. They argue that the five-level taxonomic ordering of plants and animals is a cultural or linguistic *universal* (Berlin, Breedlove, & Raven, 1973). Subsequently, Brown has found that the five-level taxonomy is appropriate to several *nonbiological* domains as well (C. H. Brown *et al.*, 1976).

However, there is some evidence (e.g., Hunn, 1976) that tempers this view. Rosch's studies (1978; Rosch, Mervis, Gray, Johnson, & Boyes-Braem, 1976) seem to show that in many domains fewer than five levels are adequate for purposes of representing the domain (see also Lachman & Lachman, 1979). Among the Bunaq, a Timorese mountain society, "plants appear to be organized more according to a complex web of resemblances and affinities in which individual plants belong to several categories, rather than according to a tree-like system of hierarchical categories and mutual exclusion [Friedberg, 1979, p. 85]." Hays finds that the Ndumba—a society in the Eastern Highlands of Papua New Guinea—utilize nontaxonomic representations of the plant world parallel to a taxonomic representation, and these "models are inevitably very shallow in depth and the membership of the categories is often overlapping [1979, p. 257]." Finally, several investigators (e.g., Bright & Bright, 1969; Rosaldo, 1972; Gardner, 1976) have noted considerable interinformant variability in the structure of elicited taxonomies. In particular, they have noted that informants either fail to supply higher order (superordinate) terms or disagree on the choice of the appropriate term.

Although we used conventional ethnoscientific procedures, we were alert to the possibility of interinformant variability. These procedures involve an interview format in which questions like the following are used: "An x is a kind of ____?" The aim is to discover contrast sets and hierarchical relationships among sets. Our questioning centered on the domain of *food*, which is not usual for this type of study, but we did so for two reasons. First, we wanted to concentrate on an area with a high degree of salience for all of our potential subjects. We were concerned that knowledge of terms in the domain of *botany*, for example, might be restricted to a few extremely experienced adults. Second, we were intent on comparing classification systems from societies in drastically different ecological niches. Thus the "ethnobotany" of Ponam Island, by necessity, would be impoverished, while the "ethnoichthyology" would be very rich—just the opposite of the Imonda, whose subsistence is based on hunting and gathering in the forest rather than in the sea.

Data-gathering sessions were conducted with the aid of a native speaker who was also fluent in English or *Pisin*. A rough outline of the food domain was obtained from a single informant. This would be filled in and modified in a group interview in which both young and mature men and women participated. A supporting cast of children brought exemplars when verbal description alone was insufficient to identify an item. (My scuba-diving and bird-watching hobbies and consequent knowledge of the more common species was enormously helpful here.) The group interview proved to be essential, as there was in fact a fair bit of disagreement, which was followed by eventual consensus. Consensus was reached fairly quickly on the existence of particular contrast sets and on questions pertaining to which contrast set a particular item belonged. Consensus was obtained more slowly on questions related to the name of a contrast set and the appropriate nesting of contrast sets. Informants often approached a contrast set from the standpoint of a particular function or situation (see also Hays, 1979). Further discussion might or might not lead to a "big" name (size was often used as a metaphor) for a particular set.

Our pilot work with Kewa and Ponam informants revealed a sharp divergence in the degree of structure in the food domain. Our lack of success in finding much of a taxonomy in Kewa led to a modification of our methods whereby I would create a display of, for example, garden crops and ask whether they belonged together, hoping to uncover a category, or perhaps a covert category. These procedures failed to generate any "missed" categories. Skeletal diagrams of Ponam and Kewa "food" taxonomies illustrate this divergence (see Figure 5.6). The designations for levels are slightly modified from the standard (Berlin, Breedlove, & Raven, 1973). Categories with fewer than three species that lack a generic term are not included. Each branch represents a coherent contrast set— those that have a consensually established label are marked with an *x*; others are included as *covert* categories.

The Ponam taxonomy resembles those previously reported in the literature in having four to six levels, with distinctions between contrast sets being based largely on morphology. The major division is between seafood on the left and land food on the right. Typical families are *ni* ("fish"), *kane-i* ("shellfish"), and *bua* ("plant food"). Typical genus level terms are *peo* ("shark"), *ool* ("lobster"), and *maf* ("taro"). Species-level terms include *ora* ("hammerhead"), *ool paropat* ("lobster" sp.), and *maf puka* ("taro" sp.). The major divisions in Kewa are between animal and plant foods. The language has one life form, *arile*, which is somewhat forced, because it means *meat* and is based more on function than on morphology. Interestingly, *meat* had this broader meaning in English at one time (R. Brown, 1958). There are no terms for *animal* or *plant*. A typical family-level term is *yapa* ("arboreal mammals"); at the genus level we have *kai* ("banana"); and at the species level *yapa-pasolo* ("cuscus"

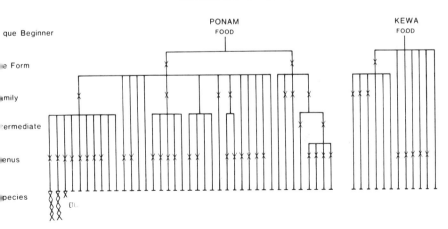

Figure 5.6. Taxonomic structure.

sp.) and *kai-konda* ("banana" sp.). Note that there are only genus-level terms in the plant portion of the domain and only family-level terms in the animal portion. However, in Rosch's scheme (Rosch *et al.*, 1976) these would all be at the "basic" level.

As it happened, Kewa and Ponam represent points on a continuum. Subsequent study in the eight remaining sites produced taxonomies that varied between these two extremes in the sheer number of items that people mentioned as foods and in the degree of hierarchicalization or structure that ordered these items. We found no support for the claim that folk taxonomies have identical structures across societies (e.g., that they derive from some universal template). As part of our overall ethno-scientific survey we also probed several other (e.g., nonfood) domains for the purposes of selecting stimuli for the free-recall and picture-sort experiments. These attempts failed to tap rich areas of taxonomic complexity. Societies with shallow food taxonomies have a paucity of named classes *in general,* and vice versa.

Cecil Brown (1977, 1979) has undertaken extensive reviews of the ethnographic record concerning plant–animal nomenclature, and his find-ings also call into question the "universal" position. Specifically, he finds that societies vary in the availability of life-form terms and their frequency is correlated with several measures of societal complexity.

With this view in mind, we undertook to create an index of complexity for the 10 food taxonomies. This was derived by assigning a score of 1 to each term at the family level and a 2 to each term at the life-form levels and summing. Other levels were excluded for various reasons: (*a*) failure to reach consensus (unique beginner); (*b*) doubts about the extent to which the terms collected exhausted the set (genus, species); and (*c*) doubts about the appropriate placement of a term (intermediate). This exercise yielded a range from 4 to 12. Since we have every reason to believe the index represents an interval scale, it was used in regression equations with the cognitive tasks as dependent variables. Age, grade, and classification index were entered in that order into the regression equa-tion. In every case, the change in R^2 after entering the classification index reached significance (.001 level or beyond).

Table 5.3 presents the beta weights for age, grade, and classification index over the seven dependent measures. It is clear that the index is especially effective in predicting performance on those tasks that measure the ability to use categories (e.g., picture-sorting and free-recall tasks) to solve a problem. Table 5.4 shows the relationship between performance and index a little more clearly. The "total-score" variable has been described on page 96.

The weight of evidence—at least prior to 1976—from cognitive studies

TABLE 5.3
Regression Analysis: Test Performance as a Function of Age, Grade, and Classification Index (Expressed as Beta Weights[a])

Task	Age	Grade	Class index
Matrix total	.266	.168	.120
Flap-board total	.239	.251	.217
Picture-sort	.150	.127	.442
Total superordinate			
Free recall			
Average recalled	.038	.161	.277
Average clustering	—	—	.215

[a]*Note*: Betas significant at the .001 level or better only are reported.

in anthropology and psychology suggested that taxonomizing is a universal phenomenon and of high importance in the routine information-processing activity of individuals. While taxonomizing is undoubtedly important in complex societies, it is not the only or even the preferred mode for representing and processing information for humans. Just as societies may forego quantification, we believe they can and do forego hierarchicalization.

Conducting the research on taxonomies, we often found it extremely difficult to get informants to move up or down the food taxonomy (e.g., "X is a kind of ____?" and "What are the different kinds of x?"). Rather, they kept going "sideways" on us. Figure 5.7 illustrates this phenomenon schematically for three hypothetical Kewa informants. Terms seem to be

TABLE 5.4
Classification Index and Overall Performance on Cognitive-Test Battery

Society	Classification index	Frequency for total score expressed as percentage			
		2–5	6–10	11–15	16–21
Ponam	12	4.2	12.5	22.9	60.4
Toaripi	11	0	33.3	52.1	14.6
Mandok	10	2.1	16.7	62.5	18.8
Kiwai	9	4.2	25.0	50.0	20.8
Oksapmin	9	12.5	41.7	37.5	8.3
Kilenge	8	6.3	41.7	50.0	2.1
Tauade	7	10.4	54.2	33.3	2.1
Melpa	6	16.7	68.8	10.4	4.2
Kewa	5	10.4	35.4	43.8	10.4
Imonda	4	16.7	58.3	20.8	4.2

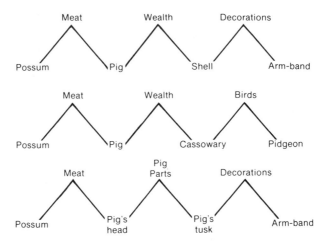

Figure 5.7. Kewa classification. (From Lancy, 1978a.)

treated inevitably as pairs, while the basis for making a pair shifts continually. What this illustrates is that, while there are categories, these are not mutually exclusive: They are not nested in a hierarchy, and the mention of a category name creates no press to list exemplars of a category. The next item mentioned (associate) might as likely belong to a different category, and shared morphology is by no means the most salient aspect of likeness judgments. This initial and tentative exploration of alternative modes of representation in Kewa was carried out much more extensively with the Melpa, and these results are reported in the next chapter.

Children's Play

After counting and classification systems, we considered play as a possibly rich source of alternative pathways to cognitive development. Vygotsky believed that "the influence of play on a child's development is enormous [1978, p. 96]." He saw play as the first step toward abstract thought in that action and meaning become separated. He was most impressed with the process whereby a stick becomes a horse and what this transformation revealed about the child's cognition. Bruner (1972, 1975) concurs with and amplifies this view. Piaget, on the other hand, (1948, 1962) saw play as merely the visible manifestation of the child's underlying cognitive potential rather than the driving force behind the development of this potential (see also the debate between Piaget & Sutton-Smith, reprinted in Herron & Sutton-Smith [1971]).

Studies have shown that play facilitates the acquisition of the conservation-of-length (Golomb & Cornelius, 1977) and number concepts (Dienes, 1963). These studies *imposed* particular play activities on children. In free play, "evidence for effects of particular games on particular learnings are few [Sutton-Smith, 1971, p. 256]." I conducted an extensive study of free play and child development among the Kpelle (1976, 1980b, 1980c, 1980d; reviewed and summarized in Schwartzman [1978]). Links between various play activities and adult skills and roles were rather easy to elucidate. Links to specifically cognitive skills were more elusive.

Evidence for interspecies (Lancy, 1980e), cross-cultural (Roberts, Arth, & Bush, 1959), and subcultural variation in qualitative aspects of play is substantial. The Roberts *et al.* study, in particular, found a high correlation between complex game configuration and other measures of cultural complexity. In addition, Smilansky (1968) and Bruner (1972) link this variation directly to the ability to use abstract reasoning.

It seemed worthwhile, then, to devote some of our energies to the study of children's play. This was accomplished by Pensa Roleasmalik, a recent anthropology graduate from the University of Papua New Guinea. He collected children's games (Roleasmalik, 1979) from 8 societies, 6 of which were among the 10 original IMP sites. Initially he would interview adults and children about the games that they knew about; then he arranged for demonstrations that permitted a fuller description of details and photographs.

The six societies were Mandok, Tauade, Toaripi, Melpa, Ponam, and Imonda. Roleasmalik collected from 25 to 27 games from each society. I used the Roberts *et al.* (1959) games taxonomy with two additional categories—"fantasy" and "discovery"—in an analysis of game types. There was almost no variation across societies. Seventy-five percent of the games in every society were games of physical skill; the remaining 25% were about evenly divided between fantasy and discovery. There were no games of strategy or chance. Some examples follow.

Physical skill: Mandok: *Avabuti*
In the game female players attempt to break through a strong line of men to collect items of their desire, in a sand model of a dugong. Two teams usually play the game with 10 to 15 players each. One team for males and the other for females. The players have to be between 10 to 20 years of age. It is played at any part of the year, during the day, on the beach.

At the beginning of the game, the sand dugong is built by the males. They then line around the model, making sure there is no space left for the charging female to pass through who should be 30 to 60 yards away. A song associated with the game is sung by both teams. After being gone through several times (4), the females rush towards the model, knocking down any weak males as they go. Very often the females win and get everything buried in the model [Roleasmalik, 1979, p. 11].

Physical Skill: Melpa: *Kupanda monumba*
The aim of this game is to train young boys to be accurate when using their spears. In the game, they try to get their 6 to 9 feet long wooden spears pierced into a rolling target which is the stalk of the banana tree cut up in the shape of a wheel or ball. Usually, two teams of about 5 to 6 players in each take part. Those who participate are aged between 11 and 15. It is played in the day time, during the dry season at slopy grounds near the village.

At the start of the game, the team of throw the target down the hill have to go to the top and wait for a signal to let go the target. As the signal is given, the target is let go and it rolls down the hill towards the receiving team. As soon as it reaches them they have to try and get as many of their spears pierced into it. After counting their scores, the two sides then change places. This may continue for quite a while. At the end, the team with most points wins [p. 111].

Fantasy: Tauade: *Iva valit*
In this game players act out an incident where a fight broke out after a man attempted to steal another man's wife. Both sexes play this game and usually 7 players participate. Those who participate are usually between the ages of 8 and 15. From the seven players, 1 has to be a prowler, 2 as a man and his wife and 4 as villagers. Implements used in this game include bow and arrows for 6 players and a bilum (local bag) for the player acting the part of the woman. The game is played in both day and night at the village square.

At the start of the game the player acting the part of the woman has to go and sit at the place of play by herself and pretend to be weeding in her family garden. Slowly and carefully, the prowler advances towards the woman. To show his presence, he first whistles and then do [sic] other signs like rubbing his feet and clapping his hands.

When the woman has finally noticed him, she invites him. They talk for a while in a manner lovers normally do. And after planning a later meeting between them, the man decides to leave. As he is several yards away from the woman, he is confronted by the husband of the woman and 4 other man who briefly question him and then start attacking him. Usually the prowler looses [sic] which means he is over powered and his weapons taken from him and destroyed [pp. 29–23].

Fantasy: Imonda: *Pinda*
In this game, players imitate a group of hunters climbing after a cuscus on a tree. Boys of the ages 8 to 15 play it. The number of players is 4. Out of the 4 players, one is to act the cuscus. The game is played in the day time during the dry season at bushes where trees grow near to each other.

At the start of the game, the one to act the cuscus climbs up to a branch and waits. Upon hearing a signal, the three other players who act the hunters climb up the tree and chase the cuscus. The chase always goes on for quite a while. In most cases, the hunters always win. They catch the cuscus and carry it home [p. 139].

Discovery: Toaripi: *Mai fako*
The aim of this game is to guess which person has got a pebble in his or her hand. It is played by both male and female especially those between the ages of 8 and 15. The game is played in both day and night at the village square.

It starts off by members of the two teams sitting and facing each other. The hands of the players should be at their backs. The distance between the two teams has to be at least 9 feet. A pebble is then given to one of the teams. After passing it back and forth among themselves, a member of the opposing team is asked to guess which person has got the pebble. If the guess was right, then the opposing team wins. The possessing team also wins, when the other team guessed on the wrong person. A win would mean scoring a point for a team and taking possession of the pebble [p. 51].

Discovery: Ponam: *Narombusi*
The aim of this game is for a player to find his or her opponent at part of the reef which is impossible to look through due to floating dirt and flooded water from rivers and small streams. Both sexes play the game, especially those between the ages of 10 and 15. 2 to 5 players usually compete. It is played in the day time during the wet season.

At the start of the game, a player goes into the water and ask his or her opponent to search for him or her. The one to search must stay on land until the one to hide has dived into the water. At a signal, the player dive into the water and start searching. If the player is able to locate his or her opponent than he or she wins. A win also means, the two players have to change sides. One rule here, is that a player has to be searched and touched while under water and not when he or she is surfacing to breath [p. 126].

The game inventories give rise to a theme to which I shall return in earnest in Chapter 8. That is, they give evidence for universal competencies at one level of cognitive development and no evidence of competencies at some higher level of development. There is an enormous "vertical" spread and almost no "horizontal" spread. By *vertical spread*, I mean, for example, that the games are highly similar across societies. All have bow-and-arrow or spear-and-target games; mock battles with mud, sand, and water; sliding games in grass, mud, and water with leaves or boards as the sliding devices; string figures and tops; mock hunting exercises; singing–dancing lines; hide and seek; and hand-hidden pebbles or shells. The differences in games and game inventories are trivial in comparison to the similarities. On the other hand, not one has games with elements (Roberts *et al.*, 1959) that would seem to tax higher order problem-solving or memory skills on the order, for example, of *mankala*, a game that is widespread in non-Western societies (Townshend, 1979). Less systematically, we also observed one other aspect of children's play—namely, activities that modeled or reproduced in truncated form various adult tasks. I shall discuss this in the next section.

Technological Complexity

Many theories of cognitive development are historically based. Soviet theories (Vygotsky, 1962; Luria, 1976) have this quality, as do French theories (Lévy-Bruhl, 1926; Durkheim & Mauss, 1963; Bourdieu &

Passeron, 1977). Differences in cognitive functioning are attributed to the nature of society, which in turn is influenced by an inevitable historical progression. Scales have been developed to describe this progression. One recently developed scale (Lomax & Arensberg, 1977) is based on the nature of the society's subsistence systems and would rank the IMP sites approximately as follows: Imonda (bottom), Ponam, Mandok, Oksapmin, Tauade, Toaripi, Kilenge, Kewa, and Melpa (top). Placement depends on the particular mix of subsistence resources—collecting, hunting, fishing, animal husbandry, horticulture, agriculture, etc. Societies low on the scale depend primarily on gathering, while those at the other extreme depend on mixed horticulture and animal husbandry. This kind of scale is not, however, very useful for our purposes. It does not correlate particularly well with cognitive-skill development, or with classification-system and social-structure complexity (see also Levinson, 1980). Furthermore, all of the Papua New Guinean societies are grouped together at the low end of the Lomax–Arensberg scale. In these societies, there are no pastoralists, no use of animals or mechanical devices in agriculture, and no industry or specialization—all activities that tend to move a society to the top of their scale.

An alternative scale is suggested by Oswalt's work (1973, 1976) on the complexity of tools and tool inventories. Oswalt, in turn, was motivated by Leslie White's dictum that "the technological factor determines, in a general way at least, the form and content of the social, philosophic, and sentimental sectors [1959, p. 19]." Oswalt's approach is direct and extremely powerful. He argues that "subsistants" (tools, weapons, implements, etc.) can be analyzed in terms of their complexity, broken into "technounits" that are in turn made up of "components," and thus compared intraculturally and interculturally:

> [that] man is first and foremost a technological animal and that the major distinctions among lifeways should be made on the basis of manufactured forms. Thus, it basically is, and was, technoculture that made man what he is or is not [1973, p. 21].

> As the most precise planters, the John Deere Number 33 and the Stanhay 5870 have an average of seventy-seven technounits compared with an average of 1.0 for the digging sticks used in farming by the aboriginal peoples sampled [1976, p. 224].

Oswalt's orientation is comparative, evolutionary, and also implicitly cognitive:

> It will be recalled that if 100 stones were employed in a weir, the stones are judged as . . . representing a single component. . . . To make or use the duplicative components of facilities did not require a *mental template* which was meaningfully different from that necessary to make or use one duplicative component [1973, p. 158; italics added].

I did not read Oswalt's books until the Indigenous Mathematics Project had been underway for nearly 18 months, but his approach fit very well with my own observations. Recall that the two societies where we conducted the initial and most extensive research were Kewa and Ponam. All the evolutionary theories would place the Kewa above the Ponam on the basis of the fact that the former practice horticulture and animal husbandry whereas the latter subsist entirely on fishing and gathering. However, casual observation and a reading of the sparse ethnographic information then available suggested just the opposite. I was struck in particular by the differences in the daily round of activities for children. Children are treated very indulgently by adults in both societies but are expected to share or mimic adult responsibilities from an early age. For Kewa children this means digging and weeding in the garden, weaving *bilums*, carrying firewood, and little else (see Figure 5.8). On Ponam, by contrast, children are engaged in a host of multifaceted activities. They help to build and then learn to handle variously sized canoes, and they work various sections of the reef with different tools and techniques. They make rope; work with wood (see Figure 5.9); make a variety of

Figure 5.8. Kewa boy gardening with digging stick. (Courtesy of R. Souviney.)

Figure 5.9. Ponam boys learning to play *garamut* drums.

traditional ornaments, costumes, and *bilums*; and mend and make various nets, spears,and other fishing gear (see also Mead, 1963; Schwartz, 1978, 1979).

Furthermore, from an evolutionary perspective, Yesner (1980) argues persuasively that maritime hunting and gathering (e.g., Ponam and Mandok) as a way of life is unstable and will change continuously in the direction of greater complexity. On the other hand, Highland horticulture and pig husbandry have persisted virtually unchanged for centuries. If anything, they have declined in complexity. The Tauade (White, Crook, & Buxton, 1970) and the Melpa (Golson, 1977) have both lost technologies (or subsistants) once used by their distant ancestors.

Unfortunately, I have not yet mustered the resources to conduct a thorough observational study to document this contrast nor to support a field-based study using Oswalt's analytical procedures. Nevertheless, I have little doubt that an index based on the number of "technounits" available in each society would predict cognitive-task performance even better than the classification index. This is because handling various tools may not only have a direct impact on cognition—a view that runs implicitly throughout Piagetian theory (Brainerd, 1978a)—but also because, as Satterthwaite has shown for Australian aboriginal societies: "More complex technologies [are] generally associated with more involved social arrangements for their use [1980, p. 314]."

Urban Residence

In virtually every theory of cultural evolution, urban Western society occupies the end-point position. Whether one looks at technology, social roles, or the demands to quantify and classify items in the environment, this kind of society would seem to require cognitive-processing strategies of the highest order. Indeed, studies in Australia (de Lemos, 1969; de Lacey, 1970; Dasen, 1974) have shown that contact with the Western urban sector has an enormous impact on the cognitive abilities of aboriginals. Buck-Morss (1975), in a critique of Piagetian theory, points out that concrete and formal operations are adaptive in modern urban societies that are dominated by scientific modes of thought but not necessarily elsewhere. Therefore, we might expect to see shifts in patterns of cognition as traditional societies become more Westernized or as children migrate to urban areas. This conclusion would be premature, however. It is possible to imagine urban residents who, by virtue of their poverty, participate to only a limited degree in the technologically and informationally rich urban society (Deutsch & Associates, 1967). Stevenson and his colleagues (Stevenson, Parker, Wilkinson, Bonnevaux, & Gonzalez, 1978) compared the performance of urban and rural Quechua Indians in Peru on a battery of cognitive tasks. While attendance at school had a positive impact on performance for all groups on all tasks, residence alone yielded mixed results. On several of the tasks, the rural children scored significantly higher. Although we are far from determining what aspects of culture have a critical influence on cognitive performance, it is clear that these may be present in varying degrees in both urban and rural environments.

Port Moresby, the capital of Papua New Guinea, is a large and rapidly growing town (population 150,000). It has most of the features one associates with an urban center: cinemas (but not TV), department stores and supermarkets, mass transportation, some high-density housing, individuals employed for wages, including white-collar and technical employees, and unfortunately, a very high rate of violent crime. Except for this last item, however, access to these features of urban life is sharply delimited. There are, throughout the city, village-like enclaves where electric lights and water—let alone department stores, toys, and films—never penetrate. One such enclave is Kaugere, a slum settlement composed of extended-family dwellings in various states of neglect. Kaugere is home to a substantial population of migrants from the same area in the gulf that served as our site for testing Toaripi-speaking children. As an outpost of Toaripi society, Kaugere has a long history (Ryan, 1965, 1971). Kin ties, language, and social obligations, to a lesser extent, carry over

TABLE 5.5
Toaripi Children in the Village, in School, and in Town

Samples	Conserve length (percentage)	Matrix total	Flap-board total	Picture-sort superordinate nominal total	Free recall average three trials	Age	Grade	N
Village								
10–13 years	30.3	3.9	1.0	5.1	6.4	10.4	0	16
	*	*	**	NS	**			
10–13 years in school	62.6	5.0	2.8	5.7	8.1	10.8	5.4	16
	**	*	**	**	**			
Town								
10–13 years in school	12.5	4.6	1.6	3.9	5.3	11.6	5.0	16

*$p < .05$.
**$p < .01$.

from village to urban settlement. But as an environment for children, Kaugere is unattractive in the extreme, not only by comparison with the more affluent sections of Port Moresby, but with the Toaripi villages on the coast. The same kind of striking contrast in opportunities to learn from and manipulate the natural and manmade environment that I observed in Ialibu and Ponam was apparent from visits to Kaugere and the Gulf villages. In the village, children fish, garden, and participate in ceremonies and crafts of various kinds, and social interchange occurs in the village square—always a riveting show for children. None of these activities are available to children in Kaugere.[2] Thus the pattern of results displayed in Table 5.5 was fully expected. Toaripi-speaking children from Grades 5 and 6 from the Kaugere Community School were chosen for testing. The only stipulation was that they had to have been urban residents for at least the previous 4 years. The table shows that while attending school leads to fairly consistent gains in performance, living in an urban slum leads to

---

[2]Louise Morauta, an anthropologist who has studied urban and rural Toaripi for many years, made these additional points after reviewing my comments:

1. The urban physical environment is impoverished. It is not safe to roam around. Backyards are tiny or nonexistent. There are no opportunities to fish, swim, or sail.
2. Houses are overcrowded, and there is little privacy.
3. There are few public play areas for the children.
4. There is a great admixture of spoken languages and dialects. Children do not develop strong competence in any single language.

decrements across the board. The most "stimulating" environment for the Toaripi child is the village, augmented by the Community School.

While there are urban migrant populations from most of our sites (all except Imonda and Oksapmin), none occur in numbers sufficient to form a second, urban village. Hence we were unable to see whether urban residence—even slum-dwelling—might enhance performance for some groups.

A second small-scale study looks at the impact of social class and race. Sprinkled throughout the urban centers of Papua New Guinea one finds International Primary (elementary) schools. These serve the same age range as Community Schools, but a very different population of children. International schools are located in relatively affluent suburbs and follow the Australian curriculum. Material inventories are far richer than in the Community Schools, and teachers are far better educated and are native-speakers of English—the language of instruction in both types of schools. Tuition for Community Schools is about $5 a year compared to $400 for International Schools, thus creating a sharp differential in the socio-economic status (SES) of pupils. A substantial proportion of the student body is composed of the children of Papua New Guinean civil servants and politicians who live in government-built Western-style homes with most of the comforts associated with living in, say, Darwin. They can afford to dress their children in store-bought clothing and amuse them with store-bought books, games, and toys. The remainder of the pupils are the children of expatriate (from Australia, England, and Southeast Asia) technocrats who have an even higher standard of living than the Papua New Guineans. But note that, by the standard of living prevailing among white-collar communities in other third-world countries, the Port Moresby elite can best be characterized as occupying the lower middle to middle classes. Random samples of 20 were chosen for testing from the Papua New Guinean and expatriate populations in a single International School. Stimuli for the free-recall and picture-sort experiments were chosen to reflect items common in an urban, Western culture. Results are shown in Table 5.6. First, note that the differences in performance between our "best" rural group and the high SES urban group are either absent or are multidirectional. Second, note that high SES[3] urban children are dramatically superior on every task when compared to the low SES urban (e.g., Kaugere) group. Clearly "urban" and "rural" have very low values as currency in understanding environmental influences on cognitive develop-

[3]Because of the rapidity of Papua New Guinea's march to nationhood, 90% of the inhabitants of Port Moresby are first-generation urbanites. The high SES children, therefore, speak a vernacular language and spend a substantial part of their childhood in their "home" village.

TABLE 5.6
Urban Residence, Social Class, and Race

Samples	Conservation of length	Matrix total	Flap-board total	Picture-sort superordinate nominal total	Free recall average three trials	Age	Grade	N
Village (Ponam)	87.6	5.2	2.9	4.8	11.9	11.9	5.0	16
	NS	NS	**	NS	**			
Urban high SES	85.0	5.6	4.0	5.1	8.6	10.9	5.5	20
	**	**	**	**	**			
Urban low SES	12.5	4.6	1.6	3.9	5.3	11.6	5.0	16
High SES	85.0	5.6	4.0	5.1	8.6	10.9	5.5	20
	NS	NS	NS	NS	NS			
Non-Papua New Guinean	100.0	5.6	4.0	5.7	9.2	10.7	5.6	20

$**p < .01.$

ment (see also Wagner, 1978). Both cities and villages offer a panorama of opportunities to children. Finally, note that the Papua New Guinean children exposed to an environment similar to that of middle-class Western children do not differ from such children in terms of performance on our battery of tests, despite racial and linguistic (a far higher proportion of the non-Papua New Guineans are monolingual English speakers) differences.

Malnutrition

Our pilot research indicated that cross-cultural differences in cognitive development might be expected, and the 10 society survey described in the previous chapter confirms that indication. We were concerned also at the outset with explaining such differences. Various ideas drawn from theories in anthropology, developmental psychology, and linguistics have been and will be discussed and tested. There is, however, a large and unrelated body of work that drew our attention—namely the study of malnutrition and its effects, especially childhood malnutrition.

The Papua New Guinea Departments of Health and Education have both been concerned with documenting and ameliorating malnutrition in Papua New Guinea. In a recent survey (Nutrition Section, 1977), it was reported that, in the country as a whole, 38% of children under 5 are malnourished, and in some localities this figure climbs to 80%. Several studies (e.g., McKay, 1960) had uncovered cases of severe malnutrition, including marasmus and kwashiorkor in village populations. The subsistence patterns in several of our sites—Kewa, Imonda, Golke, and Oksapmin, in particular—produce a diet that appears to be grossly unsuited to children. This diet consists almost entirely of tubers—sweet potatoes, taros, and yams. These foods are notoriously low in vitamins, minerals, and proteins, and the caloric value per unit of volume is also very low (Powell, 1976). Children are fed these starches from about 6 months, and their stomachs and intestines are too small to permit them to ingest the quantities necessary for adequate growth. At the same time, numerous reports had appeared that showed a relationship between malnutrition and mental development (e.g., Cravioto & De Licardie, 1975; Monckberg, 1968, 1975; for a review, see Winick, 1976). No such study had been done in Papua New Guinea, but one study in Australia had found a connection between malnutrition and lowered IQ scores among aboriginal children (Edwards & Craddock, 1973).

So, with guidance from the Department of Health, we took a mid-upper-arm-circumference (MUAC) measure for each subject in the survey.[4] This measure is normed for age and allows one to make a rough estimate of the nutritional status of the child. If the circumference is smaller than expected for a given age, the child is judged to be malnourished. As it turned out, MUAC was not of great value for our purposes, because age must be determined precisely. In only a single site was there enough variance in the MUAC, coupled with precise age information, to permit us to use the MUAC as an independent variable. Some years ago, the French Catholic missionaries were more active among the Tauade than they are today. For a period, they recorded the names, parents' names, and the birthdates of all children born in the parish, and, miraculously, all of our subjects were listed. With exact ages we were able to determine that 13 of the 32 Tauade subjects had MUAC scores below the norm. Table 5.7 shows the performance of malnourished and satisfactory Tauade subjects on our cognitive tasks. A brief inspection is sufficient to show that there is no difference between the two groups.

Although the nutritional situation in parts of Papua New Guinea is problematic overall, numerous studies (reviewed in Norgan, Ferro-Luzzi, & Durnin, 1974) have focused attention on the very low levels of protein in the diet, especially among Highlanders. Except where hunting and gathering still make a substantial contribution to the diet (e.g., Imonda, Oksapmin), Highland groups are largely dependent on the occasional pig

---

[4]I would like to thank Paul Songo for collecting MUAC scores on Ponam Island for us.

TABLE 5.7
Tauade Ten through Thirteen Year Olds

	Conservation of length	Matrix total	Flap-board total	Picture-sort superordinate nominal total	Free recall average three trials	Age	Grade	N
Malnourished	15.0	4.3	2.4	3.2	6.9	13.4	3.4	13
	NS	NS	NS	NS	NS			
Satisfactory	9.0	4.7	2.6	3.0	7.5	13.3	2.4	19

feast for protein (P. Brown, 1978). Children may be as much harmed as aided by this meat bounty, for they are liable to a disease called *pik bel*—a kind of shock syndrome brought on by the huge and unaccustomed intake of flesh and fat. We were in no position to undertake a direct study of protein intake with measures of cognitive growth and development, but an indirect approach seemed feasible. In most of Papua New Guinea, habitat and culture are closely intertwined. However, along the eastern portion of the northern coast there are isolated villages inhabited by "inland" peoples. That is, the normal tensions that tended to keep coastal and inland societies separated were broken by German, and later, Australian pacification efforts, and migrants from inland groups have filtered down to the coast. One such group, split between coastal and inland settlements, is the Mahwauké people. (See Figure 5.10.) Part of the Mahwauké live in a cluster of three villages (the largest is Meriman) on the sea, and part live 2–5 km inland in the hills. The coastal population, using simple gathering techniques on the reef, harvest a fair amount of seafood, thus earning a supply of protein not available to the inland population. The children in particular are very adept at catching fish and mollusk snacks for themselves. Thirty-two children from each population were tested with the battery by Herman Toalam—a native of the area. An inspection of Table 5.8 indicates that there is no difference between the two populations. MUAC ratings did not differ either. Anthony Ades carried out an as yet unpublished follow-up to the original study. He substituted height for age for MUAC and school exam results for the cognitive battery. Data from 159 pupils in the Behir Community School (not far from the Mahwauké area) were collected and subjected to an analysis of covariance. The results for H–A main effect F $(3, 150) = .83$ were not significant.

The final study in this series was carried out in the Jimi River valley (see Figure 5.11) with Maring-speakers. Early patrols in the Jimi region had located obvious signs of iodine deficiency in terms of both endemic goiter

TABLE 5.8
Mahwauké Inland and Coastal Populations

	Conservation of length	Matrix total	Flap-board total	Picture-sort superordinate nominal total	Free recall average three trials	Age	Grade	N
High protein	3.0	4.7	1.1	4.3	8.0	11.9	3.1	32
	NS	NS	NS	NS	NS			
Low protein	3.0	4.7	1.3	4.3	6.3	11.4	1.7	32

and cretinism. This deficiency was attributed to the practice of gardening on steep slopes which exposes the soil to leaching of trace elements, including iodine. The Public Health Department introduced iodized salt to the area in the 1950s, but the salt was promptly traded out of the valley for other, more valued commodities (John Gunther, personal communication). Therefore in 1966 they began to inject alternate families with either iodized oil or saline solutions. The incidence of goiter and cretinism dropped markedly in the treated population, and in 1978 the iodine injections were administered to the entire population. Cretinism is brought about by inadequate levels of iodine in utero, and follow-up study had shown almost a complete elimination in the iodine-treated population. However, the original investigators, augmented by Kevin Connolly, wanted to know whether endemic cretinism is an all-or-none phenomenon or rather does it "result in a range of abnormality from the severe form of endemic cretinism through to subclinical conditions in which the child manifests no obvious signs but is developmentally disadvantaged in comparison with appropriate control children who have not been subject to dietary iodine deficiency during fetal life? [Connolly, Pharoah, & Hetzel, 1979, p. 1149]."

Records were available that indicated a birth date and whether the child's mother had been administered the iodine or the saline injection. Samples from these two populations—excluding cretins—were tested with our battery and a sensorimotor battery developed by Connolly. Results on the sensorimotor tasks were not clear-cut, but the authors concluded that where the tasks required both speed and accuracy, the offspring of iodine-treated mothers were favored (Connolly et al., 1979; Pharoah, Connolly, Hetzel, & Ekins, 1981).

There are no differences in cognitive-task performance (see Table 5.9). Other research has found a similar differential impact of malnutrition on sensorimotor and cognitive development (Werner, 1979). However, scores

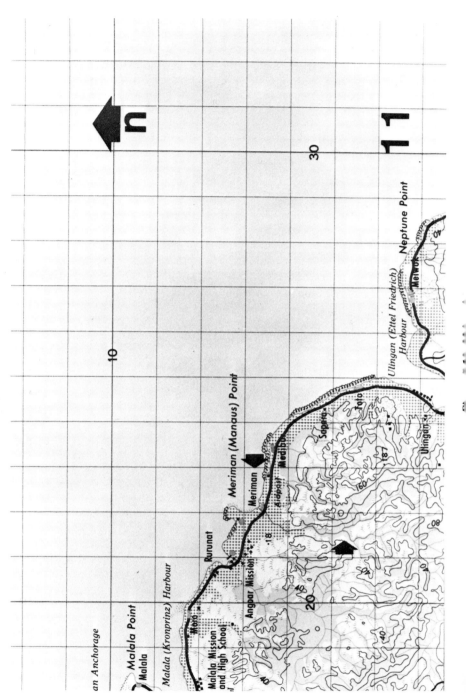

TABLE 5.9
Jimi Valley Samples

	Conservation of length	Matrix total	Flap-board total	Picture-sort superordinate nominal total	Free recall average recall	Mean age	Mean grade	N
Iodine	0	2.5	1.0	2.0	6.5	10.5	.3	24
	NS	NS	NS	NS	NS			
Saline	4.0	2.8	.8	2.0	5.0	10.9	.1	24

are extremely low for both groups when compared with those obtained in other sites. One possible explanation is that protein–calorie malnutrition is sufficiently acute so as to lead to real intellectual deficits. Seventy-five percent of the combined samples were below the norm on the MUAC—a much higher percentage than we have found elsewhere. Unfortunately, we have insufficient ethnographic data from the Jimi to permit an examination of alternate explanations.

We have consistently failed to find malnutrition effects, which at first seemed surprising, but events have caught up with us. I prepared a report in 1977 (reprinted in Lancy, 1979a) that argued that we were unlikely to find direct effects of malnutrition on mental development and school performance for several reasons. Children who are severely malnourished in infancy are unlikely to survive to school age; those who survive but suffer obvious signs of mental retardation will not be sent to school; and malnutrition probably works indirectly anyway. That is, inactivity caused by a poor diet—reduced even further by the greater incidence of ill health to which the malnourished are exposed—means that the child will grow up in an extremely impoverished stimulus environment. Where the environment is impoverished to begin with (see discussion, p. 121), such inactivity could lead to an approximation of the "child-in-the-attic" syndrome (Kagan, 1977; Kagan, Klein, Finley, Rogoff, & Nolan, 1979). The notion that malnutrition decreases interaction and activity level[5] is supported by

---

[5]Studies on the diet, physiology, and behavior of peoples from interior New Guinea have consistently challenged some fundamental assumptions. Carleton Gajdusek (1970), for example, was struck by the incredibly high tolerance for pain among the many Melanesian groups he visited. I was struck by the tolerance for boredom. That is, I have frequently noted individuals sitting for hours almost completely inactive. Gajdusek cites possible neuroanatomical differences for the pain tolerance. I believe that high levels of internally produced opiates might provide a complementary explanation for both phenomena. Whatever the case may be, I cannot help but wonder what implications a possible "motivation" or "arousal" factor might have on cognitive development.

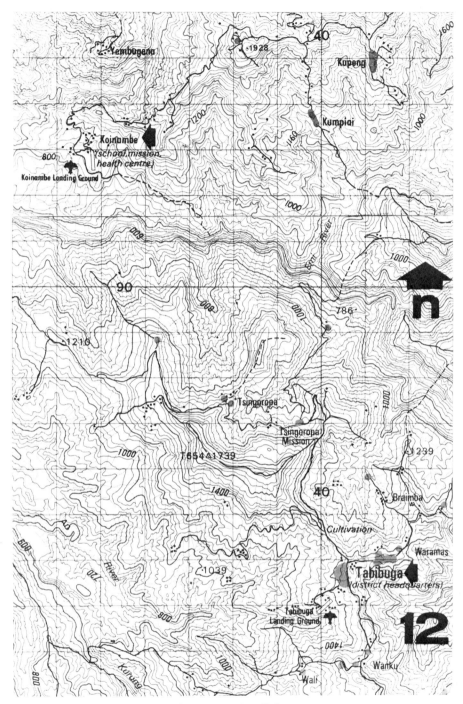

Figure 5.11. Jimi Valley.

research from Africa (Rutishauser & Whitehead, 1972) and elsewhere (Latham, 1969).

Piaget's colleagues have undertaken a study of physical and sensori-motor growth and development in matched samples of moderately malnourished (75–80% weight for age) and normal (90–100% weight for age) Baoulé infants. (The Baoulé are rural horticulturalists in the Ivory Coast.) They note no differences in behavior beyond a slight tendency for the malnourished infants to be somewhat more passive vis-à-vis the manipulation of objects (Dasen, Inhelder, Lavallée, & Retschitzki, 1978; Inhelder, 1979).

Warren (1973) has reviewed the extensive literature on malnutrition and mental deficits and finds it critically flawed by the consistent failure to control for the quality of the child's environment. Monckberg (1975), for example, found that the mothers of malnourished infants have substantially lower IQs than the mothers of normal infants, and there are other studies that show a negative correlation between malnutrition and the quality of the home environment (e.g., Cravioto & De Licardie, 1975). In those few cases where malnutrition is not correlated with SES or other indicators of environmental quality, intellectual development is unimpaired. The age of onset of malnutrition is also a critical factor. If it begins after 6 months of age, the effects on physical and intellectual growth are easily reversed (Cravioto & Robles, 1965). This finding is especially relevant, because in Papua New Guinea malnutrition usually appears only after the breast-milk diet is supplemented (e.g., after 6 months).

Ultimately, the very definition of malnutrition is open to question. One of the most consistent findings of nutritionists in Papua New Guinea in recent years (Ferro-Luzzi, Norgan, & Durnin, 1975, 1978; Rhoads & Friedlander, 1980; Heywood, personal communication) is that World Health Organization standards do not accord very well with the data. Despite "substandard" nutrition and "substandard" growth rates, Papua New Guinean children grow into healthy and well-muscled—spectacularly so in most of the Highlands—adults. At present, the questions of what constitutes adequate nutrition and what follows from inadequate nutrition are undergoing a radical reassessment (Winick, 1976, 1980):

> In the past thirty years we have come full circle. Whereas initially we believed that early malnutrition invariably led to structural and chemical changes in the brain that, in turn, left permanent scars, the current data suggest that the behavioral changes are caused by a different mechanism and, much more important from a practical standpoint, that the changes are potentially reversible [1980, p. 13].

The "different mechanism" is "the interaction of malnutrition with *environmental deprivation* [Winick, 1980, p. 13; italics added]."

I obtained dramatic evidence for this kind of interaction at Imonda in the West Sepik (see Figure 2.8), the site where we tested Waris-speaking children. As part of our standard procedure, we photographed common items from the village. In the Imonda village, we had no difficulty finding appropriate items until we asked for foods (*nneh*). Much discussion between myself, an interpreter, and village leaders led to this enigmatic statement: "There's none available in the village." Offers to pay for whatever they let me photograph brought no movement, but an impassioned plea had the effect of sending children scurrying off in various directions. Gradually, samples of several species of tubers and some sagos filtered into the village, but these were pitiful specimens—tiny and misshapen. We proceeded with the photographs, but I did not let the issue rest entirely. A second strange thing about Imonda was the widespread evidence of malnutrition among the children—pronounced abdominal oedema and dry, sandy hair in a large proportion of the children. Age was estimated in every case; hence the MUAC record is meaningless. Further inquiry among patrol officers and others who knew the area gradually led to an understanding of the situation. Aside from their exploitation of wild stands of sago palms, Imondas are (or were) hunters and gatherers. Consequently, they moved around a lot, which was a decided inconvenience in an area that has become politically sensitive due to the proximity to the border between Papua New Guinea and the Indonesian colony of Irian Jaya. Questions relating to border demarcation, to say nothing of sporadic guerrilla activity aimed at the Indonesian overlords, meant that authorities on both sides applied pressures to get people not to migrate. Agricultural extension services to support the changeover to a more sedentary way of life have not been conspicuously successful, as we have seen. Imonda children are doubly deprived: Not only is their nutrient intake even less satisfactory than it might have been in the past, but their interaction with the natural environment and the tools (traps, weapons, nets, etc.) used to exploit that environment has been sharply curtailed as well. The parallels with the Ik—an East African group that was also forced to shift suddenly from hunting and gathering to horticulture (Turnbull, 1972)—are obvious. Indeed, Imonda children do rather poorly on the cognitive tests: Less than 6% of the 8–13-year-old children conserve length, for example. However, schooling improves the situation considerably. One third of the fifth and sixth graders conserve length.

Conclusion

The main reason that consistent and widespread findings of cross-cultural differences in patterns of cognitive behavior have failed to gain acceptance is that culture is usually treated as a kind of black box. That is, there have been too few attempts to probe more deeply into the societies under comparison. In this chapter we have been concerned with a set of variables that are part of culture, that potentially can be scaled, and that might interact with patterns of cognition. I do not think we have exhausted the potential set of such variables here, nor have we thoroughly tested them for their possible explanatory power. But we have at least made a little progress in the right direction.

6

The Development of Counting and Classification Skills

As Shea (1978a) points out, the earliest "cognitive" research in Papua New Guinea was firmly based in the Western tradition of intelligence testing. The aim of this research was very straightforward—to identify "natives" who would perform adequately as infantrymen in the Pacific Islands Regiment. The authors of this research were unconcerned about why many individuals were identified as "unfit" on the basis of tests, nor were they concerned with the relationship between "cognitive skills" imbedded in the tests and the individual's potential for training beyond the rudimentary skills required of a foot soldier.

The demands on researchers in more recent years have increased in keeping with the twin goals of an education system that now produces highly skilled technicians and bureaucrats and a political philosophy that espouses equal access to these new employment opportunities. The present objective is to produce a model of cognitive development that is adequate to meeting these goals. It would be nice if a prepackaged model developed in the West could be borrowed, suitably modified, and then implemented in PNG—much as pedagogical models have been. Unfortunately, cognitive psychology is in as great a state of flux at present as at any time in its history. The majority of the Indigenous Mathematics Project research was carried out in isolation from this state of flux, relying mainly on the well-established theories of Piaget and Bruner. However, in the research to be reported in this chapter, a deliberate attempt was made to confront some of the more prominent issues in contemporary cognitive psychology, and at the same time to augment and refine the evidence gathered with a "standard" test battery.

The focus of present controversies concerns the relationship between language and thought, and the conceptual armory includes such terms as *surface structure, deep structure, competence,* and *performance.* The classic formulation is attributable to Chomsky (1968)—the originator of "transformational grammar." Chomsky argues that language is characterized by a "deep structure," which is governed by a set of rules that are all unconscious to the individual. What the individual actually says is characterized by a certain "surface structure." Chomsky believes that earlier linguistic formulations were faulty because analysis was based on surface rather than deep structure. Surface structure is an unreliable guide to deep structure because the speech of individuals is usually incomplete and inaccurate. By the same token, speech can be taken as indicative only of an individual's performance and not his competence, because it is quite likely that most of the incomplete and inaccurate utterances we record are temporary aberrations. An individual's linguistic ability (*competence*) will at all times be superior to the quality of his or her speech (*performance*). This formulation is directly relevant to cognitive psychology and especially to cross-cultural cognitive psychology.

At one extreme, Chomsky (1968) argues for the complete independence of language and thought (see also Malinowski, 1952); at the other extreme, Whorf (1956) argues that language equals thought. Vygotsky (1962, 1978) lies somewhere in the middle: He sees language and thought as originating in independent structures, that become increasingly interrelated as the individual matures. Piaget (1972) believes in independent origins, but he goes further in claiming the priority of logic or cognition, so that the child's cognitive stage determines the nature of his language. Finally, Bruner (1966b) reverses this argument completely. For him, the young child's cognitive skills are rudimentary and incomplete until the full acquisition of the structures inherent in language facilitate the deployment of truly advanced cognitive behavior in "symbolic thought." The same sort of continuum can be seen in the status accorded to evidence gleaned from language samples as opposed to test results. Although they assign different importance to language in their theories, in their research Piaget and Bruner rely heavily on what the child says to draw inferences about his or her cognitive level. Other cognitive researchers—especially American students of Piaget—tend to rely far less on language data, suspecting, like Chomsky, that what the child says is a poor guide to his or her thoughts. The bulk of cognitive research (and this is certainly true in

Papua New Guinea) has, therefore, righteously adhered to experimental tests of cognitive development. As esoteric as these issues may seem, the lack of agreement points to some potentially serious problems in the interpretation of the kinds of evidence we have presented thus far.

A proponent of Chomsky's ideas might claim that we are misguided in trying to infer cognitive processes from the purely linguistic picture-sorting and free-recall tasks. A Whorfian would claim that we are misguided in using cognitive tests: The language data (especially folk taxonomies) should be sufficient evidence for inferring cognitive processes. A Piagetian would see the linguistic data as virtually worthless and would argue for complete reliance on the cognitive tests. Recent research suggests that our hypothetical critics are all guilty of unwarranted reductionism. Anglin (1977) has been perhaps the most thorough of recent critics of "language-free" cognition. It is clear also from the burgeoning literature on language acquisition that many of the changes in the maturing individual's use of language cannot be accounted for solely by his increasing competence in the use of purely linguistic structures. Cole and Scribner (1974, Chapter 3) review cross-cultural studies that find that predictions of test behavior derived from an analysis of the native's language (a la Whorf) are not often supported (but see Bloom, 1979, 1981). They imply that competence can best be assessed through cognitive tests rather than descriptions of language. Yet, one line of investigation has yielded results critical of cognitive skills assessed through Piagetian tests. Hood and Bloom (1979), for example, find that Piagetian procedures fail to reveal the child's underlying cognitive competence that is more accurately reflected in his or her speech.

It was not our aim to try and resolve these controversies. But we were sensitive to them and tried to integrate them into the research at various points. The first series of studies to be described was carried out by Geoffrey Saxe, and is concerned with two issues. First, to what extent does variation in surface structure (in this case, counting systems) reflect deep-structure differences in patterns of thought? Second, to what extent does competence in an underlying cognitive operation (conservation of number) affect performance on a routine mental operation (counting)?

Randall Souviney was responsible for the second study, which was designed to assess the effects of varied task structure on cognitive performance. We wanted to address the possibility that our initial choice for conservation of length may have been invalid as a measure of competence because the operation employed was unfamiliar to our subjects. The final series of studies was carried out by Andrew Strathern and myself, and these studies go directly to the heart of the language-and-cognition issue. Several interacting rounds of experimental and ethnographic research served to test and retest the proposition that within Papua New Guinea different societies promote different world views that influence the cognitive makeup of individuals.

Studies of Numerical Reasoning

We start with what can only be described as a "meaty" problem in terms of the previously reviewed issues—namely, what is the relationship between indigenous counting systems, cognitive skill, and numerical reasoning? A number of authors (Menninger, 1969; Brainerd, 1979) have suggested that some societies lack true counting systems and, therefore, an abstract conception of number (see also Gay & Cole, 1967). These people do not count many things, they do not count very often, and when they do, the activity is directed entirely toward visible objects. As we have seen in the previous chapter, many of the counting systems found in Papua New Guinea (especially Types I and II) must be included in the concrete category. Following Whorf, we might predict that individuals from those societies would do poorly on various tests of the symbolic use of number. More than likely, a generative linguist would see number names as surface-structure phenomena that vary widely but that mask the underlying unity in the deep-structural conception of number or order and numerosity. Piaget, too, (1952, p. 4) would expect little connection between the particular counting system and the symbolic use of number. For him the necessary precondition for quantifying activities is the achievement of quantitative invariance (especially conservation of number).[1] Just the opposite view has been expressed by Gelman and Gallistel (1978), who see numerical operations as indicators of logical operations— in particular, that conservation of number is mediated by the child's counting the items in the array and noticing that the number did not change (see also Klahr & Wallace, 1976; Siegler, 1981).

Geoffrey Saxe has developed through a series of studies a model of how the young American child learns to use symbolic counting (1977, 1979a, 1979b). He joined us in 1977 and carried out research on the child's acquisition of symbolic counting in three of our groups: the Oksapmin, Melpa, and Ponam. The Oksapmin body-counting system was described in the previous chapter (see Figure 5.2). The Melpa have a base 4–8 system with some body-counting features (Strathern, 1977). The under-

---

[1] Geneva has begun to retreat from this position. Hermina Sinclair admitted in a 1980 speech that "conservation of number is not the watershed it's supposed to be."

lying principle is pairing (Lancy & Strathern, 1981). These two systems meet the criteria for concreteness in that neither can accommodate large numbers and both are used exclusively in concrete situations. Ponam has a base-10 counting system (see Chapter 5) that, while capable of a full range of abstract applications, apparently is not used this way very often (A. H. Carrier, 1979). Ponam children should show accelerated development in symbolic counting relative to children from the other two sites because of the more abstract counting system available to them, and also because (following Piaget) their grasp of quantitative invariance (as measured on a test of conservation of length) appears much stronger than that of either Oksapmin or Melpa children.

Saxe (1977) has shown that before children use numbers as a notational system, they exhibit various kinds of "premediational" strategies. For example, a child who is perfectly capable of counting a row of eight stones accurately may not use this skill to count out eight stones from a pile of stones to "match" the experimenter's row of eight. The child tries to make the match by some form of global correspondence: He lays out stones successively until both rows—his and the experimenter's—look about the same. He does not, in other words, use counting to mediate his solution of the problem. However, by the age of 6, the American child has abandoned these "premediational" strategies and is either in the transitional or the symbolic stage. In the PNG studies, Saxe used the following tests to probe the child's acquisition of abstract counting. In the *comparison* tasks, the child had to compare two rows of items on three occasions (3 versus 4, 6 versus 7, 8 versus 9) and tell the experimenter whether there was the same number or a different number of items in the two rows. Note was made of whether the child used counting (they were prompted to do so) to solve this problem. In the *reproduction* task, the children had to look at an array and then, no longer looking at it, had to make an identical-sized set from a group of similar items that were made available. This procedure was also repeated three times with the three set sizes. All the subjects were administered the conservation-of-number task; approximately half of the Oksapmin-speaking subjects were administered Piaget's tests for conservation of mass (clay) and seriation. All of the Ponam-speakers and half the Melpa-speakers were given the seriation task.

Eighty-six children aged 5–16 ($\bar{X} = 9$) were selected for the study: 17 Ponam-speakers, 40 Oksapmin-speakers, and 29 Melpa-speakers. None had attended school. All were tested in their home villages by a resident who used the vernacular throughout. The results indicated that counting develops much as had been found in the United States. Counting accuracy gradually improves, and older children tend to use mediational strategies more often than younger children (Saxe, 1979c). There appears to be about a 2-year delay, so that fully mediated counting is present only at age 8 in the Papua New Guinean children. Contrary to expectations raised by the abstract-versus-concrete counting-system distinction and the conservation-of-length results, there are no differences interculturally in this developmental process (Saxe, n.d.). Furthermore, contrary to Piagetian theory, conservation of number appears *after* symbolic counting—if at all. Only 1 of the 33 subjects who conserved number failed to use counting to mediate problem solution. At the same time a little over one half (36 out of 66) of those children who do mediate fail to conserve number. Despite this, any theory that suggests that symbolic counting is a necessary and sufficient condition for the appearance of conservation of number is also without support. As Figure 6.1 shows, conservation of number lags too far behind symbolic counting for any direct relationship to be operative.

A third alternative—the ordinal theory of number development (Brainerd, 1979)—also receives no support. This theory claims that an understanding of the number concept grows from the notion of *ordinality*—that things can be arranged in order of magnitude. The seriation task, which Saxe employed, is a direct test of this, supposedly underlying ability, and he found that less than 5% of the subjects succeeded on this task (the same held true for conservation of mass [Saxe, n.d.]). We must conclude that symbolic counting is a universal skill that develops gradually with age and is relatively unaffected by variations in the counting system employed, culture, cognitive development, or schooling. This is not to say that culture-specific numerical systems do not present particular obstacles for those who would learn them, as Saxe (1979c, 1981a, 1981b, in press a, in press b) has shown.

In the body-parts counting system, identical parts of the body may be used to represent different numbers. For example, in Oksapmin, the neck represents both 11 and 17, if you start counting from the right side of the body. Saxe (1981b) asked children a series of questions to see if this phenomenon created difficulties for them. They were told that a man was counting sweet potatoes in his garden. ("One day he counted to here [a part of the body is indicated], and another day he counted to here" [another part of the body is indicated]). Children were then asked whether the amounts were the same, and if not, which was the larger. There were six questions; in three of them the two parts indicated were symmetrical (e.g., right shoulder = 10; left shoulder = 18); and in the remaining three the two parts were asymmetrical (e.g., right wrist = 6; left ear = 16). As Saxe had expected, children did much better on the questions in which asymmetrical parts were used ($p < .001$). All of the 12–16-year-old children ($N=16$) answered these questions correctly, whereas only half answered all of the symmetrical questions correctly. Furthermore, he

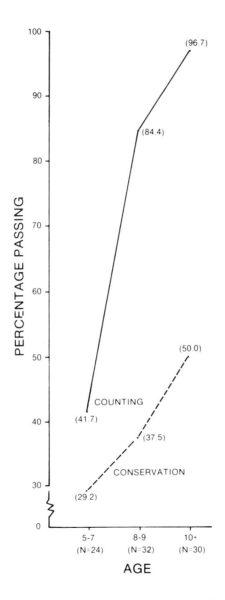

Figure 6.1. Quantitative counting and number conservation. (From G. B. Saxe, n.d.)

found developmental effects for both types of questions. Saxe also probed the child's understanding of the fact that among many arbitrary features in the body-counting system some are necessary (order), while others are not (direction).

This study was, in a sense, a replication of a study done in the United States. In that study, Saxe (1979a) had shown that young children consistently claimed that a puppet who counted with conventional number names was accurate, when compared to a puppet who counted with letter names, even when the reverse was true. In the Oksapmin study, children had to decide who had more sweet potatoes, a man from their own village who counted from right to left to the wrist, shoulder, and nose (in subsequent questions), or a man from another village who counted to the same parts but started from the *opposite* side of the body. To be successful, a child had to indicate that the sweet potatoes were the same when both men counted to the nose, but were different when they counted to the wrist and shoulder, and to indicate who was favored by the difference. Developmental effects were again obtained, but only about half (8 out of 15) of the 12–16-year-old children were completely successful. What these studies seem to indicate is that, while a body-parts counting system is perfectly adequate for the solution of problems in which counting is an aid (at least for amounts less than 10), it is indeed a cumbersome system and contributes to a substantial retardation in the individual's acquisition of the number concept.

The basic counting system used on Ponam is, for all intents and purposes, structurally identical to most Indo-European counting systems. Furthermore, it shares its number names with Austronesian-speakers throughout the Pacific region. Other aspects of number in Ponam are more unique. They use numeral classifiers, for example (A. H. Carrier, 1979), and they have a most interesting birth-order enumeration system. The first son is conventionally named *Tol*, the second *Gnih*, and so forth up to *Sebat*, the fifth-born son. The first-born daughter is named *Pindaluh*, the second *Pitatah*, and so on. These names are applied strictly according to gender. If a family has a girl, another girl, and then a boy, they will be named *Pindalah, Pitatah,* and *Tol*. Saxe (in press b) was quick to appreciate that the birth-order naming system is strictly analogous to Piaget's double-seriation (ABaCbcDd) problem (Inhelder & Piaget, 1958). He interviewed Ponam children at three age levels—10 8–11-year-olds, 10 12–15-year-olds, and 9 16–23-year-olds. He probed their ability on a standard single-seriation task and on a double-seriation task constructed from cards with stick figures drawn on them, each labeled with one of the birth-order names. These cards were used to make several families about which the children were questioned. Developmental effects for both tasks were significant. On the single-seriation task with sticks of varying lengths, Saxe had found that only 1 of the 17 5–8-year-old Ponam children tested previously had been fully successful. In this study the figures are 4/10, 6/10, and 9/9 for the 8–11-year-olds, 12–15-year-olds, and 16–23-year-olds, respectively. For the double-seriation task, the comparable figures are 0/10, 1/10, and 7/9. Ponam was the only one of our 10 sites where nearly 100% of the older samples achieved conservation of length. One hundred percent of the children in late adolescence were successful at the seriation task, and 75% of Ponam children, aged 13–15, were successful on a class-inclusion task. Although their development lags behind Western norms, individuals on Ponam achieve Piaget's concrete-operation stage, and Saxe (in press b) argues on the basis of the double-seriation results that they achieve formal operations as well. It is my conviction that Ponam society and perhaps several of the other societies where we have worked (e.g., Mandok, Kiwai, Toaripi) provide the necessary environmental supports for cognitive development—in Western terms. I am not as certain that this is the case in several other societies (e.g., Waris, Kewa, Melpa). Whether the poor performance seen in some societies can be attributed to a lower level of underlying competence will be taken up in the next section.

Studies of Length Conservation

In Chapter 4 I presented findings that showed the effects of age, education, and culture on performance on a conservation-of-length task. Piaget assigns minimal importance to the latter two and primary importance to the former. As has been shown (p. 84), our results contradict this prediction rather directly, with age effects being overshadowed by, in most cases, education-and-culture effects. In fact, in only one society— Ponam—does the improvement with age reach significance. Here we examine two possible sources for these findings. First, we consider that age effects were not pronounced because we tested over only a limited age range, thus missing the transition that may occur at a much later point in the developmental span than is typically found in the West (see also p. 63). Second, we consider the possibility that our measure of conservation of length is, for some reason, far too difficult and is thereby invalid as an accurate gauge of conservation.

We returned to the Southern Highlands a second time to work with Imbonggu-speaking children (see pp. 42–44). Recall that in the initial study neither age nor education effects were significant. On the second visit, we tested 16 children (8 males, 8 females) age 14–18 in each of two groups—unschooled and high schoolers (in Grades 7–10). The procedure was identical to that used in the first visit. The results for both studies are shown in Table 6.1. Examining the three age groups without formal education, a developmental trend is apparent (Pearson chi-square = 9.35, 2 df, $p < .05$), and this effect stems from the improvement made in the oldest group (Pearson chi-square = 11.26, 2 df, $p < .005$).

Adding the older samples also provides an education effect where previously there was none. The difference between the unschooled and schooled 10–13-year-olds, although in the predicted direction, is not significant (Pearson chi-square = 0, 1 df), while the difference between unschooled 14–18-year-olds and those in high school is (Pearson chi-square = 11.26, 2 df, $p < .005$).

In the Genevan approach, groups are usually compared on a "pass–fail" basis. Because of the stage feature in Piaget's theory, unless all or nearly all of the children conserve, that group is considered as not having "achieved" conservation. (*Transitional* is another category that is sometimes used.) Conservation of length is achieved by Western children between the ages of 8 and 11 (Piaget, Inhelder, & Szeminska, 1960; Pinard & Lavoie, 1974). By these criteria, only Ponam 10–13-year-olds and 14–18-year-old Imbonggus in high school have clearly "achieved" conservation of length. Dasen (1972), in a review of cross-cultural studies of conservation identifies four possible patterns of performance: (*a*) a concept might be achieved earlier than it is in Western populations; (*b*) it might be achieved at the same time; (*c*) it might be achieved later; and (*d*) some development occurs but quickly levels off, and the concept is never fully achieved. Excepting Ponam, which falls into the third category, all of our groups would seem to fall in the last category. However, with the Imbonggus, development does continue to progress into adolescence and high-school students very clearly conserve length. Note further, that in an earlier study (Kelly, 1977) of conservation of length among Highlanders in

TABLE 6.1
Success on the "Pit-Pit Horizontal" Task: First Study (Percentage)

Age	Grade		
	0	4–6	7–10
6–8	0 ($N = 16$)	—	—
10–13	19 ($N = 16$)	25 ($N = 16$)	—
14–18	43 ($N = 16$)	—	94 ($N = 16$)

Grades 8–10, all conserved length on "two-sticks" and "equal-strings" problems.

Our third study extends the search for full achievement into adulthood and also rectifies two flaws in the earlier studies. The first flaw stems from the fact that we used only a single measure of conservation of length—albeit the "standard" Genevan procedure. In the original Genevan studies (Piaget, Inhelder, & Szeminska, 1960), task effects were obtained; and task effects have been reported also from PNG. Shea (1978b), using a different procedure, obtained a success rate of 73% with 9–13-year-old Imbonggu-speakers in Grades 4–6, a figure that is considerably higher than our results with the two-stick procedure. We were equally concerned with the response of several anthropologists to our initial findings. They argued (personal communications) that if the task were imbedded in some routine operation, performance would improve markedly.

We (Lancy, Souviney, & Kada, 1981) therefore set out to design a battery of tasks, each of which would be unique in some respect, but all of which might indeed tap the same underlying concept. Ideally, we wanted not just to find an "easy" task, but to create a range of difficulty. We start with our old standby—Task A, something we have come to call *pit-pit horizontal*. We add *pit-pit-vertical* (Task B). Shea had used a race over straight and curving strings of equal lengths that we replicated individually in Tasks C and E. Tasks K and L were intended to highlight education effects, since both encourage the application of school-learned skills to a solution of the problem. Tasks D, G, and J use highly familiar situations. Digging sticks (D) are the principal horticultural implement of the Imbonggu and are used by both sexes of all ages, sometimes in pairs. Necklaces (G) are worn and made by nearly everyone and are built up from shells and bones, and now by multicolored plastic beads. The arms (J) are used as an informal "measuring stick" in Imbonggu and elsewhere in PNG. By contrast, our unfamiliar tasks used materials (clear tubing [H]; pulley [I]) that were unknown to our subjects. The individual tasks will now be described.

Task A: Pit-Pit Horizontal

The subject is presented with two pieces of pit-pit (a bamboo-like material indigenous to the Highlands region) that are equal in length (approximately 50 cm). The pieces are arranged in a parallel configuration from left to right and are positioned with collinear ends. The subject is asked to observe and touch the two pieces and is asked: "Are these two pieces of pit-pit the same length or is one piece longer?" If initial agreement cannot be reached, the subject is asked which is longer, and a small bit is whittled off that piece by the interviewer. The subject is again queried as to equivalence, and the process continues until the subject is satisfied. The interviewer then moves one of the pieces in a parallel fashion either left or right approximately 10–15 cm. The subject is then asked: "Are the two pieces of pit-pit still the same length, or is one piece longer now?" If the subject indicates that the lengths remain equivalent, justification is elicited. If the justification is logical—"they were the same before, so they are the same now; you just moved one"—the subject is considered concrete operational. If the subject indicates that one is now longer, justification is elicited, and the piece is returned to its original position. The process is now repeated; only the other piece is moved. If the subject still claims one is longer, he or she is considered "preoperational." If he or she changes his or her mind and indicates they are now equal in length, justification is elicited, and if logical, the subject is scored as "transitional."

Task B: Pit-Pit Vertical

Two pieces of pit-pit that are equal in length are presented in a manner similar to that in Task A—only the sticks are positioned across the table, pointing directly away from the subject. The procedures are parallel to those in Task A.

Task C: Pig Run

The subject is presented with two identical wooden rods (10 cm × 1 cm × 1 cm). He or she is then told the following: "Suppose we have two pigs, and we put one here [point to the end of one rod] and the other one here [point to the end of the other rod]. Now suppose they start at the same time and run at the same speed. Will they both reach the end [point to the opposite ends of the rods] at the same time, or will one get there first?" If the subject states that the pigs will arrive at the same time, continue as indicated below. If the subject says they will not, repeat the story in more detail, modeling the pigs' movements with two pencils until the subject accepts the initial conditions. Next the rods are shifted, and the story is repeated. If the subject says that the pigs will arrive at the same time, he is asked for justification. If the response is logical—"they are both running the same distance and are starting at the same time so neither will win"—the subject is classified as "concrete operational."

Task D: Digging Sticks

Two digging sticks of equal length (approximately 1.5 m and sharpened on one end) are presented by standing them vertically in front of the subject on level ground. Following the establishment of identity, one of the sticks is driven into the ground (10–15 cm), and the subject is asked: "Are the two digging sticks the same length, or is one longer now?" A subject who indicates that the two sticks are still the same length and offers logical justification is classified as "concrete operational."

Task E: Equal Strings

The subject is presented with two pieces of string of equal length (25 cm) displayed in a horizontal, parallel configuration with both ends collinear. After establishing identity, the interviewer then bends one of the strings, forming a curve with one end collinear with the corresponding end of the straight string. He then asks: "Are the two strings still the same length, or is one longer now?" A subject who indicates that the strings remain equal and offers logical justification is classified as "concrete operational."

Task F: Unequal Strings

A procedure similar to Task E is followed, except the initial condition is reversed (unequal versus equal). The long string (25 cm) is subsequently curved so that the ends are collinear with the straight string (15 cm), and the subject is queried as to equivalence after the transformation. If the subject indicates that one string is still longer and gives a logical justification, he is classified "concrete operational."

Task G: Neck Beads

The subject is presented with two parallel linear arrangements of colored rods (1 cm $\times$ 1 cm $\times$ various lengths). Both configurations consist of five rods of varying lengths and colors, but overall they are equivalent in length. The interviewer then states: "Pretend these colored rods are beads. Are these two necklaces the same length or is one longer?" After the subject agrees on the initial condition, the experimenter transforms the necklace closest to the subject by placing the second rod at a 90° angle to the end of the second, and so on in a zigzag pattern. The experimenter asks the subject: "Are the two necklaces still the same length or is one longer now?" A subject who indicates that the lengths remain the same and offers logical justification: "they both would fit around the same-size neck"—is classified "concrete operational."

Task H: Water Tube

The subject is presented with a piece of plastic tubing (1 cm in diameter × 50 cm in length) along with three identical glasses. Two glasses are partially filled with colored water (10 ml and 30 ml), and the third is empty. In front of the subject, the interviewer fills the tube from a separate source of colored water using a siphoning method and deposits the contents (approximately 20 ml) into the empty glass. The tube is tied with a simple overhand knot in front of the subject. The interviewer asks: "Which glass would fill up the tube again with nothing left in the glass?" A subject who gives the correct response (the 20-ml glass) with logical justification is classified as "concrete operational."

Task I: Pulley System

The subject is presented with a device that is composed of a red cord (20 cm) strung at right angles over a pulley, and the horizontal segment is connected to the support bracket by a rubber band. A weight pan is attached to the end of the vertical segment of the cord. By putting a 500-g weight on the pan, the rubber band stretches, allowing the string to run through the pulley about 5 cm, lengthening the vertical segment while shortening the horizontal segment. The subject is asked: "If I put this weight on the pan here [place the mass piece on the pan], does the red cord stay the same length or does it get longer or shorter?" The subject who answers the question correctly ("same") and offers logical justification is classified as "concrete operational."

Task J: Arms

The subject is asked to place his or her elbows on the table in front of him or her, with his or her forearms together, palms up. The interviewer asks: "Are your two arms from here [pointing to one elbow] to here [pointing to the tip of the fingers of the same arm] and from here to here [same procedure] the same length, or is one longer?" After the subject agrees with the initial condition, the experimenter moves one arm up, parallel to the other, approximately 15 cm. He asks the subject: "Are your two arms from here to here [pointing], and from here to here [pointing] the same length, or is one longer now?" The subject who answers correctly and offers logical justification is classified as "concrete operational."

Task K: Brown Rods

The subject is presented with a brown Cuisenaire rod (8 units long) and 14 unit cubes. The subject is asked: "How many of these little blocks will exactly fit along the edge of this brown rod?" The subject is encouraged to manipulate the blocks physically. Once the subject has determined that 8 unit blocks are equivalent to the brown rod (perhaps with the assistance of the interviewer), a second brown rod is produced, and the standard length-transformation procedures (Task A) are employed (the rods remain touching). If the subject fails to conserve, the interviewer asks: "How many little cubes does it take to make up this brown rod [point to one rod]? And this one?" The subject may need assistance recounting the units, or he or she may need to remanipulate the blocks. After the subject agrees that each brown rod is equivalent to 8 units, the standard length-transformation procedure is repeated. A subject who conserves after the first transformation procedure is classified as "concrete operational," and the procedure stops. For others, guided measuring takes place, as previously described. This is followed by a repetition of the transformation and question. If the subject is successful on the second attempt, he is classified as "transitional." If neither attempt is successful, the subject is considered "preoperational."

Task L: Ten Rods

The subject is presented with 1 unit cube and a scored 10 rod. The subject is asked: "How many of those little blocks would fit along this long rod?" Once it has been established that 10 unit cubes are equivalent to one rod, a second 10 rod is produced and the procedure, as in Task K, is followed.

For those tasks where the transitional stage is not defined in the protocol, the interviewer applies this classification when, during the justification stage, the subject seems unsure of his or her answer, and when probed, changes his or her mind one or more times.

The sample characteristics are shown in Table 6.2. We have included a range of age and education levels that overlap with the previous studies. We also included some older subjects (16–25-year-olds, N=18). In addition, we created subsamples to test for other effects. Only about 30% of the Imbonggu Community School graduates will be given an opportunity to enter high school. Selection is based on the results of an achievement test administered at the end of the sixth grade. The possibility exists that selection is, in fact, based on ability or IQ, which would tend to nullify the earlier finding that remaining in school through Grades 7–9 has a decisive impact on conservation. Therefore, we asked teachers to assign our subjects in Grades 4–6 into either a high-achievement (extremely likely to be selected for high school) or a low-achievement (extremely unlikely to be selected) group. The teachers were able to do this for 29 of the 35 subjects, 16 being assigned to the high group and 13 to the low group. Subsequent analysis showed no significant difference in conservation attainment between these two groups ($F[1, 29] = 2.13$, NS). This bolsters the earlier finding, which is replicated here, of great superiority for subjects who are attending high school.

The 12 tasks were randomly administered to all 105 subjects, interspersed with a distractor task in which the subject had to copy a geometric figure on a geo-board. Procedures followed the clinical pattern we had employed heretofore. The first results I would like to present are the pit-pit horizontal-task results alone, with a restricted sample of the subjects (see Table 6.3).

The success rates for the various groups are very close to those obtained previously (see Table 6.1), despite new test personnel (the supervisor, recorder, and experimenter were all new people), new subjects, and the confounding influence of 11 other similar tasks in the battery. As Table 6.4 shows, success is influenced by the nature of the task. Tasks J, D, C, E, B, and F (in that order) were subjected to a Gutmann-Scale analysis and produced a *coefficient of scalability* of .602, which is acceptable. The implication is that conservation is not an "all-or-none" phenomenon, and substages or transitional periods do not fit very well either. A better interpretation posits that the concept will be employed either sparingly or widely, depending on the individual's level of "certainty" (Miller, Brownell, & Zuiker, 1977). This view is strengthened when we note that only 7.6% of the sample was fully nonconserving and only 3.8% met the criteria for successful conservation on all 12 tasks (see also Saxe & Moylan, 1982).

The suggestion that our "standard" task discriminated against less

TABLE 6.2
Conservation of Length: Sample Breakdown[a]

| | Level of education | | | |
Age level	0–3 years	4–6 years	7–10 years	Total
7–10 years	30	15	0	45
13–25 years	20	20	20	60
Total	50	35	20	105

[a]Courtesy D. F. Lancy, R. Souviney, and V. Kada, 1981.

educated–acculturated individuals receives no confirmation. On the contrary, the standard task is among the easier tasks. Tasks that used highly familiar operations (D, J) were the most difficult, and Task H, which used an unfamiliar operation, was by far the easiest (cf. Price-Williams, 1961). The pattern of performance of unschooled individuals (see figures in parentheses in Table 6.4) shows no sharp divergence from the population as a whole, which again weakens a "systematic-bias" argument.

However, we were unable to replicate Shea's (1978b) results with either equal strongs (Task E) or a race (Task C). Nor did Tasks K and L particularly favor the school-children. Eighteen percent of children aged 7–15 in Grades 1–6 (N=46) gave fully conserving responses on these tasks versus 14% for 7–15-year-olds who had not attended school (N=29). As with number conservation and counting, conservation of length and measurement also seem to be relatively independent skills.

By assigning a score of 1 for every transitional response and a 2 for every conserving response and summing, we arrive at a total score, and Table 6.5 presents these results for two age levels and three grade levels. Main effects for age ($F[1, 103] = 7.14, p < .05$) and education ($F[2, 102] = 16.51, p < .0005$) are significant; the interaction ($F[4, 100] = 1.54$, NS) is not . This pattern of results is entirely consistent with those found in the

TABLE 6.3
Success on the "Pit-Pit Horizontal" Task: Second Study (Percentage)[a]

| | Grade | | |
Age	0	4–6	77–10
7–9	0 ($N = 9$)	—	—
10–12	0 ($N = 10$)	27 ($N = 15$)	—
13+	45 ($N = 20$)	—	70 ($N = 12$)

[a]Courtesy D. F. Lancy, R. Souviney, and V. Kada, 1981.

TABLE 6.4
Success across Tasks for Entire Sample (for Unschooled Subjects)[a]

Tasks	Fail	Trans.	Conserve
Water-tube (H)	32.4 (30.8)	0 (0.0)	67.6 (69.2)
Unequal strings (F)	41.9 (53.8)	8.6 (12.8)	49.5 (33.3)
Pit-pit vertical (B)	57.1 (71.8)	15.2 (12.8)	27.6 (15.4)
Equal strings (E)	62.9 (87.2)	15.2 (5.1)	21.9 (7.7)
Pit-pit horizontal (A)	63.8 (76.9)	8.6 (7.7)	27.6 (15.4)
Neck-beads (G)	66.7 (87.2)	6.7 (5.1)	26.7 (7.7)
Ten rods (L)	67.6 (71.8)	9.5 (5.1)	22.9 (23.1)
Pulley (I)	68.6 (79.5)	1.0 (0.0)	30.5 (20.5)
Pig run (C)	68.6 (87.2)	2.9 (0.0)	28.6 (12.8)
Brown rods (K)	76.2 (97.4)	1.0 (0.0)	22.9 (2.6)
Dig sticks (D)	77.1 (97.4)	1.9 (0.0)	21.0 (2.6)
Arms (J)	80.0 (97.4)	1.9 (0.0)	18.1 (2.6)

[a]Courtesy D. F. Lancy, R. Souviney, and V. Kada, 1981.

first study. Thus, while the task effects are significant, they do not alter the previous finding of weak developmental and strong educational effects. An extremely telling comparison is the one between high-school students (N=8) and unschooled adults (N=10) in the age range 16–25. The former averaged 20 points ($SD = 6$) out of a possible total score of 24, while the latter averaged 5 ($SD = 4.5$). Unschooled Imbonggu fall squarely into Dasen's fourth category, while children who go to school fall squarely into his third category.

As deviant as these findings are from the standpoint of the theory, they were somewhat reluctantly anticipated by Piaget (1966) himself. More important, they are foreshadowed by a number of recent studies in North America that show, for example, that:

1. Conservation skills can be successfully trained (Beilin, 1965; Gelman, 1969; Brainerd, 1977; Anderson & Clark, 1978).
2. Very young children can demonstrate conservation under some conditions (Siegel, 1978).

TABLE 6.5
Mean Score over Twelve Tasks[a]

	Level of education			
Age level	0–3 years	4–6 years	7–10 years	Grand means
7–12 years	4.6	4.1	—	4.4
13–25 years	6.6	9.2	16.5	10.8
Grand means	5.4	7.0	16.5	8.0

[a]Courtesy D. F. Lancy, R. Souviney, and V. Kada, 1981.

3. College students can be shown to fail a conservation task under certain conditions (Murray & Armstrong, 1978).
4. Conservation can be "extinguished" (Miller, 1976; Robert & Charbonneau, 1978).

Set against the background of these other studies, the Imbonggu data would seem to imply that conservation is learned, that not all societies provide the relevant learning opportunities, and that Western-style schooling does provide such opportunities. We need to ask, then, what skills are learned in school that facilitate the achievement of conservation. Fluency in the English language may be one such critical skill. (English is the language of instruction beginning in Grade 1.) Kelly (1973, 1977; Kelly & Philp, 1975) had tested Melpa children in 1972 on conservation of length, picture-sorting (production of superordinate nominal responses), and class inclusion. In addition to his usual samples of schooled and unschooled children tested in the vernacular, Kelly added a schooled sample that was tested in English. These children performed better on all three tasks (although the difference is significant only for superordinate nominal responses) than the schooled sample. Kelly attributes this difference to deficiencies in Melpa grammar. Other investigators confronting the same issue (Greenfield & Bruner, 1966) have pointed to deficiencies in the lexicon, especially in the area of "comparatives."

We had selected 35 Imbonggu children from Grades 4–6 for testing. Fifteen of these were taken at random and administered the 12 conservation-of-length tasks in English; the remaining 20 were tested in Imbonggu. A comparison of total scores for these two groups yielded a significant difference ($F[1, 33] = 4.55, p < .05$), favoring those tested in English. On the other hand, this group does only half as well overall as the high-school students, who were also tested in English. We believe the explanation for this discrepancy may lie in the relative fluency of the two groups. Community-school children rarely use English outside the classroom or even in the classroom when conversing among themselves. High-school students, perhaps to emphasize their distinctiveness, use English extensively in and outside the classroom.[2] The English-fluency issue is given further attention in the next chapter.

A "difference" account has little to contribute to an understanding of the development of very basic cognitive operations and skills, as we have seen in the studies of numerical reasoning. The conservation-of-length

[2]In a 1981 biography of a Papua New Guinean tutor of mathematics at the University of Technology, Clements and Jones reported that: "Atawe thinks that it was during his first or second year in high school that he first began to think in English. No longer did he find it necessary to translate in his mind from the English spoken to his *tok ples* Baruya [p. 18]."

results are more encouraging to a language-equals-cognition equation. However, it must be emphasized that our results bear entirely on the question of variation in performance. I think we have demonstrated convincingly that when the unschooled Imbonggu "fails" a conservation test, he does so because he cannot apply the "quantitative invariance" concept that he possesses to these particular tasks. His *wantok* in high school, for all intents and purposes his "racial" and "cultural" twin, can do so. More important, it is inconceivable that he really believes that the digging stick (Task D) grows shorter as it is driven into the ground.

In the next section, we take up two issues—language and cognition and competence versus performance—in several studies.

Further Studies in Classification and Cognition

The evidence we have presented thus far fairly consistently supports a "deficit" interpretation of the international and intranational variation in cognitive development that we have uncovered. Taken as a whole, we see a consistent developmental lag—with reference to Western norms—of 3 years or more on virtually every measure. Second, intranational differences show a similarly consistent pattern. Whether the categorizing behavior involves identity or equivalence, whether the stimuli are familiar or unfamiliar, children who make the expected transition to more symbolic patterns of processing on one task tend to do so on all tasks and vice versa. Evidence in support of a "difference" account (see p. 54) is slim. However, the elicitation research that we had carried out to assemble folk taxonomies of food (see Chapter 5) had provided us with a lead that we followed up in the next series of studies.

In some languages we worked with, the degree of hierarchicalization in the folk taxonomies seemed very low indeed (see also Kelly, 1977, p. 189). It was so low, in fact, that we began to search for alternative ways of representing these classification systems (Lancy, 1978a). In the case of the Melpa, we were struck by the tendency to group items in pairs—a tendency that I had previously detected among the Kpelle (Lancy, 1977). This emerged not only in the elicitation research but in the picture-sorting experiment as well, a pattern that is not unknown in studies that have used this technique in America (Goldstein & Scheerer, 1941; Olver & Hornsby, 1966). Pairing as an organizing technique contraposed to the taxonomy seems, from the American research, to be applied in situations where the information-processing load is low, a situation that characterizes Melpa society very well. (See also the discussion of color nomenclature, pp. 68–69.)

We were extremely fortunate at this stage in securing the collaboration of Andrew Strathern, an anthropologist with nearly 2 decades of experience in working and living with the Melpa. Strathern confirmed the Melpa pairing predilection and contributed to (Lancy & Strathern, 1981) the intensive research on Melpa classification and cognition that will be described here.

Three rounds of research have been carried out with the Melpa, specifically in the vicinity of Golke (see Figure 2.1) and a fourth round is underway as these words are being written. The first round was undertaken as part of the 10-society survey. In that survey, children tested in the Golke vicinity performed poorly overall, particularly on tasks that would seem to demand taxonomic ordering principles. On the matrix, their average total score of 3.3 placed them last among the 10 societies. On picture-sorting their mean scores and ranks for total superordinate, total nominal, and total superordinate nominal were 3.5/9, 3.7/8, and 1.9/8, respectively, and their groups tended not to reflect the objective category size of 4. On the free-recall test, their mean scores for total recall and total clustering and rank were 5.2/9 and .6/9, respectively.

Before describing the second round of research, I would like to review an extremely relevant study done by Max Kelly (1977) among Melpa-speakers with ages 10–14. He spread photographs (two-tree (*dey*) species, two sweet-potato (*oka*) species, two green-vegetables (*kim pompa*) species, and four (*kim kimpi*) green-vegetable species) out in front of the child. The child was asked to sort the photographs into two piles. This sort was scored as correct if the child placed the trees in one pile (nonfood) and the others in the second pile (*röng*=food). He was then asked to sort the larger pile into two piles and was scored as correct for *oka* versus *kim*. Again the larger pile had to be sorted into two piles and was scored correct for *pompa* versus *kimpi*. Only 17% of the unschooled and 46% of the schooled subjects were successful on this task, even though all of the classes were based on a careful elicitation of the Melpa folk taxonomy of plants, and pretesting had determined that children knew the names of all the plants as well as the category names.

Our second round of research involved a more focused replication of the picture-sort experiment and Piaget's class-inclusion test (Inhelder & Piaget, 1969; with modifications borrowed from Wohlwill [1968] and Wilkinson [1976]). Three language groups were selected—Ponam (complex folk taxonomy, extensive use of taxonomic organization on tests), Melpa, and Imbonggu (nearer the Melpa end of the strong–weak taxonomizing continuum [Leroy, 1975]).

Instead of sorting pictures, we had children sort objects taken from a single restricted domain. There was some evidence from the original picture-sort study that children who do not otherwise group categorically might do so in one or two domains, especially "food." Hence, we used food items in Melpa and Imbonggu. On Ponam, typical foods make poor stimuli, so we used shells. Shells are plentiful on Ponam, being used for decoration, food, and money. Adults had no trouble naming and categorizing a great variety of shells. We eventually settled on 16: 3 *paruwof* ("bi-valves"), 5 *palasapo* ("cowrie" sp.), 3 *mbuss* ("cone" sp.), 4 *djang* ("spider conch" sp.), and 1 *lal* ("trochus" sp.). All but 3 of the shells (cowries) had individual names as well (mostly secondary lexemes). The taxonomy is shown in Figure 6.2. The food items used in Melpa were *rua* ("banana," 5 varieties), *op* ("yam"), *me* ("taro," 4), *oka* ("sweet potato," 4), and *po* ("sugar cane," 1). The food items used in Imbonggu were *meali* ("banana," 4), *min* ("yam," 1), *me* ("taro," 4), *gai* ("sweet potato," 5), and *po* ("sugar cane," 3).

We will describe our procedure on Ponam, which was for all intents and purposes the same in the other sites. Children were tested individually and administered four tests in an invariant order. First, the children were asked to name the individual shells, and their performance was scored as the proportion of 13 shells correctly named. Then they were asked to arrange the shells in any way they liked. This test was given a score reflecting the proportion of shells correctly arranged by category. Then the experimenter rearranged the shells if necessary into their categories and asked the child for the name of the four (the trochus was left out)

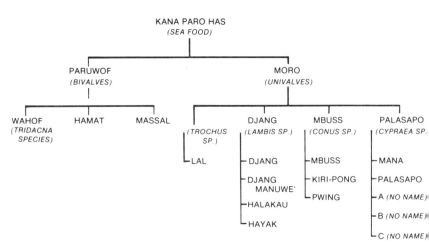

Figure 6.2. Ponam shell taxonomy.

groups. This was again scored as the proportion correctly named. Then the children were shown eight virtually identical tiger cowries and asked to name this group. Few failed to name them correctly, but if they did so, the name (*palasapo*) was provided. Then four new shells were added; these taken from each of the other four categories. This larger group was also named by the child (*moro*), or if necessary, by the experimenter. The child was then asked to point to all the *palasapo* and then to point to all the *moro*. If the child pointed to only the non-*palasapo* when asked to point to the *moro*, he or she was corrected, and the instructions were repeated. This was done as often as necessary until the child reliably pointed to all the shells when asked to point to the *moro*. The child was then asked whether there was more *palasapo* or more *moro*, and he or she was scored as "successful" for class inclusion if he or she responded *moro*. For Melpa, the subordinate category was *me tawe* ("taro" sp.) and the superordinate, *röng* ("food"); for Imbonggu we used *paka* ("taro" sp.) and *kere langi* ("food"). We tested children from four age–grade ranges. Sample-size, age, and grade means for the four groups were 1:24, 7.5/.5; 2:24, 9.5/2; 3:32, 12/5; and 4:32, 16/6. The results are shown in Figures 6.3–6.6.

Ponam children show the expected trend in the acquisition of individual names ($F = 8.3$, $p < .001$). For Melpa children, this trend is less pronounced but is, nevertheless, significant ($F = 5.1$, $p < .001$). We are somewhat surprised by the Melpa child's inability to name these very common food items—the main criteria for selection. (Compare, for example, the proficiency of a Mayan child [Stross, 1973].) We are less surprised by the Imbonggu child's poor performance. We had a very difficult time finding 17 foods in the Imbonggu area. The daily diet varies hardly at all, consisting of one or two principal species of sweet potatoes garnished with one or two species of greens. It took us 3 days traveling around the area to collect a sufficient variety of items for the Imbonggu study. The same process in Golke took 3 hours. Hence, while our adult Melpa informants could assure us that children would be familiar with all of our stimuli, Imbonggu informants could not make a similar assurance. It appears that in Melpa and Imbonggu the acquisition of the basic items in a highly salient area of the lexicon is a lifelong process, and the results from this test reinforce the comment about the information-processing load that was mentioned previously. Apparently, cultivars are known by name only to those who plant and harvest them. These people are adults in both societies.

The results of the next two tests (see Figures 6.4, 6.5) show that if you select the right domain and direct your queries to the right levels in the hierarchy, taxonomic behavior will emerge, and at a very early age. Developmental trends are significant only for Ponam, and overall per-

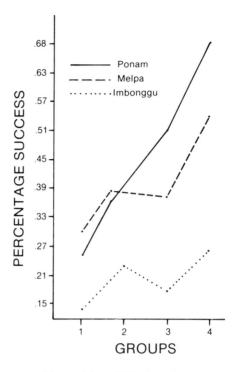

Figure 6.3. Individual naming.

formance lags behind the other two sites. (Arranging: $F = 19.7, p < .01$; naming: $F = 28, p < .001$.) Their poorer performance may be due to the lower level of salience of shells when they are compared to food. Note, however, that when Ponam children are asked to name higher order groupings (all bivalves, all univalves), they are nearly as successful at this level as at the category-name level. This is not true for the Melpa and Imbonggu children, who do much worse when asked to name higher order groups (e.g., in Melpa, *po* and *rua* are conventionally grouped as *po rua rakl*, and all the foods can be grouped as *röng*). Kelly (1977) also found that children had much more difficulty at higher levels in the taxonomy (*röng* and *mel kont* ["living things"] in his study).

Category names are learned somewhat later than the category concept itself in Ponam and Melpa, indicating that the tendency to form groups based on the shared morphology of items is not entirely mediated by the available nomenclature. This is contrary to a Whorfian prediction. The ability to form the appropriate groups without any form of prompting appears to be nearly perfect. The only deviation occurs among younger

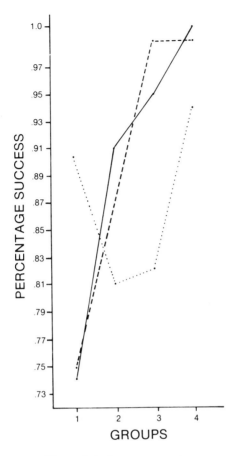

Figure 6.4. Category arranging.

children who occasionally break up a larger group into two smaller groups that differ in the relative size of items (e.g., two large/three small cowries).

In extensive research on the child's acquisition of naturally occurring taxonomies, Eleanor Rosch (1978) has found that this process takes place with considerable regularity. At some point in the hierarchy, *basic-level* terms will be found. These usually correspond to the genus level. Children acquire these terms somewhat earlier than they acquire terms superordinate to or subordinate to the basic-level terms. The same trend is apparent in these data, except that while basic-level terms are acquired at a very early age—as they are with Rosch's American subjects—subordinate and superordinate terms seem to appear very late among the Melpa and Imbonggu.

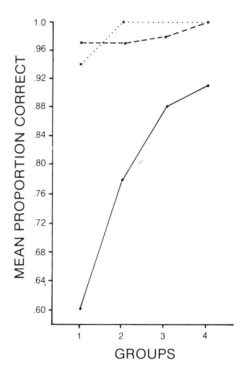

Figure 6.5. Category naming.

It may be that the notion of *certainty* introduced in the last section to explain the Imbonggu deployment of the conservation operation will be helpful here as well. It seems that the ability to form equivalence categories is universally present: What varies is the extent to which the individual utilizes this operation. We have seen Ponam children use it widely in the first and second sorting experiments—to organize randomly ordered words to aid their recall of them and in the class-inclusion task.[3] We have seen Melpa and Imbonggu children, on the other hand, use it more narrowly only in the case of arranging and naming items belonging to highly salient basic-level categories.

As Flavell points out, "For Piaget, mastery of the inclusion rela- tion . . . is the *sine qua non* of a concrete operational as opposed to late

[3]In a recent report on an island people in the Torres Strait who share a common subsistence system with Ponam (and little else), the investigators (Nietschmann & Nietsch- mann, 1981) undertook to study "how the Islanders perceive and categorize the marine environment [and found that] what began to emerge was a complex and detailed taxonomy [p. 58]."

pre-operational cognition of logical classification [1963, p. 306]." Figure 6.6 presents the class-inclusion results. Here we see again that a critical skill (in Piaget's theory) does not "develop" in some societies. The developmental trend for Ponam is significant (chi-square (2) = 16, $p <$ .001); whereas in the other societies performance *declines* with age.

In the third round of research, we focused exclusively on the Melpa. Strathern had developed a solid base in Melpa ethnography and language that permitted us to pursue the language-and-cognition issue in greater depth here than elsewhere. First, he redesigned the class-inclusion experiment.

Röng ("food") is not the perfect choice as the superordinate category. In another study (1977) using *röng* as the superordinate category and *kim* ("green vegetables") as the subordinate category, Kelly had found a

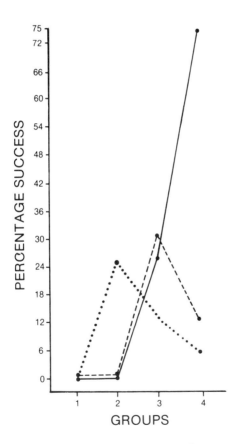

Figure 6.6. Class inclusion—I.

similarly low level of success (25% for children aged 10–14). Ideally it refers to material that is "ready for eating." The *me tawe* had been harvested and destalked, but it was still uncooked. Strathern (Lancy & Strathern, 1981) felt that a less ambiguous choice would be *moke-mel*, which includes decorations or ornaments for the body. Two examples of *moke-mel—ki rung* ("arm bands") and *ken mapa* ("gold-lip pearl-shell neck ornament")—were used for the subordinate classes, eight of the former and four of the latter. Strathern, who is fluent in Melpa, administered the test in a thoroughly clinical fashion to 10 7–9-year old, 20 10–14-year-old, and 20 16–45-year-old subjects. Because Melpa lacks comparatives, the critical question had to be phrased as "Are there many *ki rung* or many *moke-mel?*" This is the standard Melpa phrasing for quantitative comparisons. Results are shown in Figure 6.7.

Performance overall is improved as compared to performance on the *röng-me tawe* task (compare Figure 6.6). This may be due to two factors: One is that *moke-mel* is closer to being a collection than a class; members not only share attributes, but they are interdependent. The *collection* concept is acquired earlier than the *class* concept (Markman & Siebert, 1976). A second reason might be that Strathern was more successful at conveying the requirements of the task than we had been in the first study. Certainly "task effects" for the class-inclusion paradigm are widely reported (see Winer, 1980, for a review). Despite this improvement, performance over the age range tested is seen to decline again. The tendency for performance to level off or decline is best explained—we believe—by the difference model. We hope to show that for the Melpa, the preferred classification strategy is pairing rather than taxonomizing and that this tendency directly interferes with their performance on tasks that require a taxonomizing strategy for their successful solution.

Our search for taxonomies in Melpa "folk science" and cognitive development met with constant frustration. Our search for pairs was much more successful. There are a variety of expressions in Melpa that can be translated as "grouping together," "making a group," "categorizing," etc., but all contain the word for "two" (*rakl*) or the word for "partners" (*kup*). These include *wam-ambon rakl endepa ni* ("making a husband and wife two to say") and *kup endepa ni* ("making a partner to say"). The most commonly employed is a *tepa ralk ndopa ni* ("taking and making two to say" or "making twos"). Grouping in Melpa is then explicitly concerned with making pairs. And the operation is pervasive indeed, as the following examples will show. (For a full discussion, see Lancy & Strathern, 1981.)

All plants are either *mbo* ("planted") or *römi* ("wild"). Within the category of domestic plants, various pairs are formed that mitigate against a hierarchical arrangement. For example, *oka* ("sweet potato") and *kim*

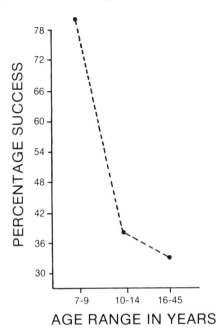

Figure 6.7. Class inclusion—II. (From Lancy & Strathern, 1981.)

("greens") are paired because they are consumed together. This pair can be contrasted with the pair of *me* ("taro") and *op* ("yam"), because the latter are luxury foods while the former are eaten daily. This pair in turn can be contrasted with the pair of "sugar cane" and "bananas" (*po-rua-rakl*), which are also luxury foods, but are planted by men, whereas *me* and *op* are planted by women. Note the importance of function as a basis for these pairs as contrasted with, say, morphology (perceptible attributes).

Kund and *pombora* are glossed as "light" and "dark." However, their use extends well beyond contrasts in which color is a salient feature. They may be used by extension to mark contrasts between "good" and "bad," and between "people," "pigs," and "spirits." Counting by pairs is the preferred method. Two sets of two fingers are bent down on the left hand (1–4), then on the right hand (5–8), at which point the two fists are brought together. The Melpa use this procedure both for traditional practices such as counting the number of pigs to be given away in a *moka* exchange (Strathern, 1971, 1977) and in dealing with modern currency as well. However, sums not divisible by 2 are explicitly disliked. The 2-Kina note (Kina = $US 1.50; it comes in 1, 2, 5, 10, and 20 denominations) is probably the preferred denomination, despite its small value relative to the other notes.

Pairs are strewn together throughout Melpa cosmology: The sky and earth are paired as are the sun and moon, night and day, months, etc. In the human sphere, every tribe has a single partner or pair-tribe; the same is true for every clan. Below the clan level are "father–son" lineage sets. Similarly, most forms of address are reciprocal. For example, father and child address each other as *ta*, indicating that any two speakers are related in some fashion, thus making a "whole pair" covered by one term. Finally, people is expressed as *wamb (wuo–amb)* or man–woman, and person as *noman–king* or character–body.

It seems safe to say that whenever the Melpa wish to generalize or to create a category, they do so not by utilizing a single superordinate lexeme but rather by specifying a pair that, by way of contrast or complementarity between members of the two halves, constitutes a totality. The taxonomy is not absent in Melpa but its use is restricted, and it is constructed from pairs. A similar conclusion seems warranted for several other Highland societies as well (Perey, 1973; Leroy, 1975; Hallpike, 1977; Biersack, 1980).

In the second class-inclusion study, Strathern noted that, despite the clear inclusion relationship between *moke-mel* against *ki rung* and *ken mapa*, many subjects tended initially to emphasize the differences between the subordinate classes rather than their similarities. Specifically, they pointed out that women usually wear pearl shells, whereas men wear armbands. This is not a hard-and-fast rule, however, and after some prodding, all subjects agreed that *ki-rung* and *ken mapa* were both *moke-mel*, but it indicates how pairing often gets in the way of taxonomizing.

Strathern also used the stimuli from our original picture-sorting study with nine adults, all of whom he had known for at least 16 years. He spread the pictures out in a random fashion on a table with as little prior instruction as possible. Subjects sensed immediately that the task was to group the pictures in some way, and they took this very seriously. Their attitude was not that of a person about to take a test, but rather of someone sitting down to do a jigsaw puzzle. They knew there was a tricky solution, and they set about to find it. Many took a long time to do this, and several of the men used the occasion to crack various salacious jokes for the benefit of Strathern and the assembled onlookers. Keep in mind that the picture set had been constructed to reflect Melpa classes: There were pictures of a man, woman, boy, and girl to represent the class of people (*wamb*); of a spear, shield, and bow and arrow to represent the class of weapons (*ell mel*); a headband, bird plumes, skirt, and *kina* shell to represent the class of decorations (*moke mel*), and so forth. Altogether, there were 28 items that were ideally groupable into seven classes. However, the only grouping principle that emerged regularly was pairing—usually on the basis of shared or complementary function. The actual pairs formed varied enormously across informants. There were no pairs that were obviously right, while others were wrong. Many people changed their pairs repeatedly during the course of the experiment. Nevertheless, two general tendencies were apparent from the comments people made before they began—"let us make them into husband–wife sets" and "let us make them into partner-helping sets."

This experiment, coupled with a broad overview of Melpa pairing that Strathern undertook at the same time (Lancy & Strathern, 1981), suggests strongly that the pairing principle derives originally from human relationships (cross-sex, cross-generation, interfamilial, etc.) and is extended to the natural world. If this conclusion proves viable, it would represent one of the few strong confirmations of Durkheim's and Mauss's theory:

> Society was not simply a model which classificatory thought followed; it was its own division which served as divisions for the system of classification. The first logical categories were social categories; the first classes of things were classes of men [1903–1963, p. 82].

The Melpa preference for pairing as opposed to taxonomizing in their equivalence-category structures and for functional as opposed to nominal or formal bases is unlikely to be unique. Nelson (1973, 1974) argues that the concepts of prelinguistic children are formed in this way, and C. H. Brown (1979; see also Lyons, 1968) indicates that category names are often created through a binary process; for example, tree-grerb from large plant, small plant. Binary opposition, pairing, "dualism," etc., is fundamental to the collective representations of many preindustrial societies (Needham, 1973).

Our intensive work with the Melpa, which is continuing, has taken us to the point where a difference model now seems more viable. From an early age some individuals see two things transposed as identical; others, the same age or even much older, insist that the two things are not identical. Some individuals when confronted with an array of items immediately set to work to categorize the items into mutually exclusive sets of a manageable (from a remembering standpoint) size; others are less willing to see the items as equivalent. Their sets are not mutually exclusive, are not easily named, and are very large or very small. The latter system for coding and grouping things in the real world is very efficient as long as the number of distinct items to be dealt with is small. It is efficient because it permits a desirably high degree of flexibility. However, when the items to be dealt with are many, the former system becomes more efficient because the fundamental capacity of human memory is limited to about 5–9 "bits" at a time. Beyond this number, items have to be "chunked" (Miller, 1956), and this is typically accomplished by the use of a taxonomy with verbal labels at each node.

A common memory-capacity test is the digit-span, where an individual is read a series of digits that he must recall in order. The span of digits that the typical individual can recall increases during childhood to about age 7, and it does not increase thereafter. In one study, however, the investigators (Ericsson, Chase, & Faloon, 1980) were able to bring an American college student to the point where, after much practice, he could accurately recall 80 digits. The authors convincingly demonstrate that the student's channel capacity had remained constant at 7 digits. His dramatic improvement was effected by his imposing spontaneously a three-level hierarchy on the digits as they were presented, and because he could "borrow" strategies he had employed to remember "running times." The authors report that the student "is a good long-distance runner who competes in races throughout the eastern United States. He classifies running times into at least 11 major categories, from half-mile to marathon with several sub-categories within each [p. 1182]." This illustration of the press to code, store, and retrieve countless bits of information is not as aberrant as it seems.

My thinking on the subject of taxonomies had been influenced by an incident that took place in 1978. I was visiting with colleagues in San Diego in the middle of my 3.5-year stay in Papua New Guinea. One of the pleasures of such home visits is eating. (PNG cuisine, whatever else it may be noted for, is not noted for its variety.) My friends obligingly took me to several nice restaurants, including a fairly posh establishment, for breakfast one morning. A casual glance at the display case on the way to the table suggested that a "Danish" would be a wise choice. "Danish" appeared nowhere on the menu, however, and in its place was a long list (with various sublists) of what I could only code as "breakfast rolls." I was saved from the agony of indecision by the welcome suggestion from one of the party that we order the "assortment basket." It remained only to order the potables. That was no problem: Before 5 o'clock, I drink only tea. This simple and apparently unambiguous request brought forth from the waitress a veritable encyclopedia of teas I might choose from. As a drowning man, I stopped her at "English breakfast," and the order was duly placed. I have not yet recovered from the shock of having to make a hurried decision with my taxonomies in a state of disarray. My point here is that the notion of *information load* as a "cultural" factor did not occur to me until I had experienced the extremes on this continuum.

There is no doubt that the information load on the typical Westerner is enormous. Carey (1978) estimates that American children have partially mastered 14,000 words at least by the age of 6. This may be an overestimate because, as several investigators (Nelson, 1973; Greenfield & Smith, 1976) have shown, some children are "expressive-language" learners: They concentrate on learning about themselves, and their vocabulary does not develop as fast as it does in "referential-language" learners. Still, half of 14,000 is a staggering figure, and it represents at least 2.5 times the number of words in the *entire lexicon* of many of the languages we have worked with.

The American situation is not entirely unique. Whereas we are innundated with breakfast rolls, running times, and dogs (Gal, 1973), the Tzeltal Maya have a huge lexicon to cover the plants and animals in their environment (Berlin, Breedlove, & Raven, 1974; Hunn, 1977). And where there are a lot of named "bits," there will be classes to group them in and names to code the classes (Berlin, 1978). Furthermore, the presence or absence of these codes is—not surprisingly—predictable from a knowledge of "cultural complexity" (C. H. Brown, 1977, 1979). However, it must be stressed that while societies vary in the depth and complexity of their taxonomies and while this is predictive of members' performance on cognitive tests (see Chapter 5), we have presented evidence in this chapter that shows that the taxonomy is available to all individuals and can be applied in the artificial setting of a cognitive test under restricted circumstances (see also Cole *et al.*, 1971, pp. 135–138).

Piaget's theory of cognitive development now seems not so much a genetic or biological theory as an historical one. Individuals are not those who achieve the concrete operational or formal operational stages, but rather, societies make such transitions (Luria, 1976). The basic building blocks of cognitive operations are available to every individual, and are possibly available at a much earlier age than Piaget suggests. Whether they are used routinely and in novel situations depends on the nature of the society and in particular on the information load (or "cognitive press") impinging on and generated by that society.

7

The Limits of
Mathematical Achievement

Some Historical Issues

Although our original goal was to study the relationship between culture, cognitive development, and the acquisition of modern mathematics, the study of the latter began fairly late during the course of the project. In fact, work on school mathematics has been very much a distinct enterprise, under the general direction of my colleagues Bob Roberts and Randall Souviney. This work is still in progress. Taking these facts into consideration, I can only attempt an overview of this research here and a preview of the major findings. A full accounting will not be available for some time.

McNamara (1979) has described three phases in the history of education in Papua New Guinea. The first phase lasted until about 1955. Papua New Guineans received very little formal schooling, and most of that consisted of the rote learning of scripture and ecclesiastical routines. As colonial subjects, Papua New Guineans received just enough education to prepare them for their new roles as Christians, clerks, soldiers, and policemen. The school system—in common with that found in many other developing countries—was primarily aimed at indoctrination rather than education (Lancy, 1975).

From 1960 onward, pressure—externally more so than internally (Jinks, 1968)—began to influence the Australian administration to prepare the territory of Papua New Guinea for independence. The timetable for granting independence was drastically shrunk. There were two principal concerns then (and now). First, schools were heavily concentrated in a few areas (especially in the far eastern section of New Britain and Port Moresby). Therefore new schools were to be built in the central portion of the country and in other "undeveloped" areas. The Highlanders in particular were especially keen to see schools established (McNamara, 1979). They were quick to appreciate that future economic opportunities (especially wage employment) would be closely tied to one's level of education. They unsuccessfully lobbied to postpone independence on the grounds that the employment vacuum created by departing Australians would be quickly filled by "coastals" who had had a head start on schooling and urban living. They were unsuccessful and are, as a consequence, grossly underrepresented as white-collar wage earners.

A second concern was to secularize the education system. Control of schools gradually passed to the government, and a Western model of public schooling was adopted. This meant an emphasis on the acquisition of basic skills necessary for employment in a modern, technologically oriented society, the use of English as the medium of instruction, competitive standards (e.g., rating exams) for advancement in the system, the use of large numbers of expatriate teachers (over 1000 at one time), the construction of school buildings along Western lines out of machine-fabricated materials, and the creation of a full-fledged bureaucracy to run everything. The crash program was spectacularly successful (McNamara, 1981). Schools were built in the remotest possible corners. Within a few short years, the system began to produce a substantial stream of fully literate and numerate graduates. Universities were established with the standard array of programs, including engineering, law, medicine, and the sciences.

This second phase lasted less than 15 years. Two problems had become apparent by the late 1960s. The expansion of the system and the drastic increase in school places at every level had gotten out of control: It had gained a momentum of its own.[1] The original goals were lost sight of, and

[1] One manifestation of this is the fact that the office responsible for monitoring enrollment occupies a division and is manned by a relatively large and well-trained staff. By contrast, the office responsible for monitoring student achievement occupies a branch in a unit that is part of a division and was—until recently—manned by one individual who was, by his own admission, untrained and wholly unsuited to the job. Thus, while various national exams are written and marked by committees and administered by teachers, no attempt is made to analyze the results (beyond assigning a grade to individual students) nor are they ever recorded in a form suitable for later analysis. Remarks about declining standards made in

expansion became an end in itself. The costs, paid largely from foreign aid, were escalating exponentially, and the returns were rapidly diminishing. That is, an increasing proportion of students leaving school were not finding jobs. Rather than halt the expansion of the system or even reduce its size to control costs and bring the system into line with manpower requirements, the initiative was taken to convert primary (Grades 1–6) schools to Community Schools (Lancy, 1979b). Community Schools were much cheaper to build because they were constructed of local materials by local labor. Wages were cut drastically, since all of the expatriate staff members were replaced by Papua New Guineans who were willing to work for much lower salaries. Subsidies of various kinds to support boarding students were eliminated; the period of primary schooling was reduced from 7 to 6 years, and pupils no longer kept back until they had mastered the material from the early grades. The supply of books and other educational materials was pared, and missions that had heretofore augmented the support structure for schools under their jurisdiction cut off virtually all such funds. Teacher-training institutions were established throughout the country to generate teachers to service the expanding student population. The number of students enrolled tripled between 1960 and 1980. To justify the drastic drop in per capita expenditures, the planners (Papua New Guinea Education Plan, 1976) redirected primary education to prepare pupils for community (e.g., village) life. Unfortunately, this goal has never been accepted by Papua New Guineans. Study after study (e.g., Thompson, 1976; J. G. Carrier, 1979; Grant & Zelenietz, 1980) have shown that Papua New Guineans are interested in schooling only insofar as it leads to wage employment. The Huli people from the Southern Highlands expect the school to "open a way for them, through their children, to a new kind of life, to enable them to get money and buy the things that they [want] [Cheetham, 1979, pp. 87–88]." Exactly the same scenario has been followed, with a lag of about 6 years, in secondary education. Here too an initial period of relatively modest growth and high per capita expenditure has been followed by a period of much more rapid growth in the number of school places and a precipitous decline in per student expenditures. The country is now experimenting with "community high schools" (Stanton, 1979). Drastic shifts in education policies have created a situation in which the quality of education varies

---

this chapter are based, therefore, on fairly flimsy evidence. Also, this explains why we had to develop a math-testing program of our own. Math-test results from the national exams were, for various reasons, inadequate for our purposes. I do not mean to imply that test scores should be treated as the only indicator of the "health" of the education system (see, for example, Lancy, 1978d), but they are an important first approximation.

widely, depending on such factors as the period during which a particular school was established, its proximity to communication centers, and so forth. The combination of expanding enrollment and declining resources has resulted in an overall decline in achievement levels (Roakeina, 1977; Lancy, 1979a; McNamara, 1981). There are serious implications for mathematics education that I will address shortly.[2]

Parallel to historical developments in the nature of schooling in Papua New Guinea have been several interesting developments in mathematics education. After plans for building and staffing schools were worked out, the Education Department in Port Moresby turned its attention to the curriculum. At the time Zoltan Dienes was active in Australia developing a "new-math" curriculum for South Australia, which was eventually published as the *Primary Mathematics Series (PMS)*. He was invited to Papua New Guinea to form a team to begin the development and trial of a new-math curriculum. Guided by Dienes during short visits in 1964 and 1965, the team produced *TEMLAB (Territory Mathematics Laboratory)* by 1967, a curriculum for Grades 1–3. *PMS* was used for Grades 4–6 when it became apparent that local resources were insufficient to carry out the development of *TEMLAB* through Grade 6. Although *TEMLAB* was commercially published and is still in use in several countries, it was considered a failure in Papua New Guinea. Development of an alternative curriculum began shortly after the completion of *TEMLAB* but was not finished until 1976. This new course, MACS, or Mathematics for Community Schools, was fully implemented by 1977, and since then has undergone continuous evaluation (Roberts, 1978, 1981; Roberts & Kada, 1979). *TEMLAB* failed because it assumed far too high a level of general knowledge and competence on the part of teachers. Essentially Dienes's theory was put forth—in language that teachers did not understand—and was coupled with various kinds of activities. Teachers had to provide their own plan of instruction. They had to use or invent particular activities to lead the child through the process of growth and development that Dienes said could be achieved. MACS formalized the instructional process, making the theory implicit rather than explicit. Teachers guides were prepared that told the teacher exactly what to do and when to do it. Later,

---

[2]Lawrence Ros (1980) of the Goroka Teachers College in the Eastern Highlands has undertaken a comprehensive study of the relationship between "transition rate" and mathematics achievement in five countries: Kenya, Liberia, Tanzania, the Solomon Islands, and Papua New Guinea. Transition rate refers to the proportion of students who continue their formal education from Grade 6 to Grade 7. Rates varied from a low of 7.56% in Tanzania to a high of 78% in Liberia. Transition rate and level of achievement on tests of numerical ability and skills (basic competencies) were perfectly correlated. Papua New Guinea falls about midway between these two extreme transition rates, and high-school students score about 15% above Liberians and 35% below Tanzanians on the same tests.

syllabuses were produced that presented some theory and outlined long-term objectives.

The Dienes approach (Dienes, 1964; Dienes & Golding, 1971) to mathematics instruction was heavily influenced by the cognitive–developmental theories of Piaget and Bruner. The central feature that makes the curriculum *cognitive* is that emphasis is given to the acquisition of general cognitive operations rather than specific mathematical operations.[3] From Piaget comes the "constructivist" principle. The child constructs cognitive tools by symbolizing and internalizing the lessons learned as he or she manipulates various concrete materials. Initially he or she is given an opportunity to explore the materials in a free-play format. Later he or she is taken through guided experiences that incorporate particular rules—e.g., set theory—or patterns. Later still, these experiences are summarized and abstracted so that the child can explicitly describe various rules, patterns, and procedures.

Dienes fully embraced the notion of enactive, ikonic, and symbolic representation, and two further principles that can be derived from the work of Jerome Bruner. First, the "multiembodiment" principle holds that any mathematical concept, no matter how abstruse, can be "embodied" in a form comprehensible to even very young children. Concepts can be broken down into constituent elements and expressed in terms of relationships among collections of concrete stimuli such as multibase blocks, balance beam and weights, attribute blocks, and so on. Gradually the child abstracts the concept after repeated exposure to it under various guises. A second theme that appears and that is emphasized in Bruner's writings (1960, 1966a, 1966b) is attention to the acquisition of appropriate language. Dienes would argue that there is no fundamental difference between the language and logic of common speech and the language and logic of mathematics—only that the latter requires greater precision. Hence all Dienes's curricula place heavy emphasis on teaching children

---

[3]Resnick and Ford (1981) make the point that the "new math" or Dienes approach has never been validated. No one has established that learning high-level principles makes it easier to learn to compute or solve problems, or that principles readily transfer from one situation to another: "Can we be sure that such an approach is not merely creating double work for the child? Will the child learn a concept one way the first time and have to relearn it in another context later? [p. 124]." Lauren Resnick suggested to me in 1978 that we should try and undertake a definitive examination of these issues, using parallel tracks in the same school. Papua New Guinea provided the perfect opportunity for such a study because the child's *only* exposure to Western mathematics occurs in school. Therefore it would be possible to create two "pure strains." I was, unfortunately, never able to muster the resources to undertake this project; thus, the studies presented in this chapter represent only a very weak test of these fundamental issues.

the precise or mathematical meaning of such critical terms as *or, and, on, square, more than, volume,* and so on.

Although the MACS course developers increased the coverage of number operations and decreased coverage of set theory, Dienes's ideas are still very much in evidence. For example, the first-grade curriculum is concerned with teaching the concepts of conservation, classification, relative "manyness," and relational terminology. Number is not introduced until the middle of the year, and by the end of the year children are expected to be able to count only to 10. The emphasis on cognitive skills and mathematically precise language continues to receive heavy emphasis at least through the fourth grade. By the end of the second grade, for example, children are only expected to count to 100 and to do single-digit addition and subtraction.

In adopting and actively promoting the Dienes approach, the Department of Education made or accepted a number of assumptions. The Department assumed that the intellectual development of children in Papua New Guinea might proceed more slowly than in the West; hence, the relatively undemanding sequence of instructional objectives in the early grades. There is considerable evidence to support this assumption, but as we have seen, there is wide intercultural variation in developmental rates. Second, the Department assumed that important cognitive operations might be slow to develop or be wholly lacking; hence the need to support cognitive development through direct instruction. This assumption too is fully supported by the data. Third, the Department assumed that high-level, abstract cognitive skills are prerequisite to the acquisition of low-level, concrete arithmetic skills. The next section presents data bearing on this assumption. Finally, the Department assumed that among these high-level skills, classification and the logic of sets were of paramount importance. We have, unfortunately, little evidence bearing on this assumption. However, Brainerd's (1979) critique is thorough and convincing.

Mathematics Achievement—First Survey

A team was constituted in 1977 under the leadership of Bob Roberts to plan an evaluation of the MACS course. Delivery of the 18 teachers' guides (3 per grade level of 120 pages each) had begun in 1976 and continued through 1977. We had several aims. Chief among these was a desire to study the implementation of the course and to determine areas in the curriculum that were being poorly covered so that in-service training could be targeted to those areas. Therefore, our first objective was to design a student test that followed the syllabus very closely. Sixty questions were devised to sample systematically the various topical strands, and five levels (Grades 1–2, 3, 4, 5, and 6). Questions were drawn entirely from material in the teachers' guides (Roberts, 1978). Hence the test measured both end-of-sequence skills (e.g., $2/10 + 5/10 =$) and preparatory skills (e.g., questions dealing with logic and relations). Reliability and validity analyses of trial versions led to a reduction in items from 60 to 50—10 for each level.

Since we were interested in studying the implementation process, testing was repeated for 3 years, at the end of the 1976–1977, 1977–1978, and 1978–1979 school years. The tests were administered to 3665 pupils from 47 schools in 14 provinces. Random samples of 20 were taken from each grade (2—6) in each school. Some schools offered no class at a particular grade level, so that level would not be represented. Some classes had fewer than 20 students, in which case all students in the class were tested.

Preliminary (ANOVA) analysis indicated that the effects of grade ($F_{5,3658} = 390.3$), gender, favoring males ($F_{1,3580} = 13.69$), and school ($F_{3,3393} = 30.76$) were all significant at the .001 level or beyond. Testing was carried out in 9 of the 10 original IMP sites (all except Kiwai). Our analyses (Lancy & Kada, 1979; Lancy, 1981) indicated that the math-test results were fairly consistent with the cognitive-test results. However, a number of other factors seemed to muddy the waters. First, scores varied as a function of the province in which the school was located ($F_{9,2912} = 43.47$, $p < .002$). Toaripi children did reasonably well on the cognitive tests, for example, but poorly on the math test. Less than one third (32.7%) of them were performing at or above grade level. But this was true of all the schools in the Gulf Province in which testing was carried out. Overall, only 36% of the children in the province were performing at or above grade level. Kewa children did better on the math test than we had expected—46% were at or above grade level, and this was true for the province as a whole (43%).

There seems to be a rural–urban dimension in the results as well (see also Cayago, 1979). Table 7.1 shows the breakdown of performance for six schools—three from the Western Highlands Province and three from the Western Province. Culturally the schools are relatively homogeneous, but they lie at varying degrees along an urban–rural continuum. The trend is quite clear: Remote rural schools appear to offer a poorer version of math instruction. Other evidence (Lancy, 1979a) indicates that teachers are more poorly trained, are absent more often, and have shorter tenures in

TABLE 7.1
Predicted versus Actual Achievement in Mathematics (Expressed in Percentages)

	Grade level				
Location	Two or more below	One grade below level	At grade level	One grade or more above	N
Urban	8.8	30.0	38.8	22.5	80
Rural	12.5	35.0	35.0	17.5	80
Remote rural	46.3	35.0	18.8	0	80

remote rural schools. The supply of materials and visits by inspectors is also sharply curtailed. Student absenteeism and poor diet and health may also be contributing factors.

Bob Roberts (1978, 1981; Roberts & Kada, 1979) has undertaken a thorough study of some of these issues, particularly teacher preparedness and the availability of materials. He used the math test just described to set up the dependent variable—mathematics achievement. His independent variables included the teacher's education history, an interview to assess the teacher's understanding of the aims and objectives of the MACS program, a classroom organization and materials-inventory checklist, and a classroom-observation schedule to monitor the teacher's performance in class. Eight hundred ninety children from 14 schools were tested for the dependent measure, and their 87 teachers were studied on the independent measures. Only two variables emerged as consistently predicting student achievement: school location (urban children did better) and the availability of classroom materials. These two items are, of course, highly correlated.

Nevertheless, some other findings are of interest. Classes were organized in a pattern that closely matched the aims of the MACS program. That is, teachers did not monopolize class time with lectures or management contacts. This contrasts sharply with their behavior in other types of instruction (Wohlberg, personal communication).[4] They let the children proceed with the business of discovery learning. Unfortunately, teachers' knowledge of mathematics was so weak that when they tried to guide students, they often sent them off in the wrong direction. Teachers averaged less than 80% on the test mentioned earlier, whereas their pupils

[4]I owe a great debt to my friend and colleague Ken Wohlberg for helping me to understand Papua New Guinea's classrooms and teachers. Ken and his wife Ruth have both taught in remote, rural primary schools and have prepared teachers at the Goroka Teachers College. Ken has undertaken systematic research on teacher values and classroom behaviors—only a fraction of which (Wohlberg, 1979), unfortunately, has been published to date.

averaged about 50%. In the upper grades the gap narrowed dangerously. In four of the Grade 6 classes, teacher and pupil scores were virtually identical, and in one class 80% of the pupils received a higher score than their teacher. Roberts's (1981) thesis contains numerous examples of faulty mathematics teaching, and equally critical, misuse of the very terms that the program attempts to convey in a precise manner.

As suggestive and interesting as these attempts to sort out what may "cause" poor or satisfactory performance in mathematics, they must be viewed in terms of the clear finding that pupils throughout Papua New Guinea—regardless of culture, province, location of residence, and access to materials—learn very little mathematics during 6 years in the Community School. As Table 7.2 shows, mastery is high on the material covered in the early grades and falls off sharply at the higher levels. Considering only the "best" province and the most "urban" location, the picture does not change much. More specifically, less than 4% of pupils in the fourth grade correctly solve problems involving single-digit multiplication and division, addition and subtraction to two decimal places (e.g., money), and telling time. Success on these same problems improves only slightly by the sixth grade (20%, 15%, and 10%, respectively). On 2-digit multiplication and division the sixth-graders' success rate is 5%. On the other hand, all children seem to do well on the items selected from the Grade 1–3 curricula. These questions primarily involve the language of mathematics and counting. We know from the results presented in Chapters 5 and 6 that children have little trouble with counting, regardless of whether or not they have been to school. Additionally, these questions were read aloud to pupils by the tester because we felt that the target

TABLE 7.2
Percentage of Students at or above Grade Level as a Function of
Grade and Location

| Grade | Overall | Location | | |
		Manus Province	Port Moresby	International School
2	85.4	98.0	100.0	100.0
3	62.0	91.6	70.0	100.0
4	34.0	81.1	44.8	100.0
5	12.8	36.2	25.0	85.0
6	5.8	0.0	6.5	89.0
Number of schools:	46	4	2	1
Number of pupils:	3,619	206	141	46

pupils—second and third graders—might not be able to read them. During the second round of testing in 1978, we decided to test for the effect of having the questions read. Two large schools (Rebiamul in Mount Hagen and Montfort in Daru) with double classes were chosen for this study. At each grade level one class was randomly assigned to the "read" condition and the other to the "nonread" condition. Performance did not differ for the two conditions at Rebiamul ($t_{97} = .07$, NS) or Montfort ($t_{93} = 1.89$, NS).

Because so very few pupils solved problems beyond single-digit multiplication, we were concerned that something might be seriously wrong with the test itself. We, therefore, administered the test in an International School in Port Moresby (see p. 125). The performance of these children is also shown in Table 7.2. Despite the fact that they follow a very different curriculum (see Leinhardt & Seewald, 1981, on the importance of "overlap" in evaluating achievement-test results), they do very well. Indeed, the 2 (out of 46) children who failed to make the grade level did not miss by much. More important, they are strong where Community-School children are weak, in such areas as 2–3-digit arithmetic, fractions, decimals, and simple measurement.

Our preliminary conclusion was that the culture, the curriculum, the teacher, and the child's own cognitive skill provide sufficient impetus to reach a stable but low level of comprehension and ability in mathematics. The chance of a child's going farther on his or her own is nil; the chance of his or her society's providing opportunities to continue the learning process is very slim in Papua New Guinea; the chances of the teacher, given the low level of his or her math ability, to guide the child further are also low. Assessing the curriculum is more difficult. We had high hopes that the low scores in 1977 could be attributed to the fact that the newly introduced program had not yet had a chance to take hold. Similarly low scores in 1978 and 1979 dashed these hopes. If we compare test performance across grade and culture, one encouraging trend does emerge. Ponam children in the second grade average 78 points; Melpa children 25. However by Grades 5–6 the gap has closed: The respective scores are 85 and 83. These scores are not high. The maximum score is 150, but there is the strong suggestion that basic quantitative and cognitive skills can be strengthened by exposure to the Dienes curriculum. It is equally clear that the curriculum alone cannot prepare the Papua New Guinean child for further study in mathematics. Brian Harrison has extensively tested students at the Balob Teacher Training College in Lae. His conclusion is that "*after four years of high school*, the potential primary school teachers of this country are equipped with arithmetical skills which are only marginally better than those of Australian grade 4 children and inferior to grade 5 children [1976, p. 19; italics in original]." Teacher training lasts 2 years during which mathematics teaching methods are taught rather than mathematics per se, and thus the circle is completed.

Mathematics Achievement—Second Survey

A second survey was undertaken by Randall Souviney (1980a; Souviney, Kada, & Malaga, 1980). Two new math tests were developed. "PMAT" was similar to the earlier achievement test in that it ranged over the whole curriculum, but it was shorter and eliminated all of the questions that had yielded very low success rates. Another test, "TAS," was a 20-question arithmetic test. Each of these came in several versions so that they could be repeatedly administered. The test battery included five "standardized" cognitive tests, including conservation of number and length, class inclusion, double seriation, and logical classification (taxonomizing). There were also tests of visual memory (Bishop, 1978), M-space (Case, 1977), and reading (Donaldson, 1978; Rawson, 1978).

Six sites were selected, including an International School (Ela Beach), a Community (Ororo) School in Port Moresby, and Community Schools near Ponam (Andra), Tekin (Divanap), Mount Hagen (Muglamp), and Ialibu (Kero). The latter three involved students from the same language groups that we had previously tested (see Chapter 2). Children in Grades 2, 4, and 6 were tested. The math and reading tests were administered to a large sample of 667 pupils. Table 7.3 presents the results in terms of percentage of success on the math and reading tests. The effects of site and grade are both significant at the .0001 level for math and reading, which are highly correlated ($r = .73$). In all the schools except Ela Beach, new curriculum and teaching were introduced (Souviney, 1980b, 1980c) that produced positive but nonsignificant gains in performance. These results parallel the earlier findings quite closely. Again the performance of International-School children is very good, and there is substantial intrasite variation among the Community Schools with the most remote, least stable schools trailing the others. Males outperform females and performance to criterion declines with increasing grade level (Souviney, 1981). Overall, Community-School children seem to make good progress on problems requiring counting and simple arithmetic, but then a plateau is reached: Skilled problem-solving and accurate work with

TABLE 7.3
Performance on Math and Reading Tests by Students in Six Schools

School	N	PMAT mean percentage	Reading mean percentage
Ela Beach[a]	91	70.0	96.6
Andra[b]	53	64.6	85.1
Kero	136	55.8	70.4
Muglamp	116	55.8	67.1
Ororo	158	54.4	76.8
Divanap	113	46.5	74.6

[a]These students have all had at least 1 year of schooling prior to Grade 1.
[b]Includes only children in Grades 4 and 6.

fractions and decimals are very rare. The new curriculum materials seem to lead to improvements in several areas but not in problem-solving (Souviney, 1981).

A subsample of 201 pupils received the math, reading, and other tests previously mentioned. Performance on the cognitive tests was comparable to the results obtained earlier (see Chapter 4). For example, success in conservation of length over all subjects was 34%, for sixth graders, 50% (compare Table 4.2), and between-site differences in performance were greater than within-site differences. Since these tests were all positively correlated, a "total-cognitive" score was created by summing over the five tests. Therefore, there were three status variables—sex, site, and grade—and four skill variables—cognitive, visual memory, M-space, and reading—to work with in explaining variation in PMAT performance. Initial analyses indicated that all the skill variables were positively correlated with PMAT, and all were subject to site and grade effects. Table 7.4 shows the interaction of PMAT with the status variables. The overall model is significant, and these variables account for 81% of the variance in PMAT. A second analysis removed the variance contributed by the status variables; and visual memory. M-space, total cognitive, and reading were regressed on this *residual* PMAT. As indicated in Table 7.5, the skill variables account for a substantial amount of the residual variance in PMAT; however, the only single variable whose effect is significant is "total cognitive." Total cognitive is correlated $+.25$, $+.29$, and $+.55$ with visual memory, M-space, and reading, respectively. Therefore visual memory and M-space can be effectively eliminated as causal agents in explaining PMAT performance.

We can be encouraged by the fact that Souviney's collection of skill and status variables accounts for over 90% of the variance in math achievement test scores. The model should give heaviest emphasis to *grade*,

TABLE 7.4
Analysis of Variance with PMAT and Status Variables

Source	df	F	p
Overall	27,172	27.7	.001
Site	4,172	17.8	.0001
Grade	2,172	226.5	.0001
Site × grade	7,172	2.1	.0460
Sex	1,172	16.8	.0001
Site × sex	4,172	3.0	.0197
Grade × sex	2,172	1.1	.3481
Site × grade × sex	7,172	0.29	.9553

which is, of course, confounded with *age*. In other words, we do not know how much mathematics skill increases, purely as a function of increased experience, and how much is due to instruction. As I indicated earlier—and Souviney's results do not contradict this—it is likely that counting and several arithmetic operations that can be effected through counting (in lieu of the algorithm) are probably available to all Papua New Guineans regardless of schooling or culture. Among the basic logical operations, some are age dependent only, for example, single and double seriation (see Chapter 4). A second level of skill is attained by all children who *attend school* for several years. They will learn to perform certain operations that will not be available to their unschooled counterparts. The distinction I make here is similar to Vygotsky's (1978) "spontaneous versus scientific concepts."

Site contributes to math performance in two ways. To the extent that progress in mathematics depends on one's level of cognitive development, site specifies culture, which affects cognitive development directly, and mathematics therefore indirectly. Second, site also specifies the quality of instruction. We do not yet have a good "fix" on which site

TABLE 7.5
Multiple Regression of Skill Variables on "Residual" PMAT

Source	df	F	p
Overall	4,172	5.2	.0006
Visual memory	4,172	0.63	.533
M-space	4,172	0.05	.964
Reading	4,172	1.4	.159
Total cognitive	4,172	2.5	.013

characteristics need attention. Sheer location is important: Remote rural schools do not do as well. The period during which a school was first established seems to be important also (Lancy, 1978c); that is, schools established during the second phase (pp. 171–174) seem to continue to operate on a more stable foundation than those that have been "thrown together" since 1970. Nor do we have a very good fix on what is significant for an analysis of the quality of instruction. However, as part of Souviney's project, sample math lessons were recorded and analyzed at each school, and there are a number of hints in these reports for an understanding of the depressed levels of achievement.

After grade and site, *sex* is an important variable to consider. Just how sex interacts with math achievement is not clear. There are no significant differences between males and females on the other skill variables. Males do not outperform females on the cognitive tests, for example (see also Table 4.9). One hint is offered by the fact that males outperformed females by a wide margin in all but one of Souviney's sites. The single exception occurred at the Andra Community School where females actually did a little better than males. Now Andra is culturally quite similar to Ponam: They are in fact only a few kilometers apart, and the subsistence systems are identical (Lancy & Madsen, 1981). Among the 10 IMP sites, I was distinctly impressed with the degree of male–female integration on Ponam. Women play important roles in the political, social, technological, and ritual spheres. The equality of the sexes is further attested to by the fact that Ponam was the only IMP site where an equal number of males and females attended school. In all the other sites the males were a clear majority, in some cases by a 4:1 margin. These attitudes undoubtedly are conveyed to teachers. Thus is may be that teachers (the majority of whom are male) pay more attention to the instruction of males in mathematics than to females, except where social mores emphasize equality. Just exactly this sort of finding has been reported in the United States (Leinhardt, Seewald, & Engle, 1979).

I must confess to a sense of disappointment that the skill variables contribute as little to mathematics achievement as they do: Indeed visual memory and M-space can be discounted altogether. I was disappointed only in that skills can be directly affected by the curriculum, by far the easiest aspect to change of the Papua New Guinean education system. Nevertheless, it is clear from this and other studies done elsewhere (reviewed in Lancy, 1981) that cognitive skills do play a role in facilitating or impeding the acquisition of mathematics. However, they do not make a contribution to very basic numerical operations like counting and simple addition (contrast with Steffe, 1968), and especially not in the way envisioned by Piaget (Piaget, 1952; Lovell, 1971; Brainerd, 1977). And we are far from finding a one-to-one correspondence between particular cognitive and mathematical skills. Perhaps it was naive to think we would: For all the parallels (Rosskoph, Steffe, & Taback, 1971; Collis, 1975; Kamii & DeVries, 1978), there is one fundamental difference between cognition and mathematics. The former involves noticing, explaining, and acting on regularities in nature whereas "mathematical concepts don't embody regularities of our sensory experiences of the physical environment, but regularities of these regularities, and relationships between them, at a high order of abstraction [Skemp, 1980, p. 9]." Before concluding this discussion of the skills that co-vary with mathematics, I would like to review an additional body of pertinent research.

Research in the Mathematics Education Centre

This program has been carried out through the Mathematics Education Centre at the University of Technology in Lae in conjunction with the Indigenous Mathematics Project. Work by Alan Bishop (1978, 1979) pinpointed difficulties that technical university students have in interpreting common graphic conventions found in drawing and technical figures. Meek and Feril (1978) found that, in effect, Grade 6 students comprehend only about 20% of the vocabulary (e.g., *corner, join, solid*) in fifth-grade math lessons; Teachers College students who will be using these same lessons for instruction understand only about 50% of the vocabulary. P. L. Jones (1981a, 1981b) has recently completed a study of the acquisition of comparative language. His questions were of three types, corresponding to three levels of difficulty. Examples of the three types are (*a*) "Which is more, 10 or 13?"; (*b*) "What is 3 less than 5?"; and (*c*) "My stick is 15 cm long. Bill's stick is 3 cm longer than mine. How long is Bill's stick?"

Mastery is achieved in the third and seventh grades for the first two types of questions, but Grade 10 students are still struggling with the third type of question. International-School students in the fifth grade achieve mastery on all three types. Other studies in which language comprehension is shown to be implicated heavily in math-test performance have been accomplished by Morrison (cited in Roberts, 1981) and Allen Thomas, and Patu (1975). Papua New Guineans must simultaneously learn *two* foreign languages—English *and* mathematics. There is some recent evidence (Fredricks, 1981; Tovirika, Korim, & Dubé, 1981), however, that suggests that English fluency and reading ability may not contribute to mathematics achievement in university-level studies. However, no one has looked at the language-related "reflective intelligence" that is a factor in high-school mathematics achievement in the West (Skemp, 1961; Jurdak, 1980).

Clements and Lean (1981) conducted extensive testing in Community Schools and International Schools in Lae and in four rural Community Schools. They employed several memory tests (including visual-memory and M-space tests), spatial-relations tests, problem-solving tests (including three tests of conservation), and several math tests, including PMAT. Most of their analyses compare the students at Community Schools and International Schools (the latter include a mix of expatriates and middle-class Papua New Guineans). Scores diverged most radically on the math and problem-solving tests. At the lower grades, performance on questions involving counting and simple arithmetic were quite comparable. They concluded that "Community School children tended to cope better with questions of the straightforward computational variety . . . , however. . . . Relative performance dropped sharply if a question required even a simple problem solving strategy to be formulated [p. 46]. . . . and they . . . had great difficulty with verbal arithmetic problems [p. 59]." On the other hand, memory, visualizing, and spatial skills were poor predictors of math-test performance. In a further study, they (Clements, 1981; Lean & Clements, in press) found that variation in spatial ability was unrelated to variation in mathematics ability among students at the University of Technology.

These studies would appear to replicate fairly closely the findings of the first and second national surveys. Sullivan (1981), reviewing this mass of results, argues that more drill and practice in basic skills is not called for (such a plan is very much on the ascendency in the country today [Edwards & Bajpai, 1979]) but rather that "teachers must be free to develop courses which place emphasis on solving new problems, applying maths to everyday situations, estimation and approximation, detecting unreasonable results, geometry, measurement, reading, interpreting and drawing graphs, statistics, the language of mathematics, as well as computational skills [p. 19]."

I could not agree more. I just wish we could offer the Department of Education something a little more definitive. We are confronted however with two fundamental problems, neither of which I fully appreciated in 1976. The first problem concerns the absence of any credible theory for the development of mathematical ability (for good reviews of this issue, see Carpenter, 1979; Shulman, 1974). Piaget's theory is the only one available. However, it leaves whole areas of mathematics untouched (e.g., numerical operations), while giving inordinate attention to a few (e.g., probability, measurement, and Euclidean geometry). Much effort has gone into "factor-analyzing" math tests to see if underlying skills might be detected. There is fairly good agreement on a family of skills that include "reasoning," "spatial," "numerical," and "verbal" skills (DeGuire, 1980). However, there is almost no agreement on what these skills should consist of. Factor analysis of the test items from the first survey did not yield usable results. The most current overview of the field (Resnick & Ford, 1981) offers a useful, but still very rudimentary, partitioning of the "mathematics space" into number facts, algorithms, and problem-solving.

Cognitive theorists have the advantage of studying processes that are not as a rule taught directly in schools. They are not influenced by variations in curriculum design. In mathematics we are fairly knowledgeable about the development process *prior to the onset of schooling* (Siegel, 1973, 1974; Gelman & Gallistel, 1978; Saxe, 1977, 1979a, 1979b). The situation during the school years has been illuminated by a few landmark studies (e.g., Paige & Simon, 1966; Wang, Resnick, & Boozer, 1971; Krutetskii, 1976), but nothing close to a coherent theory is in sight. I consider Dienes's writings to be almost entirely prescriptive.

The second advantage that cognitive theorists have had is their freedom of choice in the selection of methods. The most exciting insights into cognitive development have almost all come from the exploration of highly unusual tasks and/or the use of open-ended clinical methods with children. Individual subject's errors—unlike the situation on a group-administered math test—can be extremely informative about precursors to mature or accurate patterns of thinking. It is only very recently that extracurricular and clinical studies in mathematics have been undertaken with school-age children (Erlwanger, 1974; Ginsburg, 1975; Confrey, 1981; Resnick & Ford, 1981; Lancy & Englehardt, 1982; Carpenter, Hiebert, & Moser, 1981). These one-on-one detailed investigations show considerable promise in opening the way toward a theory of mathematical development, but it is still early, and when we began the Indigenous Mathematics Project such studies were virtually unheard of. Given the situation in Papua New Guinea, where many terminal objectives are not being met, we do not know enough about the acquisition process to make recommendations concerning the sequencing, pace, and emphasis in instruction in the early grades.

A second problem is—if anything—more intractable. In the beginning of Chapter 6, I reviewed the various strands of theory and conjecture on the relationship between language and thought, and I shall return to this issue in the next chapter. But, as we have seen here, there are urgent and extremely practical aspects of this issue that have not been addressed. (See Potter, 1979, for an introduction to the problem.) As the studies reviewed here show, we can not tell where language ends and thought begins. When children fail to answer one of Jones's (1981a) questions correctly, is it because they can not compute, lack the logical operations necessary to solve the problem, lack the appropriate concept, lack the appropriate English vocabulary, cannot read, or is it some combination of these? In Piagetian testing, the issue of language comprehension (especially *comparatives*) has become increasingly important. Siegel (1978) points out that "there seems to be no way of determining with the traditional Piagetian task, the relative contribution of cognitive or linguistic deficiencies when the child fails to achieve the correct solution [p. 45]." She and others (for a review, see Miller, 1976) have succeeded in reducing the verbal component in cognitive tests, thereby controlling for the effects of language ability (see, for example, Lancy & Goldstein, in press). To a certain extent this is what Souviney did when he created a pure arithmetic or computation test. However, even this test is correlated +.64 and +.77 with the cognitive and reading measures, respectively, and as we have seen, computation is an area of strength. Where we find that children do poorly in problem-solving, what do we recommend? Do we recommend lots of practice with multistep questions, renewed emphasis on the development of English-language fluency, more emphasis on reading, building mathematics-related vocabulary, or do we recommend "hands-on" applications? (See Souviney, 1981.) It would be nice if we could do all of these things, but as I have shown (Lancy, 1979a) the amount of time a pupil spends in instruction has been gradually declining in Papua New Guinea since the late 1960s. Nevertheless, although few concrete ideas have emerged in terms of changing the content of instruction, there is much that can be done in the methods area.

The Teaching of Mathematics

Community-School teachers in Papua New Guinea have had from 8 to 12 years of formal education. One quarter of them have had a 1-year teacher-training course, while the remainder have had a 2-year course (Roberts, 1981). The range is broad because it reflects changes in policy from 1960 to 1975. In the earliest period, teachers could practice with 7 years of education, including 1 year or less of teacher training. By 1975, the standard had become 12 years, including 2 years of training at a teachers college. In the meantime, teachers who began teaching in the 1960s have been required to upgrade their education and training through in-service and correspondence courses of various kinds. Length of service in Roberts's sample ranged from 1 to 20 years, and the median for all teachers is probably around 7 years. As I indicated before, he found that performance on a test and various other instruments designed to measure a teacher's knowledge of mathematics and the MACS course were uniformly low with little variance—a finding replicated by Souviney (1981). Like the pupils, teachers seem to have combined their formal education with experience on the job to reach a stable but low level of mathematics fluency. Roberts found almost no relationship between the teacher's level of education and his or her mathematics fluency. One reason for this anomaly is that, while the length of schooling has increased, the quality of instruction has declined.

What are the consequences for mathematics instruction? Souviney's project included the development of 125 new lessons for the MACS course. Teachers from each of his sites were given 2 weeks of in-service training in their application, and each teacher was carefully observed during a 6-week trial implementation period in the respective schools. These field reports have just become available (Gearhart, 1980; Johnson, 1980; Levin, 1980; Lineberger, 1980; Rowe, 1980; Miller-Souviney, 1981). Taken together with Roberts's work and earlier classroom studies (Lancy, 1979a), these reports begin to yield a fairly clear picture of the problems that can arise in mathematics instruction.

The most prominent issue that emerges is *time for instruction*. Studies done in the United States (Denham & Liberman, 1980) indicate, not surprisingly, that the more time that is spent in instruction in a given area, the greater are student-achievement gains. Time in instruction is a more powerful factor than the type of curriculum, the teacher's level of training, his or her teaching style, and so forth. I have tried to make a strong case (Lancy, 1979a) that time in instruction is unacceptably low for the majority of pupils in Papua New Guinea. Many factors contribute to this problem, but Gearhart (1980) touches on two of these in her report on the Divanap Community School. During 2 weeks of the 6-week observation period, students spent the majority of their time working outdoors on the school grounds and gardens. Furthermore, none of the teachers were present at the school for the entire observation period. Absences lasted from a few days to 2 weeks. The situation with respect to student attendance is much as I have described it for Golke (see pp. 25–26). Gearhart speaks of attendance as being "fairly low" and dropout rates as "fairly high" (1980, p. 8) Divanap may be the worst school in Souviney's sample, and indeed student performance on mathematics is the lowest among the six sites. It is, however, neither an atypical nor an extreme case, unfortunately.

Time for instruction is reduced in other ways. For example, the most common theme in the observer's comments on the trial lessons is that they took far longer than expected (Miller-Souviney, 1981). This seems to have been the case in virtually every lesson. Time was wasted because of, at least in part, sheer inefficiency. Great periods of lesson time were taken up with activities (e.g., materials' assembly and construction, lesson preparation, drawing or writing examples on the chalkboards, etc.) that could have been done during recess or after school. Teachers did not often delegate management tasks; thus the observers had to suggest that while they were putting examples on the chalkboard, students could pass out materials rather than the teacher doing both. Management gradually improved over the course of the study.

Lessons were slowed down also because of the teachers' very tentative understanding of the material they were to teach. It seems that they are not able to distinguish "form" from "substance." For example: "Teachers tend to view operations with each base as a terminal objective, drilling children . . . and . . . refusing to allow the class to move on until they have 'mastered' this 'modern mathematics' objective [Souviney, 1981, p. 3]." In other words, they treat many aspects of the curriculum as ends in themselves rather than only as means to an end. And Souviney states that "an unacceptable amount of time was required by grade two children in setting out their work. One of the causes seemed to be that the children had been instructed to be very accurate in their drawing and copying [1981, p. 15]." Concern with neatness and picture-perfect copying is a hallmark of Papua New Guinean teachers. I have often marveled at the visual clarity of their "board work," while at the same time feeling distinctly uneasy about the time investment such precision required. Moreover, until Souviney introduced them, student workbooks, sheets, textbooks, or whatever, were not used in math classes. Hence there is nothing for children to do during the "set-up" period. It is not that the teachers are unaware of the poor fit between the lesson and the time available to present it, but they tend to economize in the worst possible place—namely, by eliminating the introduction and demonstration of the new concept or exercise.

There is far too much of a "cooking-from-a-recipe" atmosphere about the math classes: "He repeatedly requested more explicit information on how to teach the curriculum. . . . He seemed to want a script on how to explain a concept in front of him [Lineberger, 1980, p. 8]." There is a vicious circle at work here. Each succeeding curriculum revision—including Souviney's—has sought to make instruction prescriptions more detailed and explicit or to reduce the use of broad, abstract concepts and phraseology. But what happens when teachers cannot lay their hands on copies of the various "guides"—an all too frequent occurrence (Roberts, 1981)—or fail to read them prior to class when they do have them? On

Souviney's (1981) recommendation, math textbooks and consumable workbooks will be produced for the first time. These should make a strong positive contribution to student achievement. It is my distinct impression from my observing math classes and from my reading of the reports of Souviney and his colleagues that many bright students may be "held back" by the slow pace of instruction, by their teachers' lack of mathematical fluency, and by the dearth of student-controlled materials. Ultimately, however, there is no way to create a teacher-proof curriculum. This is especially the case in Papua New Guinea where the out-of-school application of mathematics is rudimentary (see also Burstein, 1980).

Conclusion

The Indigenous Mathematics Project began with a fairly narrow focus. As the project progressed, the focus became broader and broader as new variables were introduced into the equation. To put it bluntly, we followed the ends of our noses! The successive chapters in this book trace this evolutionary process—the most recent work encompassing the broadest array of variables having been introduced in this chapter. Since Chapter 8 will be primarily concerned with theoretical issues, I shall retrace our steps here to try and pull together some of the prominent practical issues.

In Chapter 1, I indicated that Papua New Guineans want to have it both ways. They would like to have access to the most sophisticated of modern goods and services, and they want to make this essentially Western technology their own; they do not want to rely forever on expatriate technicians and managers. On the other hand, they have no desire to transform radically the village way of life (see Shankman, 1976, for a description of the comparable situation in Western Samoa). Often the most highly trained Papua New Guineans are the most vociferous opponents of change in their home villages. In practical terms this means that the education system must bear the entire burden of transporting individuals from the Stone Age into the Age of Computers. There will be no gradual evolution from the ground up. For reasons that I will review later, individuals from some societies in Papua New Guinea are better prepared than others to make that trip. Children from coastal Manus, for example, already have their bags packed, so to speak, and even with a mediocre preparation, they travel to the University of Technology and perform extremely well. For the majority, the schools must not only impart specific skills and a new language, but basic cognitive processes as well. It has been amply documented that university students are deficient in basic processes and that this impedes their progress in science, math, and engineering courses (J. Jones, 1973; P. L. Jones, 1979). Schooling does have a positive impact (see Chapter 4) but falls far short of what is needed. I do not believe that the situation is hopeless: There are far too many people who have succeeded to conclude that Papua New Guinea must be content with a gradualist policy.

We began to realize that tinkering with the curriculum and trying to pinpoint and remedy cognitive-skill deficits was not likely to be a wise use of scarce resources at this stage. Indeed, Souviney (1981) recommends removing only one piece from the MACS course: operations using different bases; and he recommends adding only two: concrete development of algorithms to strengthen basic computation skills and counting by means of the indigenous system. For one thing, the curriculum as described at the beginning of this chapter already places heavy emphasis on instruction in cognitive processes. But it is clear that the basic bricks and mortar of mathematics instruction, elements taken for granted in industrialized nations, are not in place in Papua New Guinea. Until a firm foundation is built, no evaluation of the curriculum—of its emphasis on teaching high-level, abstract cognitive skills as prerequisite to the acquisition of low-level, concrete arithmetical skills—is possible.

Primary attention needs to be paid to the basic stock-in-trade. Every classroom needs a core of appropriate materials, including course materials for the teachers, manipulatives for the students, and pencils, paper, chalk, and chalkboards. The Department is now devoting a great deal of attention to this problem (Cahill, 1980). One suggestion that I once made (Lancy, 1979a) was that materials be assigned to teachers rather than to classrooms. Given the lack of storage facilities, the poor state of building repair, the practice of the populace—including teachers—to roll their own cigarettes using whatever paper is handy, all contribute to a drastically high rate of decay and loss of materials. In fact, my impression was that the most conscientious teachers took the materials anyway, so that they were certain to have a set regardless of which classroom or school they were assigned to. (Teachers average slightly more than one "move" between classrooms or schools per year.) Additional materials are needed; recently projects have been undertaken to mass-produce meter sticks, pan balances, clock faces, etc., and student textbooks and activity books are in the works.

Teachers obviously need to know more mathematics. The department has had the practice of channeling in-service training to those teachers whose formal schooling ended after 7–9 years. The data indicate that recent graduates with 12 years of schooling are no better off—at least in mathematics. A kind of grass-roots effort has been underway since about 1978 that shows much promise (Britt & Roberts, 1979). This is a pyramid scheme where outstanding math teachers, mostly from secondary schools, are given further training and then placed at the center of a group of interested and committed Community-School teachers to go over the curriculum, create new materials, analyze test results, etc. These participants in turn take what they have learned back to the teachers in their own schools. Other small-scale programs have been introduced that exploit virtually every niche to raise teachers' consciousness and knowledge of mathematics. It remains to be seen whether these relatively low-cost, voluntary efforts will have the necessary impact. The department may need to prepare itself for a costly and prolonged program of retraining in order to bring teachers to a complete and thorough understanding of the curriculum they teach.

Much more attention needs to be paid to time for instruction. Since reading and English fluency seem to contribute to math achievement, some trade-off might be envisioned, whereby more time is given for instruction in these areas in the early grades, while math is emphasized in Grades 4 to 6.[5] Teachers must be guided toward a planning and scheduling system that highlights something like "learning time per term." Time for mathematics is allocated on a daily basis. Nothing is done to compensate for days missed on account of teacher absence. Nothing is done to compensate for a majority of the students being absent on account of bad weather, a ceremony in the village, or for garden and project days, and so forth. Teachers need to see learning time as "academic-learning time" (Fisher, Berliner, Filby, Marliave, Cahen, & Dishaw, 1980). Time taken up with making or passing out materials, writing the examples on the board, teachers' silent reading of the lesson instruction, etc., *do not count*. The math lesson lasts only as long as the majority of students are actively engaged in learning mathematics or being tested on their progress.

The results reported throughout this book point to the fact that the department's planning priorities are in sore need of redirection. For the last 20 years the main goal was to increase the number of school places. Lovely graphs showing gains over time and in remote parts of the country gave everyone something to cheer about. The celebrations were premature, to say the least. One school place is not the same as any other

---

[5]Souviney (personal communication) feels that he has uncovered a "threshold effect" in his study. If children's English and reading-comprehension skills are above some—as yet undetermined—threshold, intervention along the lines undertaken in his project will have a positive and measurable impact.

school place.[6] As these studies have shown, achievement in mathematics—and in reading, cognitive development, and everything else that has been tested—varies enormously from school to school. A school place in the Divanap Community School is worth only about half as much as a school place in the Kero Community School in terms of math and reading achievement (Gearhart, 1980; Johnson, 1980).

These problems would seem to require a more differentiated system of education for Papua New Guinea. Some thought should be given to creating special high schools that would offer accelerated education for the most able students to prepare them for postsecondary training in scientific and technical fields. At the same time, schools that serve remote areas or populations that are grossly underrepresented in the modern sector might be given special status with something more than the standard allocation of resources. They should be monitored more closely by the inspection system, and teacher-recruitment and compensation policies altered so that these schools are not wholly staffed by indifferent timeservers who leave at the first opportunity. The situation at Kero, where we have done a great deal of work, indicates that a stable and dedicated teaching staff can have a major impact on mathematics and reading achievement. Finally, I have visited enough schools elsewhere in the developing countries (Liberia, India, Indonesia, Ethiopia) to speculate that neither the results of this research nor the implications from it are uniquely applicable to Papua New Guinea.

[6]Because of the rapid proliferation of educational places, there are "disadvantaged" schools at every level in the system. In one case that I wrote about in August of 1979, two high schools, not 100 km apart in West Sepik, were virtually unrecognizable as representing the same species of institution. And the "output" of the two schools reflected the disparity in "input." On the national exams, there was virtually no overlap in scores; that is, the highest scoring Grade 10 pupils in the one school scored below the lowest scoring pupils in the other. Yet, both groups of students were *supposed to have had the same education.*

8

The Co-evolution of Culture, Cognition, and Schooling

In Chapter 1, I sketched the elongated time scale one sees in Papua New Guinea and indicated that a primary aim of our project was to aid in the process of compressing this scale. How can the education system assist individuals who want to skip over the many intervening steps from the Neolithic to the Space Age? In Chapter 7 I indicated some fairly mundane and practical steps that might be taken. Here I would like to reconsider and expand on some of the theoretical issues touched on earlier.

In their 1981 book, Lumsden and Wilson show how important it is to consider the evolution of cognitive systems in any discussion of cultural evolution and vice versa. They do not include schooling in their equations, but they probably should have. Western-style education, although part of culture, is in one sense also "supracultural." That is, at some point (probably after about 16 years of schooling) the educated individual joins a "world culture" and has far more in common with his or her similarly educated counterparts on the other side of the globe than with uneducated kinsmen in his or her hometown or village. Osgood, May, and Miron (1975) have found, for example, that college students from dozens of countries all employ the same basic dimensions in judging the connotative meaning of words. Hence I will initially review the co-evolution of culture and cognition and then later in the chapter bring formal education into the picture.

Human cognition is assumed to be linked with the growth and development of the brain, especially the cortex (Jerison, 1973). Parker and Gibson (1979) offer a thorough account of the evolution of the human brain and of language and thought. They link the various early cognitive skills identified by Piaget to particularly human activities such as gathering, butchering, food-sharing, shelter construction, tool use, and so forth. Where human activities overlap those of other primate species, the cognitive and linguistic (or protolinguistic) skills overlap as well. They go perhaps a bit too far in trying to assign a specific function for each cognitive trait (Gould, 1979), but a good case is made that human cognition evolved over 2.5 million years in the context of creatures living an omnivorous and social existence in the African savannah.

We can now ask, "At what point does genetic evolution stop and cultural evolution take over in managing the development of cognition?" Although Piaget's theory would extend the period of biologically motivated development into adolescence, cross-cultural research undertaken by his colleagues shows that only the earliest attainments associated with the sensorimotor stage are universal (Dasen & Heron, 1981). Research (Bower, 1974; Kessen & Nelson, 1978) with infants expands upon Piaget's skill inventory for the sensorimotor stage. Nevertheless, this leaves a large collection of cognitive traits as potentially malleable by culture. Even traits that are bound up inextricably with language are not immune. The very popular view first effectively promoted by Chomsky that all the important aspects of language derive from a genetically determined template or deep structure has come under attack: "The most damning evidence against the transformationalist argument . . . is that some of the so-called fundamental syntactic devices of deep structure are not available in all languages, and even when available are not equally developed or equally favored [Tyler, 1978, p. 69]."

Although the position of radical determinism is not new (see, for example, Werner, 1957), a work by Christopher Hallpike (1979) represents the most thorough treatment, and it has the added advantage of being based entirely on Piagetian theory. Hallpike develops a model for the co-evolution of culture and cognition. He says that "it seems clear that it is the transition from pre-literate and rural to literate, industrial society, rather than from hunting and gathering to agriculture, for example, that produces the really striking changes in modes of thought [p. vi]."

He argues, using three kinds of evidence, that members of primitive societies function at the preoperatory stage. He reviews much the same literature in cross-cultural psychology as Dasen did (1977a, 1977b) and comes to similar but stronger conclusions. He also reviews the ethno-graphic literature on collective representations and finds ample evidence for preoperational patterns of thought. Finally, he argues persuasively that primitive societies function very well without operational thought—that concrete and formal operational thought are really necessary only in industrialized societies. Hallpike (1977) states that,

> Because primitive technology and ecology are so simple, they can be operated in a wide variety of ways all of which are compatible with survival, but an industrial society has by its very nature to meet stringent requirements of organizational efficiency which are incompatible with an organization in terms of moral values and symbolism [p. 124].

In some respects the evidence presented in this book can be construed as supporting Hallpike's position. It is indeed the case that the majority of those tested do poorly on various tests of concrete-operational (analytical, symbolic) thought. It is also the case that a majority of our subjects are exposed to extremely primitive forms of technology. The Kewa, for example, have only five "tools": the ax, knife, digging stick, spear, and string bag—each with a maximum of two "technounits" (cf. Oswalt, 1976). However, there are far too many "exceptions." As we have seen, the data on both cultural and cognitive complexity do not, ultimately, support the kind of dichotomies used by Hallpike.[1] Rather, the evidence points overwhelmingly to a continuum in both areas. Sharply delineated changes do not appear as one moves from society to society, either in terms of the technological or cognitive repertoire of individuals.

Aside from the empirical evidence, there is an important theoretical objection to Hallpike's position that was foreshadowed in the writings of Alfred Russel Wallace over a century ago. Wallace was the co-discoverer with Darwin of the theory of evolution, and like Darwin, but more so, he had encountered and been impressed by "primitive" peoples:

> [In considering] tribes who only count to three or five and who find it impossible to comprehend the addition of two and three without having the objects actually before them, we feel that the chasm between them, and the good mathematician is so vast .... Yet we know that the mass of the brain might be nearly the same in both ... hence we may fairly infer that the savage possesses a brain capable, if cultivated and developed, of performing work of a kind and degree far beyond what he ever requires it to do. ... an organ that seems prepared in advance, only to be fully utilized as he progresses in civilization. [The human brain] ... would never have been

---

[1] Christopher Hallpike has written to me reacting to this statement: "To the extent that my book might give the impression of drawing radical dichotomies between two kinds of thought, that was not my intention, and that in addition the question of permeability deserves much more attention than I gave it."

solely developed by any of those laws of evolution, whose essence is, that they lead to a degree of organization exactly proportionate to the wants of each species, never beyond those wants [1891, pp. 191–193].

If indeed concrete and formal operational thought represent qualitatively distinct systems (according to Piaget), and if these systems are available only to individuals in industrialized societies (according to Hallpike), then we again face Wallace's quandary. There seem to be at least two ways out of this dilemma. One is that the "higher order" cognitive processes are not distinct from the "lower order" ones, and that beyond the age of about 5, there are no qualitative changes in cognitive-processing, only quantitative changes—another dichotomy that we will have to abandon some day (Brainerd, 1978b). Second, it is possible that higher order cognitive processes are indeed available to everyone, but are relied on more heavily in more complex societies.

Following Harris and Heelas (1979), I would like to juxtapose Hallpike's position with that of Michael Cole and his associates (e.g., Gay & Cole, 1967; Cole et al., 1971; Cole & Scribner, 1974; Cole & Means, 1981; Scribner & Cole, 1981; LCHC, 1979, in press). The theory that is emerging from this group owes much to research with the Kpelle and Vai in Liberia. Essentially two types of experiment were conducted in the early research with the Kpelle. One type is very similar to the procedures reported here—namely, tests developed originally in Europe and the United States and then carefully translated and adapted for implementation with nonliterate village samples. On these tests, the Kpelle did poorly when compared with Americans. However, further studies hinted that these results could be attributed to a performance deficit rather than to a competence deficit. Specifically, when Kpelle high-school students were tested, their pattern of performance did not differ from that of the American subjects; and in one of the tests, when the nonliterate subjects were given training, they began to display the Western-response pattern. A second type of experiment involved the creation of tests that reflected particular aspects of Kpelle life. For example, Kpelle adults were better able to estimate the number of cups of rice in a bowl of rice than were American Peace Corps volunteers (Gay & Cole, 1967). Another test took advantage of the ability of Kpelle adults to distinguish leaves on the basis of whether they were from trees or vines (Cole et al., 1971). Finally, a third test took advantage of a feature of Kpelle riddles—or dilemma tales—to use context in a way that virtually guaranteed that illiterate villagers would fail, while high-school students would succeed (Cole et al., 1971).

The most straightforward interpretation of these results, it seems to me, is that the cognitive processes of Americans are far less dependent on context than those of the Kpelle and that this difference may well be accounted for by the effects of schooling, a position with which Scribner and Cole (1973) at one time seemed to concur. Over time, however, Cole began to question the validity of all the results except those from the tests that had been designed to permit the specialized knowledge of the Kpelle to assist them vis-à-vis the American comparison groups (see, for example, Cole & Scribner, 1974, pp. 178–188). One reason for this shift, no doubt, stems from the results of later studies of the Vai (Scribner & Cole, 1978, 1981).

The Vai are a fairly typical group of West African slash-and-burn horticulturalists who are very similar to the Kpelle; but they have one unusual attribute. They acquired their own script 150 years ago and consequently a minority of the Vai who have never attended a Western-style school are literate in the Vai script. Here was a unique opportunity to test the frequently voiced claim (Olson, 1976; Goody, 1977; Donaldson, 1978) that literacy plays an important role in fostering higher order cognitive processes—especially decontextualized thinking. Because of the fact that individuals typically become literate while receiving instruction in a wide range of topics in the context of formal schooling, no adequate test of the effects of literacy per se had yet been done. The principal finding of their comprehensive study (Scribner & Cole, 1981) was that literacy conferred no special advantage in terms of performance on "standard" cognitive tests and other measures of modernization and Westernization. The only tests that favored the literates were those that were heavily context dependent—that called for the skills specifically implicated when one uses the Vai script. There are several possible interpretations of these results. For example, it is possible that the Vai are not truly literate in that they use their literacy in only a very narrow range of applications (e.g., letters and accounts).

The interpretation favored by Scribner and Cole is that there are no broadly applicable cognitive skills to be stimulated by the literacy experience or any other experience, such as schooling. They argue, rather, that all individuals possess the same repertoire of cognitive skills; what varies are the demands of various tasks. If one is familiar with a task, one will apply one's cognitive skills and do well on it; if unfamiliar, one will fail to apply one's skills and do poorly. American and Kpelle students do better on cognitive tests because of their greater familiarity with tests and testlike situations. Dasen (1980; see also Jahoda, 1980) sees this point of view as arguing for the "radical impermeability of contexts," as against Piaget's view that contexts are entirely permeable.[2] The results reported

---

[2] My own view lies somewhere between these two extremes. I strongly believe in something like "advanced organizers." These are essentially mental mechanisms that permit the individual to make sense of and to act upon a variety of different stimuli, situations, and so on. On the other hand, I am in general agreement with those who decry the tendency to ascribe the absence of such advance organizers to individuals or groups on the basis of very limited data.

here indicate that contexts may indeed create problems for the unprepared. We have seen (Chapter 6) that some conservation-of-length tasks are easier than others, and that conservation is attained at widely different ages, depending on the medium being tested (Chapter 3). However, it is also clear that individuals from some groups can decontextualize a wide array of problems and apply general thinking skills to their solution (p. 145).

The "contextualists" (cf. Harris & Heelas, 1979) have built their position on a careful examination of the methodological issues,[3] finding fault with any study that employs anything remotely resembling a standardized test. If one accepts the full force of their argument—and I do not—then I think one must also abandon the study of cognition as "going beyond the information given." More than this, I see a dangerous circularity in the reasoning of proponents of the contextualist position. If the only valid tests of cognitive skill are those that fully reflect the particular experiences of the testees, the resulting tests will all but preclude the application of general processes. The task will be so particularized that only low-level skills acquired in specific contexts will have an effect. General cognitive skills will not be applicable nor will we see evidence of broad experiential effects like those engendered by schooling (see for example, Lave, in press).

Any theory of the co-evolution of culture and cognition must take into account the presence of operational thought in non-Western groups (e.g., Ponam, p. 145; Eskimo [Dasen, 1975]) and its absence in a number of Western societies (e.g., southern Italians [Peluffo, 1962, 1967]; Yugoslavs [Heron & Kroeger, 1975]; and farmers in the southern United States [Graves, 1972]). The hunter–gatherer, especially the maritime hunter–gatherer, lives under an intellectually demanding regimen vis-à-vis the farmer, horticulturalist, or pastoralist (Coon, 1971; Konner, 1979). Cognitive development takes most of its cues from the daily round of human activity and is largely insensible to the surrounding ecology, national borders, gross national product, or what have you.

The plains, the desert, the ocean all provide ample but unreliable fare. There is no single species nor small collection of edibles that is available abundantly, year-round, regardless of climate, and for which there are no serious nonhuman competitors. The hunter–gatherer has to be an epicure. The sheer memory load on the really well-versed hunter–gatherer is enormous when one considers the range of plants and animals that must

[3]Cole (1972) defended his earlier position that cognitive abilities *varied* across cultures also on methodological grounds. He challenged the doctrine of *psychic unity* and critiqued the methods of anthropologists on the basis that they were suitable for a study of cognitive content but not process.

be coded and stored—with additional information about location, season, edible-versus-inedible parts, techniques and tools for extraction or capture, preparation processes, and so forth (Blurton-Jones & Konner, 1976; Premack, 1976; Parker & Gibson, 1979). Furthermore, this information must be carried around in one's head. There are no books in which to store the information. Graphic arts, while available and utilized, are usually nonrepresentational. Formal instruction including teaching occurs rarely, if at all. Finally, it may well be that language has become available only recently as a means to code, describe, and rehearse the flood of information that poured over the growing child. In fact, the hunter–gatherer way of life may have been well established before man acquired speech. Furthermore, Malinowski, for example, believed that

> language in its primitive function and original form has an essentially pragmatic character, that it is a mode of behavior, an indispensable element of concerted human action. And negatively: to regard it as a means for the embodiment or expression of thought is to take a one-sided view of one of its most derivative and specialized functions [1952, p. 316].

The maritime hunter–gatherer's engagement with the environment requires an even greater investment in information processing. Yesner (1980) sees these societies as inherently unstable and motivated by opportunity and necessity to evolve more complex subsistence practices. He points out that many marine species (e.g., turtles, sharks, migratory fish) can only be safely and reliably exploited through the use of fairly sophisticated technologies and elaborate mechanisms for specializing and dividing the labor, and hence the spoils. On the other hand, the exploitation of reef dwellers (especially shellfish) does not require tools, sophistication, strength, or cooperation, and is ideally left to children. Thus there are opportunities for a vertical division of labor as well. A final point made by Yesner is that it is very difficult, if not impossible, for maritime hunter–gatherers to find enough calories. Typically, they are forced into trading relationships with other peoples who have ready access to starches, vegetables, and grains. Such trade may encourage development and differentiation in terms of political organization. Traders are more often than not multilingual, and the trading society must cope with the constant flow of new information.

Theories of cultural evolution have been primarily concerned with explaining the origins of the state. Therefore, they place agriculturalists at a higher level than hunter–gatherers (see p. 120). This is misleading for an understanding of the co-evolution of culture and basic human traits; for, after all, history can be read as a catalog of alternatives to hunting and gathering that have *failed*. It is therefore very likely that most basic cognitive processes evolved in support of the hunter–gatherer way of life (Parker & Gibson, 1979). Language amplifies but does not fundamentally alter these processes. Many of these processes, however, go unutilized or underutilized in agricultural or pastoral societies because the activities of these people inevitably simplify the environment (Rindos, 1980). The great diversity in nature is essentially reduced to three categories— utilized, destroyed, or ignored. It is only comparatively recently that the diversity of man-produced artifacts has equaled and then eclipsed the diversity in nature. One thinks of the evolution of art, music, and architecture, for example, which have only recently begun to expand upon the range of sounds, colors, and shapes of nature. Thus Robert Ardrey (1961) may have been right for the wrong reasons: Modern man clearly reflects the traits of his ancestors, but it is the cognitive traits that are strikingly parallel, not the emotional ones.

Two of the groups that we studied stimulated my thinking along these lines; these were the Kilenge and the Mandok. I found (Lancy, 1978c) that

Figure 8.1. Kilenge children home from the garden. (Courtesy of Derk v. Groningen.)

they shared many aspects of culture such as patterns of kinship and ritual. They are also near neighbors and major trading partners, and their pattern of contact with the outside world has been very similar both in duration and extent. Yet Mandok children outperformed Kilenge children by a wide margin on cognitive tests (Lancy, 1978c) and in the first mathematics survey (Lancy, 1981). Both groups of children were healthy and well nourished. The only fundamental (see Figure 8.1) aspect of the two societies that differs is that the Mandok are maritime hunter–gatherers and traders, while the Kilenge are horticulturalists. Earlier I alluded to the probable impact these two different subsistence systems might have on children's intellectual development (see pp. 121–122).

Stage theories in developmental psychology—especially Piaget's—have come under concerted attack in recent years (e.g., Brainerd, 1978c, 1981; Boden, 1979). Piaget in his last works (e.g., Piaget, 1977) began to replace "stage" with "equilibration" as the center piece of his theory. The heuristic value of stages is still important, however, and I would like to propose a three-stage model on that basis. The first stage corresponds to Piaget's sensorimotor and preoperational stages, and partially overlaps the concrete-operational stage. It is during this stage that genetic pro-gramming has its greatest effect, at least with respect to cognition. The accomplishments of this stage are shared by all human beings.[4] Many of the experiences that Piaget describes as priming mechanisms for develop-ment at this stage are probably unnecessary. Children who are deaf (Furth, 1966), autistic (Lancy & Goldstein, in press), retarded (Weisz & Zigler, 1979), or virtually paralyzed (Jordan, 1972) all complete this stage, suffering at most a developmental lag of a few years over normal children. All of our Papua New Guinean subjects complete Stage I. Most, if not all, of the achievements in Stage I are also shared with other primates (Chevalier-Skolnikoff, 1977; Gibson, 1977; Parker, 1977). It is probably true that all important *qualitative* changes in cognition occcur during the first stage: the discovery of object permanence, the ability to form identity and equivalence classes and concepts, the ability to differentiate self from others, the beginnings of speech, and so forth. All societies will assign special statuses to individuals during this stage, and many will provide for designated ceremonies, rituals, or "rites of passage" to mark the indi-vidual's transition to the second stage (Van Gennep, 1960). Caretaker–child interaction during the first stage is characterized as *socialization*; during the second stage it is termed *enculturation* (Williams, 1972). At the

---

[4]One indirect piece of evidence that supports the notion that this stage unfolds in a preprogrammed manner comes from the "six-cultures" study (Whiting, 1963). Exhaustive data collection on socialization practices in six diverse societies failed to uncover any strong links between particular practices and later adult characteristics.

onset of Stage II the cognitive structures are in place waiting to be activated. The culture will "fill out the space permitted by the genetically determined epigenetic rules [Lumsden & Wilson, 1981, p. 21]." Process may run ahead of content: Children invent words for concepts they possess but for which they have not learned "correct" labels. They invent playmates and roles for the playmates, and they provide plausible but erroneous explanations for events. Every child is in this sense precocious. As development unfolds, differences between individuals arise. These can be either narrow or broad, depending on one's point of view. According to Greenfield and Bruner (1966), "some environments push cognitive growth better, earlier, and longer than others: what does not seem to happen is that different cultures produce completely divergent and unrelated modes of thought. The reason for this must be the constraint of our biological heritage [p. 652]."

The evidence presented in Chapters 2 and 3, while discrepant in many ways with the theories under examination, strikingly confirms that the *order* of acquisition of the concepts identified by Piaget, Bruner, and others is invariant (see also Beilin, 1971). While I emphasized the distinctiveness of Melpa thought in Chapter 6, the fact is that "making twos" is a perfectly reasonable way of creating categories and requires all the skills implicated by "decontextualizing," "generalizing," "verbally mediating," "symbolizing," "abstracting," and so forth.[5] Hallpike (1979) also shows how elementary Piagetian principles can be used to uncover the common "deep structure" underlying the widely variant surface structures of human myth, religion, and social organization (see also Murdock, 1959).

Thus development is unidirectional up to a point (see the later discussion of Stage III). The speed and extent of development in Stage II is highly variable. Wallace was correct in considering that the gulf is wide between the mathematician and the individual who finds it difficult to count when the objects to be counted are not present. He was wrong, however, in believing that the laws of evolution cannot accommodate this chasm. His assertion that every single trait must have adaptive significance represents a serious distortion of evolutionary theory (Gould, 1980). General mechanisms that permit humans to learn, to invent, and to

---

[5]While I might downplay the implications of "making twos" for a theory of the evolution of cognition, I would stress its importance for an understanding of the failure of Melpa students in school. If we view schooling as the process of leading a student from some initial configuration (cannot add) to some final configuration (can add) through a series of *steps*, it should be obvious that the Melpa child, vis-à-vis his Western counterpart, has several additional steps to worry about. The education system in PNG at present completely ignores the problem of "extra steps" for the vast majority of its pupils.

solve novel problems are adaptive (Luria, 1967; Pulliam & Dunford, 1980). Also *small* incremental changes in information-processing capacity would have conferred a small increase in fitness.[6] However, humans are by no means unique in this respect. Harry Harlow remarked as follows, after a lifetime of experimental work with nonhuman primates and other species:

> I have long been puzzled by the fact that the study of animals under laboratory conditions reveals many learning capabilities whose existence is hard to understand in terms of survival value.... As an example, the earthworm can learn a spatial maze ... it is hard to see how this feat of learning legerdemain aided the earthworm, or any other animal so endowed, to survive at the expense of less gifted associates [Harlow & Mears, 1979, pp. 46–49].

Dolphins and chimpanzees are two well-known cases of animals that are "much smarter than they ought to be." On the basis of phylogeny, gorillas should be more nearly comparable to humans in terms of cognitive development than baboons. And yet, according to McGrew (1979), "in the real world, baboons appear to be much more intelligent than gorillas ... baboons show more intelligence because they are opportunistic, omnivorous generalists subsisting in the widest range of marginal habitats. Gorillas are conservative, herbivorous specialists restricted to certain suitable habitats [p. 393]." Dumb baboons are thriving worldwide, while all but one of the smart apes is threatened with extinction.[7]

What happens to cognition during Stage II, then, has much to do with culture and environment and less to do with genetics. I have argued that maritime hunting and gathering and modern industrialized society test the limits of Stage II development, while other lifeways may not. In earlier chapters I identified some of the characteristics of "environments that push cognitive growth better, earlier, and longer [Greenfield & Bruner, 1966, p. 652]." These include the range and complexity of the tool inventory, the complexity of folk category systems, schooling (including literacy), the use of English, the prevalence of referential speech, characteristics associated with social class, and so on. It is unlikely that any single aspect of culture (e.g., literacy) is, by itself, sufficient to drive

[6]The benefits to humans—and other great apes—must have been great, because they had to outweigh some very substantial costs. The price paid for increased cognitive capacity is a prolonged period of immaturity during which this capacity can be nurtured and developed. Prolonged immaturity, in turn, requires increased energy expenditure in foraging for additional food, carrying the infant, maintenance of vigilance, and the need to defend oneself and one's offspring from prey.

[7]Dan Freedman has cautioned me that the case for intelligence can be easily overstated. The fossil record and contemporary population studies show that there are far more A grades awarded to "dumb" than to "smart" species.

cognitive development to great heights. On the other hand, aside from urban residence, I do not see that we can easily eliminate any potential causal factor. These various experiences affect cognitive development in one of two ways. Some experiences bring with them a ready-built pattern that can be incorporated almost whole into one's cognitive repertoire, as in McLuhan's "the medium is the message" (1964). Chi (1978), in an ingenious series of experiments, shows how young children who are expert chess players acquire various skills and strategies that aid their performance on tests for remembering configurations of chess pieces. Adult nonexperts, despite superior memory capacity and a greater range of general strategies and skills, do not do as well on these tests. Our research with the Ponam and Melpa (Lancy & Strathern, 1981) shows a similar phenomenon at work.

Chi used the chess experiments to make another point—namely, that it is the variation in the amount of knowledge an individual acquires that governs cognitive development, not maturation, memory capacity, or specific training. I concur with this view so long as we limit its application to Stage II. In the Indigenous Mathematics Project and in cross-cultural psychology in general, we are far more likely to see the effects of this process than the medium-as-message effect (see, for example, Greenfield & Childs, in press). The effect that any input to the cognitive system has depends less on the physical nature of the input than on its "volume" (in an information-processing sense), and on the consequences for misperceiving, misinterpreting, or forgetting it. When the flow of information is heavy and/or particularly critical, we can expect the individual to make various accommodations. These accommodations almost inevitably involve the use of more efficient strategies for perceiving, coding, retrieving, and transforming information. Similarities are emphasized over differences; two and three dimensions are processed simultaneously rather than serially; "steps" are minimized; the ends are emphasized over the means; stimuli are decomposed into "dimensions," and so forth. As Brent, following Prigogine, points out, "There is a close theoretical and mathematical relationship between the level of order and complexity of a given [cognitive] structure ... and its information storage capacity [1978, p. 382]."

Information flow can affect information-processing strategies in three distinctive ways. First, the culture may provide specific information or experience that has a direct impact on a specific cognitive skill. Mexican children exposed to pottery-making are more likely to conserve weight (but not other substances) than children without such experience (Price-Williams, Gordon, & Ramirez, 1969). Second, the information flow in a society affects the overall use of particular strategies. Identity categorization (conservation, for example) may be employed in many or only a few contexts. In Imbonggu society conservation of length is employed sporadically by adults. Third, information flow affects the rate at which more efficient strategies will be acquired by individuals. Genevan children acquire the conservation concept at a very early age, and its predominance in their thinking is reflected in the fact that they learn to apply it reliably over a wide variety of contexts within a short span of time. In other societies the initial conservation strategy is acquired much later, and it is generalized much more slowly. Therefore we see marked horizontal *décalage* where conservation of area, for example, appears 8 to 10 years after conservation of number.

There is nothing inherently "advanced" about these gains in information-processing efficiency. In fact, for solving certain kinds of problems, they can be downright dysfunctional (see, for example, Gaines, 1973). It is a little like the difference between art and illustration. Attending to the changes that occur when the experimenter starts to move the sticks around is far more stimulating and interesting than attending to the mundane facts of unchanged relative length. One of the enduring attractions of Piaget is his compelling description of children *getting it wrong*. Similarly, we see Marvin Harris as a killjoy when he demonstrates (1966, 1974) that the wonderfully inefficient and illogical sacred cow of starving India is, upon closer analysis, just the opposite. Another point that needs to be stressed is that societies are just as likely to impose restraints as they are to provide incentives to cognitive development. Much information is "owned" by individuals and/or groups and can be accessed only under highly controlled circumstances (Lancy, 1975, 1980c). Learning by discovery, a hallmark of liberal theories of education in the West (including Piaget's) may be discouraged by dangers present in the environment or by caretakers.[8] Obedience to authority may be heavily emphasized in child-rearing, with the consequent retardation of skill-learning and cognition (Munroe & Munroe, 1975). In Papua New Guinea the government's policy of introducing change and development to villages through the knowledge and initiative of "school-leavers" has been hindered by the villagers' obstinate refusal to grant any significant status to these "children" or to their knowledge (J. G. Carrier, 1980). Nor are these restraints on who may acquire and use cognitive skills limited to village-based societies. Bowles and Gintis (1976) describe how minority groups in the industrialized nations have been victimized by such restraints that operate as national policy.

---

[8]This point applies to nonhuman primates as well. Chimpanzees are far more inventive and exploratory in the laboratory colony than they are in the wild (Beck, 1975).

Although an information-processing model takes us fairly far in understanding the co-evolution of culture and cognition, it falls short. Hence the need for a third stage. Stage III also involves development, but it begins in infancy and continues throughout adulthood. Qualitative changes are probably nonexistent, nor are notions like *efficiency, cognitive structure,* or *information-processing capacity* very helpful for understanding development during Stage III. In addition to developing cognitive and linguistic strategies, individuals acquire "theories" of language and cognition (see Bernstein, 1971). They learn what kinds of knowledge are important for what purposes; they learn the relationship between knowledge and status; they learn the appropriate occasions for knowledge acquisition and display; and so forth. An example might be Robin Horton's (1967) belief that the realm of nature is essentially knowable and manageable whereas the human realm is confusing and unmanageable. His Nigerian students firmly expressed that just the opposite is true.

Despite Chomsky's (1965) claim that speech is thoroughly innate, there is evidence from widely divergent societies that parents do, indeed, attempt to teach language, especially during the earliest phase of development. Two very thorough studies illustrate that it is a *theory of language use* that is being taught rather than language per se. In Britian (Ninio & Bruner, 1978) parents teach their children that the most important function of language is reference. They prepare their children for a society that places a premium on knowing the names and classes for things. The Kaluli of the Southern Highlands of PNG (Schiefflin, 1979) invest—if anything—more time in teaching language to their children than do the British, but their aim is very different. The Kaluli child learns that the most important language functions are expressive; specifically, that the competent language user is one who can use speech to manipulate and control the behavior of others.

Similarly, some societies teach young children that knowledge is best acquired through observation and imitation. Others encourage children to actively question adults about what they are doing, while still others inculcate respect for contemplation, meditation, and dream interpretation as pathways to knowledge.

Societies hold different models of how the thinker–problem-solver should go about his or her business (Horton & Finnegan, 1973). In Western society the model is that of the scientist who uses formal, logical principles to solve problems and make inferences (Inhelder & Piaget, 1958). As rarely as this ideal is achieved by actual problem-solvers confronted with specific reasoning problems (Wason & Johnson-Laird, 1972), the model nevertheless exerts a profound influence on the societies that have adopted it. If culture takes over the cognitive processes that nature provides after Stage I and shapes them to its own ends during Stage II, the processes that are engendered in Stage III have the potential to supersede the culture that bred them and begin to take over as steering mechanisms as in Huxley's *Brave New World* (1949). The Confucian model of the nature and function of cognition still dominates Chinese society after centuries, despite Mao's best efforts to destroy this model and its influence during the Cultural Revolution. Likewise, there is an interesting battle going on in the United States today over the ascendancy of evolutionary biology as *the* cognitive model for organizing our knowledge about many processes—biological and otherwise. Finally, both the Nigerian civil war and Iranian revolution can at least partially be attributed to discrepancies between "introduced" and "native" Stage III processes.

It is difficult to say just how important Stage III effects are in accounting for the results of our research in Papua New Guinea. My impression is that Ponam and Mandok adults are more likely than Highlands parents to teach their children various skills and encourage them to ask questions. But this difference is too slight to account for the differential success of these groups with respect to the cognitive tests. In other words, while I have no doubt that we could identify aspects of Papua New Guinean societies that fall into the third stage, I doubt that there is much interaction between Stage III ideals and Stage II achievements.

On the other hand, for those children who attend the Community Schools, there is a decided Stage II–Stage III interaction. The school not only pushes cognitive development through the sheer force of new, critical information, but it also imposes a model of language and cognition that, for many of the children, is quite foreign (Scribner & Cole, 1973; Singleton, 1974; Goodnow, 1976). The particular function of English as the language of knowledge acquisition is emphasized by when it is used— namely, during "lessons." Elsewhere *Pisin* and the vernacular are used (Lancy, 1979a). Knowledge is defunctionalized, and children learn things in school that are not applied to the solution of practical problems outside of school. Constraints are—ideally—removed from knowledge acquisition. Whereas most out-of-school skills are joint accomplishments of the child and his caretakers (Greenfield & Childs, in press; Greenfield & Lave, 1982), the child is expected to go it alone in school. Socially situated and constituted knowledge is replaced by knowledge that is private and cognitively constituted. The pace of learning is dramatically increased, and areas of knowledge (e.g., biology, arithmetic) that the villager spends a lifetime learning in a leisurely fashion must be acquired within months in the school. Little provision is made (at least in PNG's schools) for children who are not ready or who are "slow learners." Nor is there the explicit division of labor one finds in the village. All children at a given grade level are expected to master the same material, regardless of gender, talent, or interest. Children are taught to use devices that are themselves "information generators." Unlike learning to make pots that, once mastered, ceases to yield new information, reading and writing are open ended, continuing to convey new information even (or especially) after mastery. To sum up, Western-style schooling represents a highly refined and peculiar view of what knowledge is for and how to obtain it. As researchers, we are apt to be critical of schools, whether they be in Papua New Guinea or in the United States, but we cannot escape the fact that the enterprise has been around for a long time,[9] all the while getting better and better at guiding cognitive development. We may debate the efficiency of the Dienes approach, but no one debates the boost that "manipulatives" have given to instruction in mathematics, for example.

But perhaps the most important aspect of the "hidden curriculum" is the view that Stage I capacities cannot be left to the imperfect mechanisms of society at large to insure their orderly development. To the extent that the future course of Western industrialized societies (with the developed countries struggling to keep up) depends increasingly on the labor of skilled information-processors (as opposed to artisans, mystics, warriors, hod carriers, farmers, etc.), we can never have enough of them.[10] One can be in sympathy with the spirit of Illich's (1971) ideas, while recognizing their futility.

The previous prime minister of Papua New Guinea, Julius Chan, took as his credo the phrase: "There's no 'Melanesian Way' to pilot a plane." What he meant by this is that many aspects of Papua New Guinea's traditional cultures can and should be integrated into national life, but to the extent that this national life includes Western technology, the country must also adopt the forms of education and cognition that go along with it (Lancy, 1980a). At the same time, Papua New Guinea's policy of *universal* schooling is creating an extremely dangerous situation. While the Stage II and III processes associated with schooling may be necessary for the production of airplane pilots, they are unnecessary or even harmful for the production of subsistence horticulturalists. How far

[9]But not that long either. The goal of universal schooling to achieve truly fluent literacy and "numeracy" in the population at large dates only from about 1920 (Resnick & Resnick, 1977). This most recent model of schooling is the one that is being promoted around the globe, however.

[10]The most modern microcomputer hardware and software is now available in several PNG high schools and in the secondary-teacher preparation center (Goroka Teachers College), and a network has been formed to share insights and problems among instructors using the new technology (Harold Fredricks, personal communication).

would a child progress in mastering the village way of life if he firmly believed that answers are found in books, that problem-solving is an individual, intellectual activity, that effort is always and promptly rewarded, that the sexes are equivalent, and so forth? In the towns and in the villages, one of the most frequently voiced concerns is the proliferation of *bik-hets* ("big heads"). The success of Papua New Guinea's evolving philosophies of development and education will be—to a large extent— charted in the output of *bik-hets* and pilots. We hope that in the years to come the former will decline in number while the latter will increase.

References

Allen, A. L., Thomas, N. D., & Patu, P. Abilities of newly trained indigenous secondary mathematics teachers in Papua New Guinea. *PNG Journal of Education*, 1975, *11*(1), 1–7.

Allen, J. Sea traffic and trade. In J. Allen, J. Golson, & R. Jones (Eds.), *Sunda and Sahul: Prehistoric studies in Southeast Asia, Melanesia, and Australia*. New York: Academic Press, 1977.

Anderson, D. R., & Clark, A. T. Comparison of conservation training procedures. *Psychological Reports*, 1978, *43*, 495–499.

Anglin, J. M. *The growth of word meaning*. Cambridge, Mass.: MIT Press, 1970.

Anglin, J. M. *Word, object and conceptual development*. New York: Norton, 1977.

Ardrey, R. *African genesis*. London: Collins, 1961.

Beck, B. B. Primate tool behavior. In R. H. Tuttle (Ed.), *Socioecology and psychology of primates*. The Hague: Mouton, 1975.

Beilin, H. Learning and operational thought convergence and logical thought development. *Journal of Experimental Child Psychology*, 1965, *2*, 317–399.

Beilin, H. Developmental stages and developmental processes. In D. R. Green, M. P. Ford, & G. S. Flamer (Eds.), *Measurement and Piaget*. New York: McGraw-Hill, 1971.

Bellwood, P. *Man's conquest of the Pacific: The prehistory of Southeast Asia and Oceania*. New York: Oxford University Press, 1979.

Berlin, B. Ethnobiological classification. In E. Rosch & B. B. Lloyd (Eds.), *Cognition and categorization*. Hillsdale, N. J.: Erlbaum, 1978.

Berlin, B., Breedlove, P. E., & Raven, P. H. Some general principles of classification and nomenclature in folk biology. *American Anthropologist*, 1973, *75*, 214–242.

Berlin, B., Breedlove, P. E., & Raven, P. H. *Principles of Tzeltal plant classification: An introduction to the botanical ethnography of a Mayan-speaking community in highland Chiapas.* New York: Academic Press, 1974.

Berlin, B., & Kay, P. *Basic color terms: Their universality and evolution.* Berkeley: University of California Press, 1969.

Bernstein, B. *Class, codes and control* (Vol. 2). London: Routledge & Kegan Paul, 1971.

Berry, J. W., & Annis, R. C. Ecology, culture and psychological differentiation. *International Journal of Psychology,* 1974, *9*, 173–193.

Biersack, A. *The hidden god: Communication, cosmology and cybernetics among a Melanesian people.* Unpublished doctoral dissertation, University of Michigan, 1980.

Birdsell, J. B. The recalibration of a paradigm for the first peopling of Australia. In J. Allen, J. Golson, & R. Jones (Eds.), *Sunda and Sahul: Prehistoric studies in Southeast Asia, Melanesia, and Australia.* New York: Academic Press, 1977.

Bishop, A. Spatial abilities and mathematics in Papua New Guinea. In D. F. Lancy (Ed.), *The Indigenous Mathematics Project,* special issue of *PNG Journal of Education,* 1978, *14*, 172–200.

Bishop, A. J. Visualizing and mathematics in a pre-technological culture. *Educational Studies in Mathematics,* 1979, *10*, 135–146.

Bloom, A. H. The impact of Chinese linguistic structures on cognitive style. *Current Anthropology,* 1979, *20*, 585–586.

Bloom, A. H. *The linguistic shaping of thought: A study of the impact of language on thinking in China and the West.* Hillsdale, N. J.: Erlbaum, 1981.

Blurton-Jones, N., & Konner, M. J. !Kung knowledge of animal behavior. In R. B. Lee & I. DeVore (Eds.), *Kalahari hunter–gatherers.* Cambridge, Mass.: Harvard Unversity Press, 1976.

Bobrow, D. G. Dimensions of representation. In D. G. Bobrow & A. Collins (Eds.), *Representation and understanding: Studies in cognitive science.* New York: Academic Press, 1975.

Boden, M. *Piaget.* London: Fontana, 1979.

Bourdieu, P., & Passeron, J. C. (Trans. R. Nice). *Reproduction in education, society and culture.* London: Sage, 1977.

Bovet, M. C. Cognitive processes among illiterate children and adults. In J. W. Berry & P. R. Dasen (Eds.), *Culture and cognition.* London: Methuen, 1974.

Bower, T. G. R. *Development in infancy.* San Francisco: W. H. Freeman, 1974.

Bowles, S., & Gintis, H. *Schooling in capitalist America.* London: Routledge & Kegan Paul, 1976.

Brainerd, C. J. Feedback, rule knowledge and conservation learning. *Child Development,* 1977, *48*, 404–411.

Brainerd, C. J. *Piaget's theory of intelligence.* Englewood Cliffs, N. J.: Prentice-Hall, 1978. (a)

Brainerd, C. J. The stage question in cognitive-developmental theory. *The Behavioral and Brain Sciences,* 1978, *1*, 173–182. (b)

Brainerd, C. J. "Stage," "structure" and developmental theory. In G. Steiner (Ed.), *The psychology of the twentieth century.* Munich: Kindler, 1978. (c)

Brianerd, C. J. *The origins of the number concept.* New York: Praeger, 1979.

Brainerd, C. J. Stages II (Review of *Beyond universals in cognitive development* by D. H. Feldman). *Developmental Review,* 1981, *1*, 63–81.

Brent, S. B. Prigogine's model for self-organization in non-equilibrium systems. *Human Development,* 1978, *21*, 374–387.

Bright, J. O., & Bright, W. Semantic structures in northwestern California. In S. A. Tyler (Ed.), *Cognitive anthropology.* New York: Holt, Rinehart & Winston, 1969.

Britt, M., & Roberts, R. E. (Eds.), *Report of the Second National Workshop for Mathematics Groups.* Port Moresby, Papua New Guinea: Department of Education, 1979.

Brookfield, H. C., & Hart, D. *Melanesia: A geographical interpretation of an island world*. London: Methuen, 1971.

Brooks, L. Nonanalytic concept formation and memory for instances. In. E. Rosch & B. B. Lloyd (Eds.), *Cognition and categorization*. Hillsdale, N. J.: Erlbaum, 1978.

Brown, C. H. Folk-botanical life-forms: Their universality and growth. *American Anthropologist*, 1977, *79*, 317–342.

Brown, C. H. Folk-zoological life-forms: Their universality and growth. *American Anthropologist*, 1979, *81*, 791–817.

Brown, C. H., Kolar, J., Torrey, S. J., Truong-Quang, T., & Volkman, P. Some general principles of biological and non-biological folk classification. *American Ethnologist*, 1976, *3*, 73–85.

Brown, P. *Highland peoples of New Guinea*. Cambridge: Cambridge University Press, 1978.

Brown, P., & Brookfield, H. C. *Struggle for land*. Melbourne, Australia: Oxford University Press, 1963.

Brown, R. *Words and things*. Glencoe, Ill.: Free Press, 1958.

Bruner, J. S. *The process of education*. Cambridge, Mass.: Harvard University Press, 1960.

Bruner, J. S. The course of cognitive growth. *American Psychologist*, 1964, *19*, 1–15.

Bruner, J. S. *Toward a theory of instruction*. Cambridge, Mass.: Harvard University Press, 1966. (a)

Bruner, J. S. On cognitive growth: I and II. In J. S. Bruner, R. R. Olver, & P. M. Greenfield (Eds.), *Studies in cognitive growth*. New York: Wiley, 1966. (b)

Bruner, J. S. *The relevance of education*. New York: Norton, 1971.

Bruner, J. S. Nature and uses of immaturity. *American Psychologist*, 1972, *27*, 687–708.

Bruner, J. S. Play is serious business. *Psychology Today*, 1975, *8*(1), 81–83.

Bruner, J. S., Goodnow, J. J., & Austin, G. A. *A study of thinking*. New York: Wiley, 1956.

Bruner, J. S., & Kenney, H. J. On multiple ordering. In J. S. Bruner, R. R. Olver, & P. M. Greenfield (Eds.), *Studies in cognitive growth*. New York: Wiley, 1966.

Bruner, J. S., Olver, R. R., & Greenfield, P. M. (Eds.). *Studies in cognitive growth*. New York: Wiley, 1966.

Buck-Morss, S. Socio-economic bias in Piaget's theory and its implications for cross-cultural studies. *Human Development*, 1975, *18*, 35–49.

Bulmer, R. N. H. Worms that croak and other mysteries of Karam natural history. *Mankind*, 1968, *6*, 621–639.

Bulmer, R. N. H., & Menzies, J. I. Karam classification of marsupials and rodents. *Journal of the Polynesian Society*, 1972, *81* (4), 472–499.

Bulmer, R. N. H., & Menzies, J. I. Karam classification of marsupials and rodents. *Journal of the Polynesian Society*, 1973, *82* (1), 86–107.

Bulmer, R. N. H., Menzies, J. I., & Parker, F. Kalam classification of reptiles and fishes. *Journal of the Polynesian Society*, 1975, *89*, 267–308.

Bulmer, R. N. H., & Tyler, M. J. Karam classification of frogs. *Journal of the Polynesian Society*, 1968, *77*, 333–385.

Burstein, L. The role of levels of analysis in the specification of educational effects. In R. Dreeben & J. A. Thomas (Eds.), *The analysis of educational productivity: Issues in microanalysis* (Vol. 1). Cambridge, Mass.: Balinger, 1980.

Campbell, D. T. The mutual methodological relevance of anthropology and psychology. In F. L. K. Hsu (Ed.), *Psychological anthropology*. Homewood, Ill.: Dorsey, 1961.

Cahill, B. Distribution problems. In *Curriculum unit status report*. Port Moresby, Papua New Guinea: Department of Education, 1980.

Carey, S. The child as word learner. In M. Halle, J. Bresnan, & G. A. Miller (Eds.), *Linguistic theory and psychological reality*. Cambridge, Mass.: MIT Press, 1978.

Carpenter, T. R. Cognitive development research and mathematics education. *Theoretical*

Paper No. 73, 1979. Madison, Wis.: University of Wisconsin, Wisconsin Research and Development Center for Individualized Schooling.

Carpenter, T. P., Hiebert, J., & Moser, J. M. First-grade children's initial solution processes for simple addition and subtraction problems. *Journal for Research in Mathematics Education*, 1981, *12*, 27–39.

Carrier, A. H. *The structure and substance of counting on Ponam*. Port Moresby, Papua New Guinea: University of Papua New Guinea, Education Research Unit Seminar, August, 1979.

Carrier, J. G. School and community on Ponam. In D. F. Lancy (Ed.), *The Community School*, special issue of the *PNG Journal of Education*, 1979, *15*, 66–77.

Carrier, J. G. Knowledge and its use: Constraints on the application of new knowledge in Ponam society. *PNG Journal of Education*, 1980, *16*, 102–126.

Carrier, J. G. Education as investment: Education, economy and society on Ponam Island. *PNG Journal of Education*, 1981, *17*, 17–35. (a)

Carrier, J. G. Labour migration and labour export on Ponam Island. *Oceania*, 1981, *51*, 237–255. (b)

Case, R. Responsiveness to conservation training as a function of induced subjective uncertainty, M-space and cognitive style. *Canadian Journal of Behavioral Science*, 1977, *9*, 12–25.

Cayago, S. Community school characteristics. In D. F. Lancy (Ed.), *The Community School*, special issue of the *PNG Journal of Education*, 1979, *15*, 27–37.

Cheetham, B. School and community in the Huli area of the Southern Highlands province. In D. F. Lancy (Ed.), *The Community School*, special issue of the *PNG Journal of Education*, 1979, *15*, 78–96.

Chevalier-Skolnikoff, S. A Piagetian model for describing and comparing socialization in monkey, ape, and human infants. In S. Chevalier-Skolnikoff & F. E. Poirer (Eds.), *Primate bio-social development: Biological, social and ecological determinants*. New York: Garland, 1977.

Chi, M. T. H. Knowledge structures and memory development. In R. S. Siegler (Ed.), *Children's thinking: What develops?* Hillsdale, N. J.: Erlbaum, 1978.

Chomsky, N. *Aspects of the theory of syntax*. Cambridge, Mass.: MIT Press, 1965.

Chomsky, N. *Language and mind*. New York: Harcourt Brace Jovanovich, 1968.

Churchill, L. *Notes on everyday quantification practices*. Paper presented at the Annual Meeting of the American Sociological Association, Miami, August 1966.

Ciborowski, T., & Cole, M. A developmental and cross-cultural study of the influences of rule structure and problem composition on the learning of conceptual classifications. *Journal of Experimental Child Psychology*, 1973, *15*, 193–215.

Clements, M. A. *Spatial ability, visual imagery, and mathematical learning*. Paper presented at the Annual Meeting of the American Educational Research Association, Los Angeles, April 1981.

Clements, M. A., & Jones, P. L. *The education of Atawe* (Tech. Rep. 18). Lae, Papua New Guinea: Papua New Guinea University of Technology, Mathematics Education Centre, 1981.

Clements, M. A., & Lean, G. A. *Influences on mathematical learning in Papua New Guinea: Some cross-cultural perspectives* (Tech. Rep. 13). Lae, Papua New Guinea: Papua New Guinea University of Technology, Mathematics Education Centre, 1981.

Cohen, B. H. An investigation of recoding in free recall. *Journal of Experimental Psychology*, 1963, *65*, 368–375.

Cole, M. *Toward an experimental anthropology of thinking*. Paper presented at the Joint Meeting of the American Ethnological Society and the Society for Applied Anthropology, Montreal, April 1972.

Cole, M., & Bruner, J. S. Cultural differences and inferences about psychological processes. *American Psychologist*, 1971, *26*, 867–876.

Cole, M., Gay, J., Glick, J., & Sharp, D. *The cultural context of learning and thinking.* New York: Basic Books, 1971.

Cole, M., & Means, B. *Comparative studies of how people think.* Cambridge, Mass.: Harvard University Press, 1981.

Cole, M., & Scribner, S. *Culture and thought: A psychological introduction.* New York: Wiley, 1974.

Cole, M., Sharp, D. W., & Lave, C. The cognitive consequences of education: Some empirical evidence and theoretical misgivings. *The Urban Review*, 1976, *9*, 218–233.

Collis, K. F. *A study of concrete and formal operations in school mathematics: A Piagetian viewpoint.* Hawthorn, Australia: Australian Council for Education Research, 1975.

Confrey, J. *Using the clinical interview to explore students' mathematical understandings.* Paper presented at the Annual Meeting of the American Educational Research Association, Los Angeles, April 1981.

Connolly, K. J., Pharoah, P. O. D., & Hetzel, B. S. Fetal iodine deficiency and motor performance during childhood. *The Lancet*, 1979, *2*, 1149–1151.

Coon, C. S. *The hunting peoples.* Boston: Little, Brown, 1971.

Cravioto, J., & DeLicardie, E. R. Neurointegrative development and intelligence in children rehabilitated from severe malnutrition. In J. W. Prescott, M. S. Read, & D. B. Coursin (Eds.), *Brain function and malnutrition.* New York: Wiley, 1975.

Cravioto, J., & Robles, B. Evolution of adaptive and motor behavior during rehabilitation from Kwashiorkor. *American Journal of Orthopediatrics*, 1965, *35*, 449–464.

D'Albertis, L. M. *New Guinea: What I did and what I saw.* London: Low, Marston, Searles, & Rivington, 1880.

Dantzig, T. *Number: The language of science* (4th ed.). New York: Macmillan, 1954.

Dark, P. J. C. *Kilenge life and art.* New York: St. Martin's Press, 1974.

Dasen, P. R. Cross-cultural Piagetian research: A summary. *Journal of Cross-Cultural Psychology*, 1972, *3*, 23–39.

Dasen, P. R. The influence of ecology, culture and European contact on cognitive development in Australian aborigines. In J. W. Berry & P. R. Dasen (Eds.), *Culture and cognition.* London: Methuen, 1974.

Dasen, P. R. Concrete operational development in three cultures. *Journal of Cross-Cultural Psychology*, 1975, *6*, 156–172.

Dasen, P. R. Are cognitive processes universal? In N. Warren (Ed.), *Studies in cross-cultural psychology.* London: Academic Press, 1977. (a)

Dasen, P. R. Introduction. In P. R. Dasen (Ed.), *Piagetian psychology.* New York: Gardner Press, 1977. (b)

Dasen, P. R. Psychological differentiation and operational development: A cross-cultural link. *Quarterly Newsletter of the Laboratory for Comparative Human Cognition*, 1980, *2*, 81–86.

Dasen, P. R., & Heron, A. Cross-cultural tests of Piaget's theory. In H. C. Triandis & A. Heron (Eds.), *Handbook of cross-cultural psychology: Developmental psychology* (Vol. 4). Boston: Allyn & Bacon, 1981.

Dasen, P. R., Inhelder, B., Lavallée, M., & Retschitzki, J. *Naissance de l'intelligence chez infant baoulé* de côte d'Ivoire. Bern: Hans Huber, 1978.

DeGuire, L. J. *A review of the factor analytic literature on mathematical abilities.* Paper presented at the Fourth International Congress on Mathematics Education, Berkeley, California, August 1980.

de Lacey, P. R. A cross-cultural study of classificatory ability in Australia. *Journal of Cross-Cultural Psychology*, 1970, *1*, 293–304.

de Lemos, M. M. The development of conservation in aboriginal children. *International Journal of Psychology*, 1969, *4*, 255–269.

Denham, C., & Liberman, A. (Eds.). *Time to learn.* Washington, D. C.: National Institute of Education, 1980.

Deutsch, M., & Associates. *The disadvantaged child.* New York: Basic Books, 1967.

Diamond, J. M. Zoological classification system of a primitive people. *Science*, 1966, *151*, 1102–1104.

Dienes, Z. P. *An experimental study of mathematics learning.* London: Hutchinson, 1963.

Dienes, Z. P. *Mathematics in the primary school.* Adelaide, Australia: Macmillan, 1964.

Dienes, Z. P., & Golding, E. W. *Approach to modern mathematics.* New York: Herder & Herder, 1971.

Donaldson, M. *Children's minds.* New York: Norton, 1978.

Doob, L. Exploring eidetic imagery among the Kamba of Central Kenya. *The Journal of Social Psychology*, 1965, *67*, 3–22.

Douglas, M. *Purity and danger.* London: Routledge & Kegan Paul, 1966.

Durkheim, E., & Mauss, M. *Primitive classification* (R. Needham, trans.). Chicago: University of Chicago Press, 1963. (Originally published, 1903.)

Durrenberger, E. P., & Morrison, J. W. Commentary. *American Ethnologist*, 1979, *6*, 408–409.

Dwyer, P. The rediscovery of Lufi. *Australian Natural History*, 1976, *18*(9), 317–323. (a)

Dwyer, P. Beetles, butterflies and bats: Species transformation in a New Guinea folk classification. *Oceania*, 1976, *46*(3), 188–205. (b)

Edwards, A., & Bajpai, A. *Preliminary report on the basic arithmetic test carried out in post-secondary institutions in Papua New Guinea* (Tech. Rep. 6). Lae, Papua New Guinea: Papua New Guinea University of Technology, Mathematics Education Centre, 1979.

Edwards, L. D., & Craddock, L. J. Malnutrition and intellectual development: A study in school age aboriginal children at Walgett, N. S. W. *Medical Journal of Australia*, 1973, May, 880–884.

Elkind, D. Conservation and concept formation. In D. Elkind & J. M. Flavell (Eds.), *Studies in cognitive development.* New York: Oxford University Press, 1969.

Ericsson, K. A., Chase, W. G., & Faloon, S. Acquisition of a memory skill. *Science*, 1980, *208*, 1181–1182.

Erlwanger, S. *Case studies of children's conceptions of mathematics.* Unpublished doctoral dissertation, University of Illinois—Urbana, 1974.

Ferro-Luzzi, A., Norgan, N. G., & Durnin, J. V. G. A. Food intake and its relationship to body weight and age and its apparent nutritional adequacy in New Guinea children. *American Journal of Clinical Nutrition*, 1975, *28*, 1443–1453.

Ferro-Luzzi, A., Norgan, N. G., & Durnin, J. V. G. A. The nutritional status of some New Guinea children as assessed by anthropometric, biochemical and other indices. *Ecology of Food and Nutrition*, 1978, *7*, 115–128.

Fisher, C., Berliner, D., Filby, N., Marliave, R., Cahen, L., & Dishaw, M. Teaching behaviors, academic learning time and student achievement, an overview. In C. Denham & A. Liberman (Eds.), Time to learn. Washington, D. C.: National Institute of Education, 1980.

Flavell, J. M. *The developmental psychology of Jean Piaget.* Princeton, N. J.: Van Nostrand, 1963.

Frake, C. O. The ethnographic study of cognitive systems. In S. A. Tyler (Ed.), *Cognitive anthropology.* New York: Holt, Rinehart & Winston, 1969.

Frazer, J. G. *The golden bough.* New York: Macmillan, 1922.

Fredricks, H. R. A test of measurement—or is it? In P. Clarkson (Ed.), *Research in mathematics education in Papua New Guinea*. Proceedings of the First Mathematics Education Conference. Lae, Papua New Guinea: Papua New Guinea University of Technology, Mathematics Education Centre, 1981.

Friedberg, C. Socially significant plant species and their taxonomic position among the Bunaq of Central Timor. In R. F. Ellen & D. Reason (Eds.), *Classifications in their social context*. London: Academic Press, 1979.

Furth, H. *Thinking without language*. New York: Free Press, 1966.

Gaines, R. Matrices and pattern detection by young children. *Developmental Psychology*, 1973, *9*, 143–150.

Gajdusek, D. C. Physiological and psychological characteristics of Stone Age man. *Engineering and Science*, 1970, *33*(6), 26–62.

Gal, S. Inter-informant variability in ethnozoological taxonomy. *Anthropological Linguistics*, 1973, *45*, 203–219.

Gardner, P. M. Birds, words and a requiem for the omniscient informant. *American Ethnologist*, 1976, *3*, 446–468.

Gay, J., & Cole, M. *The new mathematics and an old culture*. New York: Holt, Rinehart & Winston, 1967.

Gearhart, M. Divanap Community School Field Report. *Indigenous Mathematics Project Working Paper Number 8*. Port Moresby, Papua New Guinea: UNESCO/Education, 1980.

Gell, A. F. *Society, ritual and symbolism in Umeda village*. Unpublished doctoral dissertation, London School of Economics, 1973.

Gell, A. F. *Metamorphosis of the Cassowaries: Umeda society, language and ritual*. London: Athlone Press, 1975.

Gelman, R. Conservation acquisition: A problem of learning to attend to relevant attributes. *Journal of Experimental Child Psychology*, 1969, *7*, 167–187.

Gelman, R., & Gallistel, C. R. *The child's understanding of number*. Cambridge, Mass.: Harvard University Press, 1978.

Gibson, K. R. Brain structure and intelligence in macaques and human infants from a Piagetian perspective. In S. Chevalier-Skolnikoff & F. E. Poirer (Eds.), *Primate biosocial development: Biological, social and ecological determinants*. New York: Garland, 1977.

Ginsburg, H. Young children's informal knowledge of mathematics, unpublished manuscript, Cornell Univ., 1975.

Ginsburg, H. *Children's arithmetic*. New York: Van Nostrand, 1977.

Gladwin, T. *East is a big bird: Navigation and logic on Puluwat Atoll*. Cambridge, Mass.: Harvard University Press, 1970.

Glick, L. B. Categories and relations in Gimi natural science. *American Anthropologist*, 1964, *66*(4), 273–280.

Goldstein, K., & Scheerer, M. Abstract and concrete behavior: An experimental study with special tests. *Psychological Monographs*, 1941, *53*(2, Serial No. 239).

Golomb, C., & Cornelius, C. B. Symbolic play and its cognitive significance. *Developmental Psychology*, 1977, *13*, 246–252.

Golson, J. No room at the top: Agricultural intensification in the New Guinea Highlands. In J. Allen, J. Golson, & R. Jones (Eds.), *Sunda and Sahul: Prehistoric studies in Southeast Asia, Melanesia, and Australia*. New York: Academic Press, 1977.

Golson, J., & Hughes, P. Ditches before time. *Hemisphere*, 1977, *21*(2), 13–21.

Goodenough, W. Componential analysis and the study of meaning. *Language*, 1956, *32*, 195–216.

Goodenough, W. Cultural anthropology and linguistics. In P. L. Garvin (Ed.), *Report of the Seventh Round Table Meeting on Linguistics and Language Study*. Washington, D. C.: Georgetown University Monograph Series on Language and Linguistics No. 9, 1957.

Goodnow, J. J. Problems in research on culture and thought. In D. Elkind & J. M. Flavell (Eds.), *Studies in cognitive development*. New York: Oxford University Press, 1969.

Goodnow, J. J. The nature of intelligent behavior: Questions raised by cross-cultural studies. In L. B. Resnick (Ed.), *The nature of intelligence*. Hillsdale, N. J.: Erlbaum, 1976.

Goody, J. *The domestication of the savage mind*. Cambridge: Cambridge University Press, 1977.

Gould, S. J. Panselectionist pitfalls in Parker and Gibson's model for the evolution of intelligence. *The Behavioral and Brain Sciences*, 1979, *2*, 385–386.

Gould, S. J. Wallace's fatal flaw. *Natural History*, 1980 *89*(1), 26–40.

Grant, J. *Struggling with dependency: Melanesian strategies for self-reliance*. Paper presented at the Annual Meeting of the Association for Social Anthropology in Oceania, Galveston, Texas, February—March 1980.

Grant, J., & Zelenietz, M. *The current state of artifact production in Kilenge, West New Britain*. Paper presented at the Second International Symposium on the Art of Oceania, Wellington, New Zealand, February 1978.

Grant, J., & Zelenietz, M. Changing patterns of wage labor migration in the Kilenge area of Papua New Guinea. *International Migration Review*, 1980, *14*, 215–234.

Graves, A. J. The attainment of conservation of mass, weight and volume in minimally educated adults. *Developmental Psychology*, 1972, *1*, 223–224.

Greenfield, P. M. On culture and conservation. In. J. S. Bruner, R. R. Olver, & P. M. Greenfield (Eds.), *Studies in cognitive growth*. New York: Wiley, 1966.

Greenfield, P. M., & Bruner, J. S. Culture and cognitive growth. In D. A. Goslin (Ed.), *Handbook of socialization theory and research*. New York: Rand McNally, 1966.

Greenfield, P. M., & Childs, C. P. Weaving, color terms and pattern representation: Cultural influences and cognitive development among the Zinacantecos of southern Mexico. *International Journal of Psychology*, in press,.

Greenfield, P. M., & Lave, J. Cognitive aspects of informal education. In D. A. Wagner & H. Stevenson (Eds.), *Child development in cross-cultural perspective*. San Francisco: W. H. Freeman, 1982.

Greenfield, P. M., Reich, L. C., & Olver, R. R. On culture and equivalence. In J. S. Bruner, R. R. Olver, & P. M. Greenfield (Eds.), *Studies in cognitive growth*. New York: Wiley, 1966.

Greenfield, P. M., & Schneider, L. Building a tree structure: The development of hier-archical complexity and interrupted strategies in chidlren's construction activity. *Developmental Psychology*, 1977, *13*, 299–313.

Greenfield, P. M., & Smith, J. H. *The structure of communication in early language development*. New York: Academic Press, 1976.

Grieve, R. Decentralization and the community school in Northern Province, In D. F. Lancy (Ed.), *The Community School*, special issue of the *PNG Journal of Education*, 1979, *15*, 97–102.

Griffen, J., Nelson, H., & Firth, S. *Papua New Guinea: A political history*. Richmond, Australia: Heinemann, 1979.

Groube, L. M., Tumbe, J., & Muke, J. *Recent discoveries on the Huon Peninsula*. Paper presented at the 53rd ANZAAS Congress, Brisbane, Australia, August 1981.

Hallpike, C. R. *Bloodshed and vengeance in the Papuan Mountains*. Oxford: Oxford University Press, 1977.

Hallpike, C. R. *The foundations of primitive thought*. New York: Oxford University Press, 1979.

Harding, T. G. *Voyagers of the Vitiaz Straits*. Seattle: University of Washington Press, 1967.

Harlow, H., & Mears, C. *The human model: Primate perspectives*. Washington, D. C.: Winston, 1979.

Harris, M. The cultural ecology of India's sacred cattle. *Current Anthropology*, 1966, *7*, 51–59.

Harris, M. *Cows, pigs, wars and witches: The riddles of culture*. New York: Random House, 1974.

Harris, P., & Heelas, P. Cognitive processes and collective representation. *Archives of European Sociology*, 1979, *20*, 211–241.

Harrison, B. Naught for our comfort—Some indication of mathematical standards in PNG primary schools and teachers colleges, *Math News*, 1976, *1*, 18–26.

Hays, T. E. Plant classification and nomenclature in Ndumba, Papua New Guinea highlands. *Ethnology*, 1979, *18*, 253–270.

Heron, A., & Kroeger, E. The effects of training on uneven concrete operational development in Yugoslav migrant children. In J. W. Berry & W. J. Lonner (Eds.), *Applied cross-cultural psychology*. Amsterdam: Swets & Zeitlinger, 1975.

Heron, R. E., & Sutton-Smith, B. (Eds.). *Child's play*. New York: Wiley, 1971.

Hood, L., & Bloom, L. What, when and how about why: A longitudinal study of early expressions of causality,. *Monographs of the Society for Research in Child Development*, 1979, *44*(6, Serial No. 181).

Horton, R. African traditional thought and Western science, Part II: The closed and open predicaments. *Africa*, 1967, *37*, 155–187.

Horton, R., & Finnegan, R. (Eds.). *Modes of thought: Essays on thinking in Western and non-Western societies*. London: Faber & Faber, 1973.

Hughes, I. *New Guinea Stone Age Trade*. Canberra: Research School of Pacific Studies, 1977.

Hunn, E. Toward a perceptual model of folk biological classification. *American Ethnologist*, 1976, *3*, 508–524.

Hunn, E. *Tzeltal folk zoology: The classification of discontinuities in nature*. New York: Academic Press, 1977.

Huntsman, R. W. Some aspects of children's ability to form equivalence categories. *PNG Journal of Education*, 1973, *9*(3), 1–8.

Hutchins, E. *Culture and inference*. Cambridge, Mass.: Harvard University Press, 1980.

Huxley, A. *Brave new world*. New York: Harper, 1949.

Illich, I. *Deschooling society*. New York: Harper & Row, 1971.

Inhelder, B. Naissance de l'intelligence et malnutrition. *Revue de Psychologie Appliqué*, 1979, *29*, 153–159.

Inhelder, B., & Piaget, J. *The growth of logical thinking from childhood to adolescence*. New York: Basic Books, 1958.

Inhelder, B., & Piaget, J. *The early growth of logic in the child*. New York: Norton, 1969.

Jahoda, G. Theoretical and systematic approaches in cross-cultural psychology. In H. C. Triandis & W. W. Lambert (Eds.), *Handbook of cross-cultural psychology: Perspectives* (Vol. 1). Boston: Allyn & Bacon, 1980.

Jerison, H. J. *Evolution of the brain and intelligence*. New York: Academic Press, 1973.

Jinks, P. (Ed.). *Readings in New Guinea history*. Sydney, Australia: Angus & Robertson, 1968.

Johnson, K. Kero Community School field report. *Indigenous Mathematics Project Working Paper No. 9*. Port Moresby, Papua New Guinea: UNESCO/Education, 1980.

Jones, J. *Proportionality as a predictor of success at the University of Papua New Guinea* (Working Paper No. 8). Port Moresby, Papua New Guinea: University of Papua New Guinea, Education Research Unit, 1973.

Jones, J. *Cognitive studies with students in Papua New Guinea* (Working Paper No. 10). Port Moresby, Papua New Guinea: University of Papua New Guinea, Education Research Unit, 1974.

Jones, P. L. *A study of proportional reasoning* (Tech. Rep. 12). Lae, Papua New Guinea: Papua New Guinea University of Technology, Mathematics Education Centre, 1979.

Jones, P. L. *Mathematical language and the learning of mathematics in Papua New Guinea* (Tech. Rep. 16). Lae, Papua New Guinea: Papua New Guinea University of Technology, Mathematics Education Centre, 1981. (a)

Jones, P. L. Solving word problems in a second language and reading proficiency. In P. Clarkson (Ed.), *Research in mathematics education in Papua New Guinea*. Proceedings of the First Mathematics Education Conference. Lae, Papua New Guinea: Papua New Guinea University of Technology, Mathematics Education Centre, 1981,(b)

Jordan, N. Is there an Achilles' heel in Piaget's theorizing? *Human Development*, 1972, *15*, 379–382.

Jurdak, M. Reflective intelligence and mathematics. In R. Karplus (Ed.), *Proceedings of the Fourth International Conference for the Psychology of Mathematics Education*. Berkeley: University of California Press, 1980.

Kagan, J. Resilience and continuity in psychological development. In A. M. Clarke & D. B. Clarke (Eds.), *Early experience: Myth and evidence*. New York: Free Press, 1977.

Kagan, J., Klein, R. E., Finley, G. E., Rogoff, B., & Nolan, E. A cross-cultural study of cognitive development. *Monographs of the Society for Research in Child Development*, 1979, *44*(5, Serial No. 180).

Kamii, C., & DeVries, R. *Physical knowledge in pre-school education: Implications of Piaget's theory*. Englewood Cliffs, N. J.: Prentice-Hall, 1978.

Kearins, J. Skills of desert children. In G. E. Kearney & D. W. McElwain (Eds.), *Aboriginal cognition*. Canberra, Australia: Institute for Aboriginal Studies, 1975.

Kelly, M. *Some cognitive variables of New Guinea children*. Paper presented at the 42nd Congress. ANZAAS Melbourne, August 1970.

Kelly, M. Some aspects of conservation of quantity and length in Papua New Guinea in relation to language, sex and years in school. *PNG Journal of Education*, 1971, 7(1), 55–60. (a)

Kelly, M. *Some comparative results on Piaget and Bruner measures from the 4-culture study on cognitive development*. Paper presented at the 43rd ANZAAS Congress, Brisbane, Australia, May, 1971. (b)

Kelly, M. A two-criteria classification matrix with some Papua New Guinea children. *PNG Journal of Education*, 1971, 7(2), 46–49. (c)

Kelly, M. The validity of Bruner's concept of modes of representation of reality with a sample of Papua New Guinea children. *PNG Journal of Education*, 1971, 7(3), 33–37. (d)

Kelly, M. Differential cognitive development of children exposed to a bilingual and bicultural situation. *PNG Journal of Education*, 1973, 9(2), 44–47.

Kelly, M. Papua New Guinea and Piaget: An eight-year study. In P. R. Dasen (Ed.), *Piagetian psychology: Cross-cultural contributions*. New York: Gardner Press, 1977.

Kelly, M., & Philp, H. Vernacular test instructions in relation to cognitive task behaviour among highlands children of Papua New Guinea. *British Journal of Educational Psychology*, 1975, *45*, 189–197.

Kennedy, J. Lapita colonization of the Admiralty Islands? *Science*, 1981, *213*, 757–759.

Kessen, W., & Nelson, K. What the child brings to language. In B. Z. Presseisen, D. Goldstein, & M. H. Appel (Eds.), *Topics in cognitive development: Language and operational thought* (Vol. 2). New York: Plenum, 1978.

Kettenis, F. Traditional food classification and counting system of Kilenge—West New

Britain. In D. F. Lancy (Ed.), *The Indigenous Mathematics Project*, special issue of *PNG Journal of Education*, 1978, *14*, 31–46.

Klahr, D., & Wallace, J. G. *Cognitive development*. Hillsdale, N. J.: Erlbaum, 1976.

Konner, M. Origins of language: A proposed moratorium. *The Behavioral and Brain Sciences*, 1979, *2*, 391.

Krutetskii, V. A. *The psychology of mathematical abilities in school children*. Chicago: University of Chicago Press, 1976.

Laboratory for the Comparative Study of Human Cognition. Cross-cultural psychology's challenges to our ideas of children and development. *American Psychologist*, 1979, *34*, 827–833.

Laboratory for the Comparative Study of Human Cognition. Culture and cognitive development. In W. Kessen (Ed.), *Mussen handbook of child development* (Vol. 1). New York: Wiley, in press.

Lachman, J. L., & Lachman, R. Theories of memory organization and human evolution. In C. R. Puff (Ed.), *Memory organization and structure*. New York: Academic Press, 1979.

Lancy, D. F. *An experimental analysis of riddles and rule-based problem solving*. Paper presented at the Annual Meeting of the Society for Applied Anthropology, Montreal, April 1972.

Lancy, D. F. The social organization of learning: Initiation rituals and public schools. *Human Organization*, 1975, *34*, 371–380.

Lancy, D. F. The play behavior of Kpelle children during rapid cultural change. In D. F. Lancy & B. A. Tindall (Eds.), *The anthropological study of play: Problems and prospects*. West Point, N. Y.: Leisure Press, 1976.

Lancy, D. F. Studies of memory in culture. *Annals of the New York Academy of Sciences*, 1977, *285*, 297–307.

Lancy, D. F. Indigenous mathematics systems. In D. F. Lancy (Ed.), *The Indigenous Mathematics Project*, special issue of *PNG Journal of Education*, 1978, *14*, 15–18. (a)

Lancy, D. F. Introduction to part II: Culture, schooling, and the development of symbolic thought. In D. F. Lancy (Ed.), *The Indigenous Mathematics Project*, special issue of *PNG Journal of Education* 1978, *14*, 85–88. (b)

Lancy, D. F. Cognitive testing in the Indigenous Mathematics Project In D. F. Lancy (Ed.), *Mathematics Project*, special issue of *PNG Journal of Education*, 1978, *14*, 117–146. (c)

Lancy, D. F. The classroom as phenomenon. in D. Dar-Tal & L. Saxe (Eds.), *Social psychology of education*. New York: Wiley, 1978. (d)

Lancy, D. F. *Education research 1976–1979: Reports and essays*. Port Moresby, Papua New Guinea: UNESCO/Education, 1979. (a)

Lancy, D. F. Introduction. In D. F. Lancy (Ed.), *The Community School*, special issue of *PNG Journal of Education*, 1979, *15*, 1–7. (b)

Lancy, D. F. Some observations on technology and education in Papua New Guinea. *Catalyst*, 1980, *10*, 3–7. (a)

Lancy, D. F. Speech events in a West Africa court. *Communication and Cognition*, 1980, *13*, 397–412. (b)

Lancy, D. F. Becoming a blacksmith in Gbarngasuakwelle. *Anthropology and Education Quarterly*, 1980, *11*, 266–274. (c)

Lancy, D. F. Work as play: The Kpelle case. In H. B. Schwartzman (Ed.), *Play and culture*. West Point, N. Y.: Leisure Press, 1980. (d)

Lancy, D. F. Play in species adaptation. *Annual Review of Anthropology*, 1980, *9*, 471–495. (e)

Lancy, D. F. The Indigenous Mathematics Project: An overview. *Educational Studies in Mathematics*, 1981, *12*, 445–453.

Lancy, D. F., & Engelhardt, J. *The Navajos and geometry.* Paper presented at the Symposium on Culture and Mathematics, Annual Meeting of the American Educational Research Association, New York, March 1982.

Lancy, D. F., & Goldstein, G. I. Using non-verbal Piagetian tasks to assess the cognitive development of autistic children. *Child Development,* in press.

Lancy, D. F., & Kada, V. Report on a preliminary analysis of the 1978 primary mathematics achievement test program. Port Moresby, Papua New Guinea: Department of Education, 1979.

Lancy, D. F., & Madsen, M. Cultural patterns and the social behavior of children: Two studies from Papua New Guinea. *Ethos,* 1981, *9,* 201–216.

Lancy, D. F., Souviney, R., & Kada, V. Intra-cultural variation in cognitive development: Conservation of length among the Imbonggu. *International Journal of Behavioral Development,* 1981, *4,* 455–468.

Lancy, D. F., & Strathern, A. J. "Making twos": Pairing as an alternative to the taxonomic mode of representation. *American Anthropologist,* 1981, *83,* 389–408.

Landtman, G. *The Kiwai Papuans of British New Guinea: A nature-born instance of Rousseau's ideal community.* London: Macmillan, 1927.

Langness, L. L. Some problems in the conceptualization of highlands social structure. *American Anthropologist,* 1964, *66,* 162–182.

Lankford, F. G. Some computational strategies of seventh grade pupils (Final Report Project No. 2-c-d3). Charlottesville, Va.: HEW/DE National Center for Educational Research and Development and the Center for Advanced Studies, University of Virginia, October 1972.

Latham, M. C. Malnutrition and consequent behavioral development. *Ohio's Health,* 1969, *21,* 11–16.

Lave, J. *Tailored learning: Education and cognitive skills among tribal craftsmen in West Africa.* Cambridge, Mass.: Harvard University Press, in press.

Lawson, A. M-space: Is it a constraint on conservation reasoning ability? *Journal of Experimental Child Psychology,* 1976, *22,* 40–49.

Laycock, D. C. Observations on number systems and semantics. In S. A. Würm (Ed.), *Papuan languages and the New Guinea linguistic scene.* Canberra, Australia: ANU, 1977.

Lean, G. A., & Clements, M. A. Spatial ability, visual imagery, and mathematical performance. *Educational Studies in Mathematics,* in press.

Leinhardt, G., & Seewald, A. Overlap: What's tested, what's taught? *Journal of Educational Measurement,* 1981, *18,* 85–96.

Leinhardt, G., Seewald, A. M., & Engle, M. Learning what's taught: Sex differences in instruction. *Journal of Educational Psychology,* 1979, *71,* 432–439.

Leroy, J. D. *Kewa reciprocity: Cooperation and exchange in a New Guinea highlands culture.* Unpublished doctoral dissertation, University of British Columbia, Vancouver, 1975.

Levin, P. Andra Community School field report. *Indigenous Mathematics Project Working Paper No. 6.* Port Moresby, Papua New Guinea: UNESCO/Education, 1980.

Levinson, D. Subsistence systems as a measure of cultural complexity. *Current Anthropology,* 1980, *21,* 128–129.

Levinson, P. J., & Carpenter, R. L. An analysis of analogical reasoning in children. *Child Development,* 1974, *48,* 857–861.

Lévi-Strauss, C. *The savage mind.* Chicago: University of Chicago Press, 1966.

Lévi-Strauss, C. *The raw and the cooked.* New York: Harper & Row, 1969.

Lévy-Bruhl, L. *How natives think* (L. A. Clare, trans.). New York: Knopf, 1926. (Originally published, 1910.)

Lewis, D. *We the navigators.* Honolulu: University of Hawaii Press, 1972.

Lewis, D. Observations on route finding and spatial orientation among the aboriginal peoples of the Western Desert region of Central Australia. *Oceania*, 1976, *46*(4), 249–282.

Lewis, G., & Mulford, W. R. Conservation of time amongst Papua New Guinea school children: An exploratory study. *PNG Journal of Education*, 1974, *10*(2), 18–38.

Lineberger, J. Ororo Community School field report. *Indigenous Mathematics Project Working Paper No. 7*. Port Moresby, Papua New Guinea: UNESCO/Education, 1980.

Lomax, A., & Arensberg, C. M. A worldwide evolutionary classification of cultures by subsistence. *Current Anthropology*, 1977, *18*, 659–708.

Lounsbury, F. L. The structural analysis of kinship semantics. In S. A. Tyler (Ed.), *Cognitive anthropology*. New York: Holt, Rinehart, & Winston, 1971.

Lovell, K. *The growth of understanding in mathematics: Kindergarten through grade 3*. New York: Holt, Rinehart & Winston, 1971.

Lucy, J. A., & Shweder, R. A. Whorf and his critics: Linguistic and non-linguistic influences on color memory. *American Anthropologist*, 1979, *81*, 581–615.

Lumsden, C. J., & Wilson, E. O. *Genes, mind and culture: The coevolutionary process*. Cambridge, Mass.: Harvard University Press, 1981.

Luria, A. R. L. S. Vygotsky and the problem of functional localization. *Soviet Psychology*, 1967, *5*, 53–57.

Luria, A. R. *Cognitive development: Its cultural and social foundations*. Cambridge, Mass.: Harvard University Press, 1976.

Lyons, J. *Introduction to theoretical linguistics*. Cambridge, Mass.: Cambridge University Press, 1968.

McGrew, W. C. Habitat and the adaptiveness of primate intelligence. *The Behavioral and Brain Sciences*, 1979, *2*, 393.

McKay, S. R. Growth and nutrition of infants in the Western Highlands of New Guinea. *Medical Journal of Australia*, March 1960, *47*, 452–459.

McLuhan, M. *Understanding media: The extentions of man*. New York: McGraw-Hill, 1964.

McNamara, V. Some experiences of Papua New Guinea primary schools. In D. F. Lancy (Ed.), *The Community School*, special issue of the *PNG Journal of Education* 1979, *15*, 10–26.

McNamara, V. Practicalities. In B. Anderson (Ed.), *The right to learn*. Port Moresby, Papua New Guinea: Department of Education, 1981.

Madsen, M., & Lancy, D. F. Cooperative and competitive behavior: Experiments related to ethnic identity and urbanization in Papua New Guinea. *Journal of Cross-Cultural Psychology*, 1981, *12*, 389–408.

Malinowski, B. The problem of meaning in primitive languages. In C. K. Ogden & I. A. Richards (Eds.), *The meaning of meaning* (10th ed.). New York: Harcourt, 1952.

Mandler, J. M., Scribner, S., Cole, M., & DeForest, M. Cross-cultural invariance in story recall. *Child Development*, 1980, *51*, 19–26.

Markman, E. M., & Siebert, J. Classes and collections: Internal organization and resulting holistic properties. *Cognitive Psychology*, 1976, *8*, 561–577.

Mead, M. An investigation of the thought of primitive children with special reference to animism. *Journal of the Royal Anthropological Institute*, 1932, *62*, 173–190.

Mead, M. *Growing up in New Guinea*. New York: Mentor, 1963.

Meek, C., & Feril, N. *A pilot study into the level of comprehension of some words taken from the New Guinea Community Schools Mathematics Project* (Tech. Rep. 3). Lae, Papua New Guinea: Papua New Guinea University of Technology, Mathematics Education Centre, 1978.

Menninger, K. *Number words and number symbols*. Cambridge, Mass.: MIT Press, 1969.

Metzger, D., & Williams, G. E. Procedures and results in the study of native categories: Tzeltal firewood. *American Anthropologist*, 1966, *68*, 389–407.

Mikloucho-Maclay, N. N. *New Guinea diaries 1871–1883.* (C. L. Sentinella, trans.). Madang, Papua New Guinea: Kristen Press, 1975.

Miller, G. A. The magical number seven, plus or minus two: Some limits on our capacity for processing information. *Psychological Review*, 1956, *63*, 81–97.

Miller, S. A. Extinction of Piagetian concepts: An updating. *Merrill-Palmer Quarterly*, 1976, *22*, 257–281.

Miller, S. A., Brownell, C. A., & Zuiker, H. Cognitive certainty in children: Effects of concept, developmental level and method of assessment. *Developmental Psychology*, 1977, *13*, 236–245.

Miller-Souviney, B. Teaching school mathematics: A comparison of five sites. *Indigenous Mathematics Project Working paper No. 18.* Port Moresby, Papua New Guinea: UNESCO/Education, 1981.

Monckberg, F. Effect of early marasmic malnutrition on subsequent physical and psychological development. In N. S. Scrimshaw & J. E. Gordon (Eds.), *Malnutrition, learning and behavior.* Cambridge, Mass.: MIT Press, 1968.

Monckberg, F. The effect of malnutrition on physical growth and brain development. In J. W. Prescott *et al.* (Eds.), *Brain Function and Malnutrition: Neuropsychological methods of assessment.* New York: Wiley, 1975.

Morauta, L. Malalauas in Port Moresby. In R. J. May (Ed.), *The urban household survey: Town profiles.* Port Moresby, Papua New Guinea: Institute for Applied Social and Economic Research, 1979.

Munroe, R. L., & Munroe, R. H. Levels of obedience among U.S. and East African children in an experimental task. *Journal of Cross-Cultural Psychology*, 1975, *6*, 498–503.

Munroe, R. L., & Munroe, R. H. Perspectives suggested by anthropological data. In H. C. Triandis & W. W. Lambert (Eds.), *Handbook of cross-cultural psychology: Perspectives* (Vol. 1). Boston: Allyn & Bacon, 1980.

Murdock, G. P. Evolution in social organization. In B. J. Meggers (Ed.), *Evolution and anthropology.* Washington, D. C.: Anthropological Society of Washington, 1959.

Murphy, W. P. *A semantic and logical analysis of Kpelle proverb metaphors of secrecy.* Unpublished doctoral dissertation, Stanford University, 1976.

Murray, F. B., & Armstrong, S. L. Adult non-conservation of numerical equivalence. *Merrill-Palmer Quarterly*, 1978, *24*, 255–263.

Needham, R. (Ed.), *Right and left: Essays on dual symbolic classification.* Chicago: University of Chicago Press, 1973.

Nelson, K. Structure and strategy in learning to talk. *Monographs of the Society for Research in Child Development*, 1973, *38*(1–2, Serial No. 149).

Nelson, K. Concept, word and sentence: Interrelations in acquisition and development. *Psychological Review*, 1974, *81*, 267–285.

Nietschmann, B., & Nietschmann, J. Good dugong, bad dugong, bad turtle, good turtle. *Natural History*, 1981, *90*(5), 54–63.

Ninio, A., & Bruner, J. S. The achievement and antecedents of labelling. *Journal of Child Language*, 1978, *5*, 1–15.

Norgan, N. G., Ferro-Luzzi, A., & Durnin, J. V. G. A. The energy and nutrient intake and the energy expenditure of 204 New Guinea adults. *Philosophical Transactions of the Royal Society of London*, 1974, *268*, 309–348.

Nutrition section. *Evidence of malnutrition among children under 5 years of age attending child health clinics in Papua New Guinea.* Unpublished tables. Port Moresby, Papua New Guinea: PNG Department of Health, 1977.

Ohtsuka, R. The sago eaters: An ecological discussion with special reference to the Oriono Papuans. In J. Allen, J. Golson, & R. Jones (Eds.), *Sunda and Sahul: Prehistoric Studies in Southeast Asia, Melanesia, and Australia.* New York: Academic Press, 1977.

Olson, D. R. On conceptual strategies. In J. S. Bruner, R. R. Olver, & P. M. Greenfield, (Eds.), *Studies in cognitive growth.* New York: Wiley, 1966.

Olson, D. R. Culture, technology and intellect. In L. B. Resnick (Ed.), *The nature of intelligence*. Hillsdale, N.J.: Erlbaum, 1976.

Olver, R. R., & Hornsby, J. R. On equivalence. In J. S. Bruner, R. R. Olver, & P. M. Greenfield (Eds.), *Studies in cognitive growth*. New York: Wiley, 1966.

Osgood, C. E., May, W. H., & Miron, M. S. *Cross-cultural universals of objective meaning*. Urbana, Ill.: University of Illinois Press, 1975.

Oswalt, W. H. *Habitat and technology: The evolution of hunting*. New York: Holt, Rinehart & Winston, 1973.

Oswalt, W. H. *An anthropological analysis of food-getting technology*. New York: Wiley, 1976.

Paige, J. M., & Simon, H. A. Cognitive processes in solving algebra word problems. In B. Kleinmutz (Ed.), *Problem solving*. New York: Wiley, 1966.

Papua New Guinea Education Plan 1976–1980. Port Moresby, Papua New Guinea: Government Printer, 1976.

Parker, S. T. Piaget's sensorimotor series in an infant Macaque: A model for comparing unstereotyped behavior and intelligence in human and non-human primates. In S. Chevalier-Skolnikoff & F. E. Poirer (Eds.), *Primate bio-social development*. New York: Garland, 1977.

Parker, S. T., & Gibson, K. R. A developmental model of the evolution of language and intelligence in early hominids. *The Behavioral and Brain Sciences*, 1979, *2*, 367–381.

Pascual-Leone, J. A mathematical model for the transition rule in Piaget's developmental stages. *Acta Psychologica*, 1970, *63*, 301–345.

Peluffo, N. Les notions des conservation et de causalité chez les enfants provenant de differents millieux physiques at socio-culturelles. *Achives de Psychologie*, 1962, *38*, 275–291.

Peluffo, N. Culture and cognitive problems. *International Journal of Psychology*, 1967, *2*, 187–198.

Perey, A. *Oksapmin society and world view*. Unpublished doctoral dissertation, Columbia University, 1973.

Pharoah, P., Connolly, K., Hetzel, B., & Ekins. R. Maternal thyroid function and motor competence in the child. *Developments in Medical and Child Neurology*, 1981, *23*, 76–82.

Philp, H., & Kelly, M. Product and process in cognitive development: Some comparative data on the performance of school age children in different cultures. *British Journal of Educational Psychology*, 1974, *44*, 248–265.

Piaget, J. *The moral judgement of the child*. Glencoe, Ill.: Free Press, 1948.

Piaget, J. *The child's conception of number*. New York: Humanities Press, 1952.

Piaget, J. *Play, dreams and imitation in childhood*. New York: Norton, 1962.

Piaget, J. Need and significance of cross-cultural studies in genetic psychology. *International Journal of Psychology*, 1966, *1*, 3–13.

Piaget, J. *Structuralism*. New York: Harper & Row, 1970.

Piaget, J. Problems of equilibration. In C. Nodine, J. Gallagher, & R. Humphrey (Eds.), *Piaget and Inhelder on equilibration*. Philadelphia: Jean Piaget Society, 1972.

Piaget, J. *The development of thought: Equilibration of cognitive structures* (A. Rosin, trans.). New York: Viking, 1977.

Piaget, J., Inhelder, B., & Szeminska, A. *The child's conception of geometry* (E. Lunzer, trans.). New York: Basic Books, 1960.

Pinard, A., & Lavoie, G. Perception and conservation of length: Comparative study of Rwandese and French Canadian children. *Perceptual and Motor Skills*, 1974, *39*, 363–368.

Posner, M. I. *Cognition: An introduction*. Glenview, Ill.: Scott, Foresman, 1976.

Potter, M. C. Mundane symbolism: The relation among objects, names and ideas. In N. R. Smith & M. B. Franklin (Eds.), *Symbolic functioning in childhood*. Hillsdale, N. J.: Erlbaum, 1979.

Powell, J. M. Ethnobotany. In K. Paijmans (Ed.), *New Guinea vegetation*. Canberra, Australia: Australian National University, 1976.

Powell, J. M., Kulunga, A., Moge, R., Pono, C., Zimike, F., & Golson, J. *Agricultural traditions of the Mt. Hagen area* (Occasional Paper No. 12). Port Moresby, Papua New Guinea: University of Papua Guinea, Department of Geography, 1975.

Premack, D. *Intelligence in man and ape*. New York: Wiley, 1976.

Price, J. R. Cognitive development in Papua New Guinea: A survey of conservation research. *International Journal of Psychology*, 1978, *13*, 1–24.

Price, J. R., & Nidue, J. Conservation of area: A quantitative study. *PNG Journal of Education*, 1974, *5*(2), 17–25.

Price-Williams, D. R. A study concerning concepts of conservation of quantities among primitive children. *Acta Psychologica*, 1961, *18*, 297–305.

Price-Williams, D. R. Abstract and concrete modes of classification in a primitive people. *British Journal of Educational Psychology*, 1962, *32*, 50–61.

Price-Williams, D. R., Gordon, W., & Ramirez, M. Skill and conservation: A study of pottery-making children. *Developmental Psychology*, 1969, *1*, 769.

Prince, J. R. The effect of Western education on science conceptualization in New Guinea. *British Journal of Educational Psychology*, 1968, *68*, 64–74.

Prince, J. R. *Science concepts in a Pacific culture*. Sydney, Australia: Angus & Robertson, 1969.

Pulliam, R., & Dunford, C. *Programmed to learn: An essay in the pre-evolution of culture*. New York: Columbia University Press, 1980.

Pumuye, H. The Kewa calender. In D. F. Lancy (Ed.), *The Indigenous Mathematics Project*, special issue of the *PNG Journal of Education*, 1978 *14*, 47–56.

Rappaport, R. A. *Pigs for the ancestors*. New Haven, Conn.: Yale University Press, 1968.

Rawlinson, R. A cross-cultural study of intelligence in Papua New Guinea and Tasmania. *New Guinea Psychologist Monograph No. 6*, 1974.

Rawson, H. The function of reading in the transition to concrete and formal operations. In B. Z. Presseisen, D. Goldstein, & M. H. Appel (Eds.), *Topics in cognitive development: Language and operational thought* (Vol. 2). New York: Plenum, 1978.

Resnick, L. B., & Ford, W. W. *The psychology of mathematics for instruction*. Hillsdale, N. J.: LEA, 1981.

Resnick, D. P., & Resnick, L. B. The nature of literacy: An historical exploration. *Harvard Educational Review*, 1977, *47*, 370–385.

Rhoads, J. G., & Friedlander, J. S. *A follow-up study of child and adolescent growth in the Solomon Islands*. Paper presented at the Annual Meeting, American Association of Physical Anthropologists, Niagara Falls, April 1980.

Rindos, D. Symbiosis, instability and the origins and spread of agriculture: A new model. *Current Anthropology*, 1980, *21*, 751–772.

Rinsland, H. D. *A basic vocabulary of elementary school children*. New York: Macmillan, 1945.

Roakeina, G. (Ed.) Committee of Enquiry into Standards of High School Students Entering Colleges. Port Moresby, Papua New Guinea: Papua New Guinea Department of Education, 1977.

Robert, M., & Charbonneau, C. Extinction of liquid conservation by modelling: Three indicators of its artificiality. *Child Development*, 1978, *49*, 194–200.

Roberts, J. M. The self-management of cultures. In W. Goodenough (Ed.), *Explorations in cultural anthropology*. Chicago: Aldine, 1964.

Roberts, J. M., Arth, M., & Bush, R. R. Games in culture. *American Anthropologist*, 1959, *61*, 597–605.

Roberts, R. E. Primary mathematics in Papua New Guinea. In D. F. Lancy (Ed.), *The*

Indigenous Mathematics Project, special issue of the *PNG Journal of Education*, 1978, *14*, 205–220.

Roberts, R. E. *Primary mathematics learning: A study of the relationship between teacher preparedness and pupil achievement in Papua New Guinea primary schools*. Unpublished Master's thesis. University of Papua New Guinea, 1981.

Roberts, R. E., & Kada, V. The primary mathematics classroom. In D. F. Lancy (Ed.), *The Community School*, special issue of the *PNG Journal of Education*,1979,*15*,174–201.

Rogers, C. A. (Ed.), *National education strategy: Papua New Guinea education plan review and proposals*. Port Moresby, Papua New Guinea: Institute of Applied Social and Economic Research Monograph No. 9, 1979.

Rogoff, B. Schooling and the development of cognitive skills. In H. C. Triandis & A. Heron (Eds.), *Handbook of cross-cultural psychology: Developmental psychology* (Vol. 4). Boston: Allyn & Bacon, 1981.

Roleasmalik, P. M. *Traditional games of Papua New Guinea*. Port Moresby, Papua New Guinea: Government Printer, 1979.

Ros, L. *Transition rates and mathematics achievement in five developing countries*. Unpublished manuscript, Goroka Teacher's College, 1980.

Rosaldo, M. Z. Metaphors and folk classification. *Southwest Journal of Anthropology*, 1972, *28*, 83–99.

Rosch (Heider), E. R. Universals in color naming and meaning. *Journal of Experimental Psychology*, 1972, *93*, 10–20.

Rosch, E. Human categorization. In N. Warren (Ed.), *Advances in cross-cultural psychology*. London: Academic Press, 1977.

Rosch, E. Principles of categorization. In E. Rosch & B. B. Lloyd (Eds.), *Cognition and categorization*. Hillsdale, N.J.: LEA, 1978.

Rosch, E., & Mervis, C. B. Family resemblance: Studies in the internal structure of categories. *Cognitive Psychology*, 1975, *7*, 573–605.

Rosch, E., Mervis, C. B., Gray, W. D., Johnson, D. M., & Boyes-Braem, P. Basic objects in natural categories. *Cognitive Psychology*, 1976, *7*, 573–605.

Rosskoph, M. F., Steffe, L. P., & Taback, S. (Eds.), *Piagetian cognitive developmental research and mathematics education*. Washington, D. C.: National Council for Teachers of Mathematics, 1971.

Rowe, B. Muglamp community school field report. *Indigenous Mathematics Project Working Paper No. 10*. Port Moresby, Papua New Guinea: UNESCO/Education, 1980.

Rubel, P. G., & Rosman, A. *Your own pigs you may not eat: A comparative study of New Guinea societies*. Chicago: University of Chicago Press, 1978.

Rundus, D. Negative effects of using list items as recall cues. *Journal of Verbal Learning and Verbal Behavior*, 1973, *12*, 43–50.

Rutishauser, I. H. E., & Whitehead, R. G. Energy intake and expenditure in 1–3-year-old-Ugandan children living in a rural environment. *British Journal of Nutrition*, 1972, *28*, 145–152.

Ryan, D. *Social change among the Toaripi, Papua*. Unpublished master's thesis, University of Sydney, 1965.

Ryan, D. *Rural and urban villagers: A bi-local social system in Papua New Guinea.* Unpublished doctoral dissertation, University of Hawaii, 1971.

Sahlins, M. *Stone Age economics*. Chicago: Aldine, 1972.

Sahlins, M. *Culture and practical reason*. Chicago: University of Chicago Press, 1976.

Salzman, Z. A method for analyzing numerical systems. *Word*, 1950, *6*, 78–83.

Sankoff, G. Cognitive variability and New Guinea social organization: The Buang Dgwa. *American Anthropologist*, 1972, *74*, 555–566.

Satterthwaite, L. D. *A comparative study of Australian aboriginal food procurement tech-*

nologies. Unpublished doctoral dissertation, University of California at Los Angeles, 1980.

Saxe, G. B. A developmental analysis of notational counting. *Child Development*, 1977, *48*, 1512–1520.

Saxe, G. B. Children's counting: The early formation of numerical symbols. *New Directions for Child Development*, 1979, *1*(3), 73–84. (a)

Saxe, G. B. Developmental relations between notational counting and number conservation. *Child Development*, 1979, *50*, 180–187. (b)

Saxe, G. B. A comparative analysis of the acquisition of numeration: Studies from Papua New Guinea. *The Quarterly Newsletter of the Laboratory for Comparative Human Cognition*, 1979, *1*(3), 37–43. (c)

Saxe, G. B. The changing form of numerical reasoning among the Oksapmin. *Indigenous Mathematics Project Working Paper No. 14.* Port Moresby, Papua New Guinea: UNESCO/Education, 1981 (a)

Saxe, G. B. Body parts as numerals: A developmental analysis of numeration among the Oksapmin in Papua New Guinea. *Child Development*, 1981, *52*, 306–316. (b)

Saxe, G. B. Culture and the development of numerical cognition: Studies among the Oksapmin of Papua New Guinea. In C. J. Brainerd (Ed.), *Children's logical and mathematical cognition*. Berlin: Springer-Verlag, in press. (a)

Saxe, G. B. When fourth can precede second: A cross-cultural analysis of children's understanding of a birth order numerational system among an island population in Papua New Guinea. *Journal of Cross-Cultural Psychology*, in press. (b)

Saxe, G. B. *Culture, counting and number conservation.* Unpublished Manuscript, n.d.

Saxe, G. B., & Moylan, T. *The development of measurement operations among the Oksapmin of Papua New Guinea.* Paper presented at the Symposium on Culture and Mathematics, American Educational Research Association, New York, March 1982.

Schank, R. C., & Abelson, R. P. *Scripts, plans, goals and understanding.* Hillsdale, N. J.: Erlbaum, 1977.

Schiefflin, B. B. Getting it together: An ethnographic approach to the development of communicative competence. In E. Ochs & B. B. Schiefflin (Eds.), *Developmental pragmatics*. New York: Academic Press, 1979.

Schwartz, T. The size and shape of culture. In F. Barth (Ed.), *Scale and social organization*. Oslo: Universitets Forlaget, 1978.

Schwartz, T. *The acquisition of culture.* Unpublished manuscript, University of California, San Diego, 1979.

Schwartzman, H. B. *Transformations: The anthropology of children's play*. New York: Plenum, 1978.

Scribner, S. Developmental aspects of categorized recall in a West African society. *Cognitive Psychology*, 1974, *6*, 475–494.

Scribner, S., & Cole, M. The cognitive consequences of formal and informal education. *Science*, 1973, *182*, 553–559.

Scribner, S., & Cole, M. Literacy without schooling: Testing for intellectual effects. *Harvard Educational Review*, 1978, *48*, 448–461.

Scribner, S., & Cole, M. *The psychology of literacy*. Cambridge, Mass.: Harvard University Press, 1981.

Seagrim, G., & Lendon, R. *Furnishing the mind: A comparative study of cognitive development in central Australian aborigines*. Sydney, Australia: Academic Press, 1980.

Shankman, P. *Migration and underdevelopment: The case of Western Samoa*. Boulder, Colo.: Westview Press, 1976.

Sharp, L. Steel axes for Stone-Age Australians. *Human Organization*, 1952, *11*, 17–22.

Sharp, D., Cole, M., & Lave, C. Education and cognitive development: The evidence from experimental research. *Monographs of the Society for Research in Child Development*,

1979, *44*(1, 2, Serial No. 178).

Shea, J. Conservation in community-school children in Papua New Guinea. In D. F. Lancy (Ed.), *The Indigenous Mathematics Project*, special issue of the *PNG Journal of Education* 1978, *14*, 147–172. (a)

Shea, J. The study of cognitive development in Papua New Guinea. In D. F. Lancy (Ed.), *The Indigenous Mathematics Project*, special issue of the *PNG Journal of Education*, 1978, *14*, 89–116. (b)

Shea, J., & Yerua, G. Conservation in community-school children in Papua New Guinea. *International Journal of Psychology*, 1980, *15*, 11–25.

Shulman, L. S. The psychology of school subjects: A premature obituary? *Journal of Research in Science Teaching*, 1974, *4*, 943–948.

Shweder, R. A. Likeness and likelihood in everyday thought: Magical thinking in judgments about personality. *Current Anthropology*, 1977, *18*, 637–658.

Siegel, L. S. The role of spatial arrangement and heterogeneity in the development of numerical equivalence. *Canadian Journal of Psychology*, 1973, *27*, 351–355.

Siegel, L. S. Development of number concepts: Ordering and correspondence operations and the role of length cues. *Developmental Psychology*, 1974, *10*, 907–912.

Siegel, L. S. The relationship of language and thought in the preoperational child: A reconsideration of nonverbal alternatives to Piagetian tasks. In L. S. Siegel & C. J. Brainerd (Eds.), *Alternatives to Piaget*. New York: Academic Press, 1978.

Siegler, R. Developmental sequences within and between concepts. *Monographs of the Society for Research in Child Development*, 1981, *46*(2, Serial No. 189).

Sinclair, H. *Young children's acquisition of language and understanding of mathematics*. Plenary Address, Fourth International Congress for Mathematics Education, Berkeley, California, August 1980.

Singleton, J. Implications of education as cultural transmission. In G. D. Spindler (Ed.), *Education and cultural process*. New York: Holt, Rinehart & Winston, 1974.

Skemp, R. R. Reflective intelligence and mathematics. *British Journal of Educational Psychology*, 1961, *31*, 45–54.

Skemp, R. R. *Mathematics as an activity of our intelligence*. Paper presented at the Seventh Annual Conference for Diagnostic and Prescriptive Mathematics, Vancouver, April 1980.

Smilansky, S. *The effects of sociodramatic play on disadvantaged pre-school children*. New York: Wiley, 1968.

Smith, G. Counting and classification on Kiwai Island. In D. F. Lancy (Ed.), *The Indigenous Mathematics Project*, special issue of the *PNG Journal of Education*, 1978, *14*, 57–72.

Souviney, R. J. Assessment administration guide. *Indigenous Mathematics Project Working Paper No. 3*. Port Moresby, Papua New Guinea: UNESCO/Education, 1980. (a)

Souviney, R. J. Learning to compute. *Indigenous Mathematics Project Working Paper No. 1*. Port Moresby, Papua New Guinea: UNESCO/Education, 1980. (b)

Souviney, R. J. Strategies for mathematical problem solving. *Indigenous Mathematics Project Working Paper No. 2*. Port Moresby, Papua New Guinea: UNESCO/Education, 1980. (c)

Souviney, R. J. Teaching and learning mathematics in the Community Schools of Papua New Guinea. *Indigenous Mathematics Project Working Paper No. 20*. Port Moresby, Papua New Guinea: UNESCO/Education, 1981.

Souviney, R. J. Kada, V., & Malaga, D. *The Indigenous Mathematics Project of Papua New Guinea*. Paper presented at the Fourth International Congress for Mathematics Education, Berkeley, California, August 1980.

Stanton, R. Secondary Schools Community Extension Project SSCEP: An innovation in high school education. In B. Anderson (Ed.), *Educational innovation in Papua New Guinea*. Port Moresby, Papua New Guinea: UNESCO/Education, 1979.

Steffe, L. The relationship of conservation of numerousness to problem-solving abilities of first-grade children. *Arithmetic Teacher*, 1968, *15*, 47–52.

Stevenson, H. W., Parker, T., Wilkinson, A., Bonnevaux, B., & Gonzalez, M. Schooling, environment and cognitive development: A cross-cultural study. *Monographs of the Society for Research in Child Development*, 1978, *43*(3, Serial No. 175).

Strathern, A. J. *The rope of Moka*. Cambridge: Cambridge University Press, 1971.

Strathern, A. J. *One father, one blood*. London: Tavistock, 1972.

Strathern, A. J. Mathematics in the Moka. *Papua New Guinea Journal of Education*, 1977. *13*(1), 16–20.

Strathern, A. J. *Ongka: A self-account of a New Guinea big-man*. New York: St. Martin's Press, 1979.

Strathern, A. J., & Strathern, A. M. *Self-decoration in Mt. Hagen*. London: Duckworth, 1971.

Stross, B. Acquisition of botanical terminology by Tzeltal children. In M. Edmondson (Ed.), *Meaning in Mayan languages*. The Hague: Mouton, 1973.

Sturtevant, W. C. Studies in ethnoscience. In A. K. Romney & R. G. D'Andrade (Eds.), *Trans-cultural studies in cognition. American Anthropologist* (special issue), 1964, *66*(3), part 2.

Sullivan, P. *The standards debate: An alternative strategy* (Tech. Rep. 15). Lae, Papua New Guinea: Papua New Guinea University of Technology, Mathematics Education Centre, 1981.

Sutton-Smith, B. The role of play in cognitive development. In R. E. Heron & B. Sutton-Smith (Eds.), *Child's play*. New York: Wiley, 1971.

Thompson, N. *Colour and chaos*. London: Robert Hale, 1976.

Thune, C. Number and counting in Loboda: An example of a non-numerically oriented culture. In D. F. Lancy (Ed.), *The Indigenous Mathematics Project*, special issue of the *PNG Journal of Education* 1978, *14*, 73–84.

Tovirika, W. F., Korim, H., & Dubé, L. S. A proposed categorization system for student errors in mathematics. In P. Clarkson (Ed.), *Research in mathematics education in Papua New Guinea*. Proceedings of the First Mathematics Education Conference. Lae, Papua New Guinea: Papua New Guinea University of Technology, Mathematics Education Centre, 1981.

Townsend, P. K. Sago production in a New Guinea economy. *Human Ecology*, 1974, *2*, 217–236.

Townshend, P. African Mankala in anthropological perspective. *Current Anthropology*, 1979, *20*, 794–796.

Tulving, E. Theoretical issues in free recall. In T. R. Dixon & D. L. Horton (Eds.), *Verbal behavior and general behavior theory*. Englewood Cliffs, N. J.: Prentice-Hall, 1968.

Turnbull, C. *The mountain people*. New York: Simon & Schuster, 1972.

Turner, V. *Dramas, fields and metaphors: Symbolic action in human society*. Ithaca, N. Y.: Cornell University Press, 1974.

Tyler, S. A. Introduction. In S. A. Tyler (Ed.), *Cognitive anthropology*. New York: Holt, Rinehart, & Winston, 1969.

Tyler, S. A. *The said and the unsaid: Mind, meaning and culture*. New York: Academic Press, 1978.

Van Esterik, P. Commentary. *American Ethnologist*, 1978, *5*, 404–405.

Van Esterik, P. Commentary. *American Ethnologist*, 1979, *6*, 408.

Van Gennep, A. *The rites of passage* (2nd ed.). Chicago: University of Chicago Press, 1960.

Vygotsky, L. S. *Thought and language*. Cambridge, Mass.: MIT Press, 1962.

Vygotsky, L. S. *Mind in society*. Cambridge, Mass.: Harvard University Press, 1978.

Wagner, D. A. Memories of Morocco: The influence of schooling and environment on memory. *Cognitive Psychology*, 1978, *10*, 1–28.

Wagner, R. *The curse of Souw*. Chicago: University of Chicago Press, 1967.

Wallace, A. R. *Natural selection and tropical nature*. London: Macmillan, 1891.

Wang, M. C., Resnick, L. B., & Boozer, R. F. The sequence of development of some early mathematics behaviors. *Child Development*, 1971, *42*, 1767–1778.

Warren, N. Malnutrition and mental development. *Psychological Bulletin*, 1973, *80*, 324–328.

Wason, P. C., & Johnson-Laird, P. N. *Psychology of reasoning: Structure and content*. Cambridge, Mass.: Harvard University Press, 1972.

Weisz, J. R., & Zigler, E. Cognitive development in retarded and non-retarded persons: Piagetian tests of the similar sequence hypothesis. *Psychological Bulletin*, 1979, *86*, 831–851.

Werner, E. E. *Cross-cultural child development*. Monterey, Calif.: Brooks–Cole, 1979.

Werner, H. *The comparative psychology of mental development* (Rev. ed.). New York: International Universities Press, 1957.

West, F. *Hubert Murray: The Australian pro-consul*. Melbourne, Australia: Melbourne University Press, 1968.

White, J. P. New Guinea: The first phase in Oceanic settlement. In R. C. Green & M. Kelly (Eds.), *Studies in Oceanic culture history*. Honolulu: Pacific Anthropological Records, 1971.

White, J. P. Crude, colourless and unenterprising? Prehistorians and their views on the Stone Age in Sunda and Sahul. In J. Allen, J. Golson, & R. Jones (Eds.), *Sunda: Prehistoric studies in Southeast Asia, Melanesia, and Australia*. New York: Academic Press, 1977.

White, J. P., Crook, K. A. W., & Buxton, B. P. Kosipe: A late Pleistocene site in the Papuan highlands. *Proceedings of the Pre-Historic Society*, 1970, *36*, 152–170.

White, L. A. *The evolution of culture*. New York: McGraw-Hill, 1959.

Whiting, B. B. (Ed.), *Six cultures: Studies on child rearing*. New York: Wiley, 1963.

Whorf, B. L. *Language, thought and reality*. Cambridge, Mass.: MIT Press, 1956.

Wilkinson, A. Counting strategies and semantic analysis as applied to class inclusion. *Cognitive Psychology*, 1976, *8*, 64–85.

Williams, T. R. *Introduction to socialization*. St. Louis: Mosby, 1972.

Winer, G. A. Class inclusion reasoning in children: A review of the empirical literature. *Child Devleopment*, 1980, *51*, 309–328.

Winick, M. *Malnutrition and brain development*. New York: Oxford University Press, 1976.

Winick, M. Nutrition and brain development. *Natural History*, 1980, *89*(12), 6–13.

Witkowski, S. R., & Brown, C. H. Lexical encoding sequences and language change: Color terminology systems. *American Anthropologist*, 1981, *83*, 13–27.

Wohlberg, K. The teacher as missionary. In D. F. Lancy (Ed.), *The community school*, special issue of the *PNG Journal of Education*, 1979, *15*, 120–136.

Wohlwill, J. F. Responses to class inclusion questions for verbally and pictorially presented items. *Child Development*, 1968, *39*, 449–465.

Wolfers, E. P. Counting and numbers. In P. Ryan (Ed.), *The encyclopedia of Papua New Guinea*. Melbourne, Australia: Melbourne University Press, 1972.

Worsley, P. *The trumpet shall sound*. (2nd ed.). New York: Schocken Books, 1968.

Würm, S. A. Australian New Guinea Highlands languages and the distribution of their typological features. *American Anthropologist*, 1964, *66*(4), 77–97.

Würm, S. A. The classification of Papuan languages and its problems. *Linguistic Communication*, 1972, *6*, 118–178.

Würm, S. A. The Kiwaian language family. In K. Franklin (Ed.), *The linguistic situation in the Gulf district and adjacent areas, Papua New Guinea*. Canberra, Australia: Australian National University, 1973.

Yesner, D. R. Maritime hunter–gatherers: Ecology and prehistory. *Current Anthropology*, 1980, *21*, 727–750.

Zaslavsky, C. *Africa counts: Number and pattern in African culture.* Boston: Prindle, Weber & Schmidt, 1973.

Zelenietz, M. *After the despot: Changing patterns of leadership and social change in Kilenge.* Unpublished doctoral dissertation, McMaster University, 1980.

Zelenietz, M., & Grant, J. *The ambiguities of education in Kilenge, Papua New Guinea.* Paper presented at the International Conference on Education in Oceania, Victoria, Canada, March 1980. (a)

Zelenietz, M., & Grant, J. Kilenge *Narogo*: Ceremonies, resources and prestige in a West New Britain society. *Oceania*, 1980, *51*(2), 98–117. (b)

Author Index

Numbers in italics indicate pages on which complete references can be found.

A

Abelson, R.P., 64, *230*
Allen, A.L., 185, *213*
Allen, J., 15, 40, *213*
Anderson, D.R., 154, *213*
Anglin, J.M., 64,67,139, *213*
Annis, R.C., 74, *214*
Ardrey, R., 202, *213*
Arensberg, C.M., 120, *225*
Armstrong, S.L., 155, *226*
Arth, M., 117, 119, *228*
Austin, G.A., 64, *215*

B

Bajpai, A., 186, *218*
Beck, B.B., 207, *213*
Beilin, H., 154, 204, *213*
Bellwood, P., 15, *213*
Berlin, B., 64,67,68,111,113,169, *213,214*
Berliner, D., 193, *218*
Bernstein, B., 208, *214*

Berry, J.W., 74, *214*
Biersack, A., 166, *214*
Birdsell, J.B., 14, *214*
Bishop, A., 181, 185, *214*
Bloom, A.H., 139, *214*
Bloom, L., 139, *221*
Blurton-Jones, N., 201, *214*
Bobrow, D.G., 67, *214*
Boden, M., 203, *214*
Bonnevaux, B., 123, *232*
Boozer, R.F., 187, *233*
Bourdieu, P., 119,120, *214*
Bovet, M.C., 84, *214*
Bower, T.G., 196, *214*
Bowles, S., 207, *214*
Boyes-Braem, P., 111, 114, *229*
Brainerd, C.J., 9,86,102,105,122,140,142,
   154,176,184,198,203, *214*
Breedlove, P.E., 111,113,169, *213*
Brent, S.B., 206, *214*
Bright, J.O., 112, *214*
Bright, W., 112, *214*

Subject Index

DEVELOPMENTAL PSYCHOLOGY SERIES

Continued from page ii

RAINER H. KLUWE and HANS SPADA. (Editors).
Developmental Models of Thinking

ROBERT L. SELMAN. *The Growth of Interpersonal Understanding:
Developmental and Clinical Analyses*

BARRY GHOLSON. *The Cognitive-Developmental Basis of Human Learning*:
Studies in Hypothesis Testing

TIFFANY MARTINI FIELD, SUSAN GOLDBERG, DANIEL STERN, and
ANITA MILLER SOSTEK. (Editors). *High-Risk Infants and Children*:
Adult and Peer Interactions

GILBERTE PIERAUT-LE BONNIEC. *The Development of Modal Reasoning*:
Genesis of Necessity and Possibility Notions

JONAS LANGER. *The Origins of Logic*: *Six to Twelve Months*

LYNN S. LIBEN. *Deaf Children: Developmental Perspectives*